Why Do People Discriminate against Jews?

Why Do People Discriminate against Jews?

JONATHAN FOX AND LEV TOPOR

OXFORD
UNIVERSITY PRESS

OXFORD
UNIVERSITY PRESS

Oxford University Press is a department of the University of Oxford. It furthers
the University's objective of excellence in research, scholarship, and education
by publishing worldwide. Oxford is a registered trade mark of Oxford University
Press in the UK and certain other countries.

Published in the United States of America by Oxford University Press
198 Madison Avenue, New York, NY 10016, United States of America.

© Oxford University Press 2021

Library of Congress Cataloging-in-Publication Data
Names: Fox, Jonathan, 1968– author. | Topor, Lev, author.
Title: Why do people discriminate against Jews? / Jonathan Fox, Lev Topor.
Description: New York, NY : Oxford University Press, [2021] |
Includes bibliographical references and index.
Identifiers: LCCN 2020058616 (print) | LCCN 2020058617 (ebook) |
ISBN 9780197580349 (hardback) | ISBN 9780197580356 (paperback) |
ISBN 9780197580370 (epub)
Subjects: LCSH: Antisemitism. | Religious discrimination. | Conspiracy theories | Zionism.
Classification: LCC DS145 .F683 2021 (print) | LCC DS145 (ebook) |
DDC 305.892/4—dc23
LC record available at https://lccn.loc.gov/2020058616
LC ebook record available at https://lccn.loc.gov/2020058617

DOI: 10.1093/oso/9780197580349.001.0001

1 3 5 7 9 8 6 4 2

Paperback printed by Marquis, Canada
Hardback printed by Bridgeport National Bindery, Inc., United States of America

Contents

Acknowledgments

We would like to thank all of those who helped with this project, from the data-collection stage through the writing. We are grateful to Matthias Basedau, Daniel Philpott, Jocelyne Cesari, Lene Kuhle, Yasemin Akbabba, Chris Bader, Roger Finke, Jeff Haynes, Patrick James, Shmuel Sandler, Ariel Zellman, Torkel Brekke, Tom Konzack, Dane Mataic, Jonathan Rynhold, Baruch Susser, and Ariel Zellman, as well as the anonymous reviewers, for their advice and comments at various points in the project. Thanks to the research assistants for round 3 of the project, including Sherrie Feigelson, Mora Deitch, Tanya Haykin, and Eytan Meir.

We also thank the Israel Science Foundation (Grant 23/14), The German-Israel Foundation (Grant 1291-119.4/2015), and the John Templeton Foundation for funding this project, as well as the Association of Religion Data Archives for their help with the data. The opinions expressed in this study are solely those of the authors and do not necessarily reflect those of any of the funders.

1

Introduction

The question of why people discriminate against Jews is an age-old question. It is a seemingly simple question, but there has been considerable disagreement on the answer. This is not surprising because the causes of discrimination against any minority, religious or otherwise, are complex and often crosscutting. Social scientists have long disagreed over the root causes of the phenomenon, and discrimination against Jews is certainly no exception. The case of discrimination against Jews is further complicated by the fact that it is a controversial political issue.

This study seeks to focus on the academic aspect of the controversy. That is, we seek to avoid normative issues and instead focus on empirics. We ask empirically testable questions about what causes discrimination against Jews. We draw on several types of academic literatures to inform us on both what questions we should ask and how to understand our empirical findings.

More specifically, this study uses new data to address this question and to examine the causes of discrimination against Jewish minorities in 76 countries between 1990 and 2014. In a small number of countries, including Barbados, Luxembourg, Montenegro, Panama, and Suriname, we find no discrimination either by governments or society. This is important because the question of what causes discrimination also requires an explanation for situations where no discrimination is present. In the other 71 countries, at least some discrimination is present. Often this discrimination against Jews is quite substantial. Thus there is a great amount of variation across countries in how much discrimination is present against Jews. This makes the question of the causes of this discrimination pertinent. That is, as discrimination against Jews differs from country to country, we need to ask why there are high levels of discrimination in countries like Greece, Russia, and Turkey, on one hand, and none in Barbados, Luxembourg, Montenegro, Panama, and Suriname, on the other.

This question is also pertinent because levels of discrimination against Jews are rising. Recent country-level examinations in the United States and Europe find that levels of incidents of harassment and attacks on Jews have been rising.[1] These include high-profile lethal attacks against Jews, such as the Paris attacks in 2015 and the 2018 attack on the Tree of Life Synagogue in Pittsburgh, which are likely a consequence of this process. They also include numerous reports of harassment, vandalism, graffiti, and violence. This study's empirical results confirm this anecdotal and country-specific evidence and show that between 1990 and 2014 there has been a measurable rise in discrimination against Jews.

We examine a wide range of causes. We find that factors such as government support for religion, the presence of anti-Israel sentiments in a country's population, and anti-Israel voting by a country's government in the United Nations all predict levels of discrimination. However, the most consistent predictor of discrimination against Jews by both governments and society is the proportion of a country's population which believes in conspiracy theories of Jewish power and control over society, the economy, the media, and politics. These causes are not mutually exclusive; that is, these factors are not competing explanations. Rather, they likely work in combination to influence levels of discrimination against Jews.

It is critical to be clear that the factor we are seeking to explain in this book is discrimination against Jews, not anti-Semitism. That being said, we argue that anti-Semitism is a critical factor in explaining why people and governments discriminate against Jews, though it is certainly not the only one. In fact, there are many potential motivations for discriminating against religious minorities, which we discuss in more detail later in this chapter and in Chapter 2. These other potential causes of discrimination are common to Jews and other religious minorities. Anti-Semitism, however, is unique to Jews. Various definitions of anti-Semitism focus on "perceptions" of Jews or "hatred of Jews" that can result in negative behavior toward Jews. Thus, anti-Semitism is primarily a belief, ideology, or motivation. Discrimination, as defined in this study, constitutes concrete actions taken against a minority. Thus, while anti-Semitism is a central element of this study, we consider it an explanation or motivation for what we are seeking to explain—discrimination against Jews.

More precisely, the empirical portion of this study focuses on forms of discrimination that can and have been measured. This is because they are overt actions taken against Jews in the real world. Our independent variables—the factors which we posit cause discrimination against Jews—are also factors with tangible measurements. These include factors that theories on anti-Semitism posit are the avenues through which anti-Semitism can cause negative actions to be taken against Jews. These include religious motivations, anti-Israel sentiment, and belief in conspiracy theories about Jews.

That being said, while the purpose of this study is to explain discrimination against Jews rather than anti-Semitism per se, our findings have important implications for our understanding of anti-Semitism. That is, as discrimination against Jews is at least in part a consequence of anti-Semitism, a better understanding of the processes which result in this discrimination will inevitably shed light on the role of anti-Semitism in causing discrimination, as well as the nature of anti-Semitism itself. We discuss this issue in more detail in our concluding chapter.

This approach also has deep roots in the literature on anti-Semitism. Many writers in this literature see anti-Semitism as a negative attitude toward Jews and see discrimination, on the other hand, as a negative action against Jews. From this perspective, one can hold anti-Semitic worldviews and not discriminate against Jews, while another can discriminate against Jews but be less anti-Semitic in general (see Wistrich, 2020; Waldman, 1956; Weil, 2005).

We argue that this approach also has at least one additional advantage. It allows us to avoid many unnecessary complexities, debates, and normative conundrums on the nature and extent of anti-Semitism while trying to answer what we consider to be an empirical question—why do people and governments discriminate against Jews? In Chapter 3, for example, when we find an empirical connection between government support for religion and discrimination against Jews, this correlation exists regardless of whether these government policies and the actions taken against Jews are anti-Semitic.

We also consider the relationship between discrimination against Jews and discrimination against religious minorities in general. While we focus on discrimination against Jews, this discrimination does not occur in a vacuum. Many of the causes of discrimination against Jews are also causes of discrimination against other identity groups. Studies which compare discrimination and anti-minority sentiment across minority groups generally find that levels of discrimination and prejudice toward one minority group in a country are related to the levels of prejudice and discrimination against other minority groups in the same country (Fox, 2016, 2020; Zick et al., 2011).

Thus, theories and empirical findings which focus on other identity groups or religious minorities in general certainly can add to our understanding of discrimination against Jews. Similarly, many of the findings of this study can potentially shed light on the causes of discrimination against non-Jewish religious minorities and identity groups. In addition, some of the discrimination against Jews is likely part of larger processes that also influence discrimination against other religious minorities.

Thus our approach can be seen as shaped like an hourglass. We draw from a wide range of theories and perspectives. Then, just as the hourglass forces its sand to pass through a narrow hole at the bottom of its wider upper glass, we focus these theories on the narrower question of what causes discrimination against Jews. We then take these results and discuss their implications for discrimination against a broader range of identity groups and religious minorities, much as the sand in the hourglass fills the wider lower glass. Of course we also discuss the implications of these results for our understanding of the causes of discrimination against Jews and the nature of anti-Semitism.

Finally, we selected the three theories we test in this book based on two criteria. First, all of them are central theories within the anti-Semitism literature that have parallels within the general social science literature on the causes of discrimination. Second, they are theories which can be tested with the available data. As we note, this is not meant to imply that other factors such as populism or economic deprivation do not influence discrimination against Jews. Rather, we seek to focus on three central theories that can be tested empirically.

Perhaps one of the oldest documented discussions of discrimination against Jews is the Haggadah, the book which is read at the Passover Seder. While it focuses on the story of the Jews' exodus from Egypt, its discussion repeatedly addresses the eternal problem of enmity against Jews. Perhaps one of its most pertinent statements on the topic is that "in every generation they stand against us to destroy us and the Holy One, blessed be He, saves us from their hand."[2] History and the findings of this book demonstrate the accuracy of this statement.

The discussion at the Passover Seder begins with four questions, as do we. The rest of the discussion in this chapter seeks to provide an overview of the book by asking these four questions: What is this book about? What are the patterns of discrimination against Jews? What are the causes of discrimination against Jews? And what is unique about this book?

What Is This Book About?

It is important to reiterate that this book's focus is the causes of discrimination against Jews. This raises the issue of to what extent discrimination against Jews overlaps with anti-Semitism. There is no agreement within the literature on this issue. While some consider the two the same (e.g., Johnson, 2016; Fein, 1987; Marcus, 2013), others consider them distinct topics, at least in theory (e.g., Wistrich, 2020; Waldman, 1956; Weil, 2005). As we discuss in more detail in Chapter 4, the same is true of the overlap between anti-Semitism and anti-Zionism.

It is not the purpose of this book to settle the issue of the normative overlap between discrimination against Jews, anti-Semitism, and anti-Zionism. In fact, we do not think it is possible to do so, for two reasons. First, this is a highly politicized normative issue. Second, this study does not have the tools to settle this issue.

Given this, it is important to be transparent about how we address this issue in our study. That is, while we are unlikely to settle the debate over what anti-Semitism is and how it relates to discrimination, we can be clear on how we approach the issue in our study. Our focus is to understand the causes of discrimination against Jews. We see anti-Semitism as one of the potential causes of this discrimination. While we address many theories on the causes of discrimination which are not specific to Jews, the theoretical and empirical focus of our study are those causes related to anti-Semitism. Thus, when this study addresses anti-Semitism, it is as an independent variable that is used to predict our dependent variable, discrimination against Jews. Thus we see the relationship between the two as causal.

We posit that this approach has merit because we identify at least four interrelated differences between the two concepts. First, while there is little dispute that anti-Semitism can be defined as hatred of Jews, the devil is in the details. As we discuss in more detail in Chapter 4, there is considerable dispute over whether anti-Zionism is considered anti-Semitism and, if so, what manifestations of anti-Zionism are anti-Semitic. This dispute takes place in both the academic and political arenas. As we outline in more detail in this chapter and in Chapter 2, discrimination can be measured more objectively in a manner that avoids political disputes and, to a lesser extent, academic disputes. More specifically, while academic disputes on nearly any topic are perhaps unavoidable,[3] the discrimination data we use in this study are part of a larger project that is widely used and cited. These measures are applied to all religious minorities across the world, not just Jews (Fox, 2020). This lends our measures of discrimination a measure of neutrality and objectivity.

Second, anti-Semitism is something specific to Jews, just as the concept of Islamophobia is specific to Muslims. Discrimination, in contrast, can apply to a wide variety of groups, including Jews and Muslims. This book focuses specifically on the causes of two forms of discrimination against Jews that we measure empirically for Jewish minorities in 76 countries. Specifically, we look at government-based religious discrimination (GRD) and societal religious discrimination (SRD). These concepts are measured by variables taken from round 3 of the Religion and State-Minorities data set (RASM3). The RASM3 data set defines GRD as restrictions placed on the religious institutions or practices of minority religions that are not placed on the majority religion, and SRD as societal actions taken against religious minorities by members of a country's religious majority who do not represent the government (Fox, 2015, 2016, 2019, 2020).

We discuss these variables and their definitions in more detail in Chapter 2. What is important for our purposes here is that these variables are not intended specifically for Jews and provide objective measures of discrimination that can and have been applied to other types of religious minorities. In fact, Fox (2020) examines the general causes of discrimination against 771 religious minorities in 183 countries using this data. This includes all minorities that meet a population cutoff of 0.2% of the population of the country in which they are present, as well as some smaller minorities. The minorities studied include Christians, Muslims, Jews, Buddhists, Hindus, Zoroastrians, Bahai, and Sikhs, among others. Fox (2020) finds that most of these 771 religious minorities experience discrimination. In Chapter 2 we use this data to compare levels of discrimination against Jews to the other religious minorities present in the 76 countries in which RASM3 includes a Jewish minority.

Thus using discrimination as our dependent variable allows us to compare discrimination against Jews to discrimination against other religious minorities. We argue that this is important because discrimination rarely occurs in a vacuum. Jews are rarely the only minority that experiences discrimination in a country. This ability to compare allows us to discern what is unique about discrimination against Jews, and what is similar to discrimination against other religious minorities.

The third difference relates to the first two. It is possible to objectively measure discrimination while avoiding political and academic disputes. In addition to the data used in this study, other studies such as Grim and Finke (2011) have also developed measures of religious freedom, and several projects have developed measures of human rights, discrimination, or freedom (see, for example, Cingranelli & Richards, 2010; Gurr, 1993, 2000; Facchini, 2010). All of these measures, including this study's RASM3 measures, can be criticized for focusing on some forms of discrimination rather than others. However, as they are transparent and explicit on exactly what is being measured and how it is measured, they can be considered objective measures. While some might prefer measures with different foci or content, the measures themselves are generally accepted as valid. In contrast, there is considerable controversy on how anti-Semitism is defined beyond the simple concept of hatred of Jews.

The fourth difference between anti-Semitism and discrimination in general is normative. While few would dispute that it is morally wrong to engage in discrimination against religious minorities, the normative weight of discrimination in general and anti-Semitism is, in practice, different. As we show in Chapter 2, most countries discriminate. This includes all Western democracies other than Canada. Thus, religious discrimination is utterly common. While we may agree that discrimination is wrong, it occurs all over the world, often with little discussion or sanction. Anti-Semitism, in contrast, is currently far more likely to be criticized and sanctioned than discrimination in general.

In this context we view theories on anti-Semitism as a resource for understanding the causes of discrimination against Jews. That is, theories on why people are anti-Semitic and how this anti-Semitism can cause harm to Jews are, in effect, theories on the causes of discrimination against Jews. Given this, this study's findings on the causes of discrimination against Jews certainly have implications for our understanding of the nature and influence of anti-Semitism. Thus the two, while distinct, are fundamentally related.

Thus it is important to address the definition of anti-Semitism. The most commonly accepted definition of anti-Semitism, both in academia and politics, is the working definition adopted by the International Holocaust Remembrance Alliance (IHRA). It reads:

Anti-Semitism is a certain perception of Jews, which may be expressed as hatred toward Jews. Rhetorical and physical manifestations of anti-Semitism are directed toward Jewish or non-Jewish individuals and/or their property, toward Jewish community institutions and religious facilities.[4]

It also provides the following illustrative examples:

Manifestations might include the targeting of the state of Israel, conceived as a Jewish collectivity. However, criticism of Israel similar to that leveled against any other country cannot be regarded as anti-Semitic. Anti-Semitism frequently charges Jews with conspiring to harm humanity, and it is often used to blame Jews for "why things go wrong." It is expressed in speech, writing, visual forms and action, and employs sinister stereotypes and negative character traits.

Contemporary examples of anti-Semitism in public life, the media, schools, the workplace, and in the religious sphere could, taking into account the overall context, include, but are not limited to:

- Calling for, aiding, or justifying the killing or harming of Jews in the name of a radical ideology or an extremist view of religion.
- Making mendacious, dehumanizing, demonizing, or stereotypical allegations about Jews as such or the power of Jews as collective—such as, especially but not exclusively, the myth about a world Jewish conspiracy or of Jews controlling the media, economy, government or other societal institutions.
- Accusing Jews as a people of being responsible for real or imagined wrongdoing committed by a single Jewish person or group, or even for acts committed by non-Jews.
- Denying the fact, scope, mechanisms (e.g., gas chambers) or intentionality of the genocide of the Jewish people at the hands of National Socialist Germany and its supporters and accomplices during World War II (the Holocaust).
- Accusing the Jews as a people, or Israel as a state, of inventing or exaggerating the Holocaust.
- Accusing Jewish citizens of being more loyal to Israel, or to the alleged priorities of Jews worldwide, than to the interests of their own nations.

- Denying the Jewish people their right to self-determination, e.g., by claiming that the existence of a State of Israel is a racist endeavor.
- Applying double standards by requiring of it a behavior not expected or demanded of any other democratic nation.
- Using the symbols and images associated with classic anti-Semitism (e.g., claims of Jews killing Jesus or blood libel) to characterize Israel or Israelis.
- Drawing comparisons of contemporary Israeli policy to that of the Nazis.
- Holding Jews collectively responsible for actions of the state of Israel.[5]

It is important to be clear that this definition is not universally accepted and, as we discuss in more detail in Chapter 6, there is significant resistance both in politics and academia to elements of this definition.

While in this book we follow this definition of anti-Semitism, it is not directly relevant to the empirical portion of our study. This is because, as we note, this study's empirics focus precisely on the causes of discrimination against Jews. Both these causes, our independent variables (which we discuss in more detail in the following section), and our dependent variables—discrimination against Jews as measured by the RASM3 GRD and SRD variables—can be measured objectively. This means that when we identify empirical links between these factors and discrimination against the 76 Jewish minorities included in this study (which are all Jewish minorities included in the RASM3 data set), these findings are valid, no matter one's opinion on the definition or even existence of anti-Semitism.

Put differently, when in Chapter 2 we find, for example, that discrimination against Jews is rising, this phenomenon is occurring whether or not the discrimination is motivated in part or in whole by anti-Semitism, or whether the discrimination itself is considered anti-Semitic. Similarly, when we find in Chapter 5 that a higher proportion of a country's population which believes in conspiracy theories about Jewish power will lead to more discrimination against Jews, that finding is present and valid regardless of whether these beliefs or the discrimination are classified as anti-Semitic. Thus, the questions of what is anti-Semitism or who is anti-Semitic are not critical to the empirical portion of our research.

By analogy, it is possible to argue over why the sun rises in the east every morning and sets in the west every evening. The scientific explanation is that the sun is not actually rising and setting. Rather, the Earth is rotating on its axis so different parts of the Earth face the sun over a 24-hour period and the sun only appears to rise and set based on our point of observation. The ancient Greeks believed that the sun was the wheel of Apollo's chariot which Apollo rode across the sky each day. Yet, whichever explanation is correct, from our point of observation, the sun still rises in the east and sets in the west. We know when to expect light and when to expect dark. This observation remains identical regardless of the explanation for it.

This study similarly seeks to determine basic relationships through the use of empirical evidence and methodology. More specifically, we seek to determine whether discrimination against Jews is empirically connected to discrete independent variables, including how strongly states support a single religion, how many people in a country are religious (Chapter 3), how often states vote against Israel in the United Nations, the proportion of a country's population that holds anti-Israel sentiments (Chapter 4), and the proportion of a population that believes in conspiracy theories of Jewish power (Chapter 5). We neither seek nor claim to provide definitive answers of what is and is not anti-Semitic. However, as we discuss in Chapter 7, our study's results certainly have implications for the debate over this issue.

Accordingly, we take no stand in this book on a number of issues related to anti-Semitism. These include but are not limited to:

- *How is anti-Semitism defined?* While we follow the IHRA definition to the extent that we require a definition of anti-Semitism in this study, this specific definition in no way influences either our research design or our findings. Theories of the causes of anti-Semitism, most of which existed before the IHRA definition was created, do influence our research in that they make predictions on what causes discrimination against Jews, and we test several of these theories. However, we posit that these theories are independent of any single definition of anti-Semitism.
- *What types of actions, speech, or discrimination are anti-Semitic?* Our goal is to use objective measures of discrimination and its theorized causes to determine which of these theorized causes are accurate. Whether any discriminatory actions are themselves anti-Semitic or are caused by anti-Semitic motivations is independent of this objective.
- *What types of criticism of Israel are anti-Semitic?* Two of our independent variables include whether survey respondents have a negative view of Israel or a positive view of Palestine. Whether these variables influence levels of discrimination is independent of whether these views and actions are in any way influenced by anti-Semitism or in and of themselves constitute anti-Semitism, however defined.

Discussions of anti-Semitism can be a political and academic minefield. At least among the mainstream, no one wants to be accused of anti-Semitism (Topor, 2018). Even actions and events that most rational people would attribute to anti-Semitic motives can cause considerable controversy and emotion. One of the goals of our research design is to avoid this quagmire to whatever extent is possible. We limit our discussion to questions that can be asked objectively and answered using objective methodology and measures. While we realize that our findings will likely contribute to the larger debates surrounding anti-Semitism, between the covers of this book we seek to remain within the bounds of objective empirical social science research.

We posit that this approach has three advantages. First, it avoids the many complicated and controversial issues surrounding what is considered anti-Semitic. Second, it focuses on empirics rather than normative issues. This allows us to focus on factual issues that can be resolved objectively. Third, despite this more limited scope, the results still provide evidence that is relevant to the normative debates surrounding anti-Semitism and its definition. That is, providing empirical evidence for what does and what does not cause discrimination against Jews cannot be anything other than relevant to the academic and political discussion of anti-Semitism and its causes.

This book is also about applying the methodologies of comparative politics and the empirical social sciences to answer the question of why people and governments discriminate against Jews. This methodology assumes that it is possible to compare across cases and detect patterns. This includes comparing Jewish minorities in different countries, as well as comparing the case of Jewish minorities to the cases of other religious minorities. This is not in any way intended to deny that the case of Jewish minorities is unique. In fact, we posit that it is the uniqueness of this case which increases the power of comparative methodology. The insights gained from comparative methodology come from determining what elements are different and what elements are similar across cases.

Also, sometimes patterns that are not obvious in one case become easier to identify when they are more obvious in another. For example, in Chapter 4 we examine theories on how Muslims become stigmatized as a security threat and how this leads to discrimination against them. This, we argue, can shed light on the processes involving how tropes of Jewish dual loyalty and association with the state of Israel can stigmatize Jews and lead to discrimination. While the reasons for the stigmatization of Jews and Muslims are different, we argue that the dynamics of this stigmatization are similar. Thus, while both the Jewish and Muslim experiences as minorities are unique, comparing these cases can lead to greater insight, which involves applying theories developed to understand the Muslim case to better understand the Jewish case. In addition, this comparison also leads to insights that help to better understand the Muslim case.

Another implication of this methodology is that it is evidence-based. We collect data to test various theories on what might cause discrimination against

Jews. This includes data on levels of discrimination and data which measures the theorized causes. While no social science data can ever be called perfect, all data in this study are from recognized sources, and we are fully transparent on how the data are obtained and used. Thus, our results, in our eyes, are results based on the use of the scientific method. We start with a theory, test it, and re-evaluate it in light of the results. As we discuss in the following, some theories hold up better than others, but all of the results provide new information that allows us to add depth to our understanding of the causes of discrimination against Jews.

This is not to imply that there have been no previous empirical studies on the causes of anti-Semitism. However, the vast majority are based exclusively on survey data and look at what type of person is likely to have anti-Semitic attitudes. Some of the factors connected to anti-Semitism in these studies include religious identity, religiosity, an authoritarian personality, left-right political affiliation, sexism, racism, and other types of prejudices, among others.[6] Some compare levels of anti-Semitism to other factors, such as homophobia, anti-immigrant attitudes, racism, sexism, and anti-Muslim attitudes (Zick et al., 2011). Other studies simply track the number and type of incidents over time in a single country or group of countries, or survey what proportion of Jews have experienced anti-Semitism. While most studies in these genera do not empirically test the causes of these incidents, one study connects anti-Semitic incidents on US college campuses to the presence of anti-Israel activities and organizations on those campuses.[7]

However, our study's approach is different. Our dependent variable measures real-world discrimination, rather than attitudes, though it does look at the prevalence of some types of attitudes in society as potential explanations for discrimination against Jews. Also, most previous empirical studies focusing on anti-Semitism are limited to a single country or a small number of countries. This study of 76 countries includes nearly every sizable Jewish population in the world outside of Israel.

Finally, while this book focuses on why people discriminate against Jews, we also address larger issues. Our findings have implications for our understanding of the general causes of discrimination against religious minorities, not only Jews. An important assumption of comparative methodology is that what occurs in one case may also occur in another. If it doesn't apply in other cases, this allows us to ask why and to learn more about the general phenomenon. In addition, we posit that the general literature on the causes of discrimination against religious minorities and the anti-Semitism literature have been relatively isolated from each other. In this book we seek to increase the cross-fertilization between these literatures and believe that each can gain insight from the other.

What Are the Patterns of Discrimination against Jews?

In Chapter 2 we discuss in detail how we measure discrimination against Jews and compare the results to discrimination against other minorities in the same countries. We find that patterns of discrimination against Jews are unique. This is not, in itself, unique, as all categories of minorities experience unique patterns of discrimination (Fox, 2016, 2020). In the case of the 76 Jewish minorities included in this study, what is particularly unique is that while SRD is comparatively high, levels of GRD against Jews are mostly below the mean levels for all minorities. In Christian-majority counties, SRD is higher against Jews than against any other religious minority. In Muslim-majority countries, it is higher than against all other minorities except Christians. GRD against Jews in Muslim-majority countries is lower than against any other minority. In Christian-majority countries, GRD against Jews is lower than against all other minorities except "other" minorities—those which are not Jewish, Muslim, or Christian.

This is a particularly interesting relationship because Grim and Finke (2007, 2011) theorize that SRD should be a cause of GRD. Thus, if SRD is high, so should be GRD. Other studies find that this SRD-GRD relationship applies only under certain circumstances, particularly where the minority is seen as some form of existential threat and this threat triggers the SRD-GRD relationship (Fox, 2020). Yet, as we discuss, particularly in Chapters 4 and 5, many do see Jews as a threat, so the absence of this relationship remains interesting and indicates that it is likely that the perception of Jews as an existential threat have not yet become sufficiently mainstream for the SRD-GRD link to be activated. In addition, the question of why SRD is higher than GRD against Jews is also important. We theorize that the legacy of the Holocaust deters governments from discriminating against Jews, though while this deterrence lowers levels of GRD, it does not inhibit it altogether. However, this deterrence is less effective at the societal level.

What Are the Causes of Discrimination against Jews?

The theories on the causes of discrimination against Jews can be divided into two categories: theories which focus specifically on Jews, mostly derived from the literature on anti-Semitism, and theories which are intended to apply to all religious minorities. However, the line between these two types of theories can often be difficult to draw. This is because most theories from the anti-Semitism literature have parallel theories in the general literature on religious discrimination. Nevertheless, the application of many theories in the general literature to explain discrimination against Jews can have aspects that are unique to Jews.

This raises three additional and related questions regarding how we should understand the causes of discrimination against Jews. First, should the focus of the study be on Jews specifically, or should we examine the causes of discrimination against all religious minorities and, in this context, seek our answers to the causes of discrimination against Jews? Studies examining the general causes of discrimination against religious minorities are a valid approach. The quantitative literature includes several such studies, which we draw upon for insight in this study (e.g., Grim & Finke, 2011). In fact, as we have noted, the data used in this study comes from the RASM3 data set, which has been the basis for several such studies (e.g., Fox, 2016, 2020). However, there has been no cross-country study of this nature focusing on Jews. Thus, this study's approach of focusing on Jews is a novel approach with the potential to add a new perspective to the issue.

Second, should the study focus on general theories of the causes of discrimination to find its explanation for discrimination against Jews, or should it focus on theories specific to Jews? We consider each of these approaches valid and therefore seek to use both. In doing so, we compare and contrast the insights of these two bodies of theory and demonstrate that there is considerable overlap and agreement between them on the causes of discrimination—both against Jews and in general. However, we also find that each body of theory has much that can enrich the other.

Third, how should we address the relationship between what causes discrimination against Jews and what causes discrimination in general? We take a classic comparative politics approach to this issue. While our focus is specifically on the causes of discrimination against Jews, as we noted earlier, we believe that our findings have wider implications. An important insight of the comparative politics approach is that we can examine a specific case and use it to provide insights which may be generalizable to other cases. Accordingly, we begin by applying a mix of theories, those specific to the Jewish case and more general theories, to understand the causes of discrimination against Jews. We then take our results and ask to what extent they may shed light on the general causes of discrimination.

Theories Specific to Jews

In Chapters 3, 4, and 5 we focus on three types of causes of discrimination which we draw from the literature on anti-Semitism: religious motives, anti-Zionism, and belief in conspiracy theories about Jews. More specifically, the literature on anti-Semitism posits that these are causes or manifestations of anti-Semitism, and we argue that they can also be seen as causes of discrimination against Jews. While we derive these theories from the literature on anti-Semitism, we demonstrate that all of these potential causes and motives are addressed to some extent in the general literature. The parallels are likely more obvious and clearer in the case of religious motives than they are for anti-Zionism and conspiracy theories, but they still remain present for the latter two.

As we noted earlier, we'd like to be clear that these are not the only theories on the causes of discrimination against Jews that can be found in the anti-Semitism literature. For example, theories of the racial inferiority of Jews, such as those propagated by the Nazis, figure dominantly in that literature. This type of motivation is prominent in right-wing populist discourse. Given this, it is not surprising that there is also a growing literature on the link between populism and anti-Semitism (Wodak, 2018). While our empirical focus is on these theories, in our discussion of the literature we discuss a wider array of theories. Also, we know of no cross-country data which would allow us to test the validity of the propositions that racial ideology or populism influence discrimination against Jews.

The concept that religious exclusivism and theology can result in discrimination against religious minorities is certainly not unique to potential motives and causes of discrimination against Jews. As we discuss in more detail in Chapter 3, this is an argument found both in the general literature and the anti-Semitism literature. In fact, the existing empirical literature finds that governments which are more closely connected to religion also tend to engage in more discrimination against all religious minorities (Fox, 2008, 2015, 2016, 2020; Grim and Finke, 2011). In Chapter 3 we confirm that this finding specifically applies to GRD against Jews and, to a lesser extent, that government support for religion also predicts SRD.

However, SRD against Jews is lower in countries in which the populations are more religious. This is interesting as it means that in countries where the societal actors who could potentially engage in discrimination against Jews are more religious, they tend to engage in less discrimination. We argue that this is likely a result of two societal dynamics. First, in an age where all religions are challenged by secularism, there is more respect among religious individuals for members of other religions who are religious. Second, a major cause of discrimination against religious minorities, especially in the West, is secular ideologies which are intolerant of many religious practices, especially those of minority religions. Countries which have more religious people will likely have fewer secular people with this motivation to discriminate.

Of course, this is likely at least partially contextual; that is, in societies where secularism is on the rise, religious people may feel more threatened and thus band together to support each other. However, this is less likely to be the case in highly religious societies where secularism is not seen by religious people as a serious threat.

In contrast, societal levels of religiosity have no impact on GRD. We posit that it is logical that one aspect of government policy—state support for religion—is more likely to influence another form of government policy—government-based restrictions on the religious institutions and practices of minority religions—than are societal factors.

We posit that anti-Zionism can motivate discrimination against Jews based on two mechanisms. First, it can be a cover for other motives for anti-Semitism; that is, it can be a "politically correct" excuse or alibi for engaging in actions that have other motivations and would otherwise be seen as inexcusable. Being against Israel can be considered politically and socially acceptable, so if those with other motivations are able to frame their actions in this manner, it can provide an efficient camouflage. Yet, as we discuss in more detail in Chapter 4, many anti-Zionists place on all Jews the responsibility for the evils Israel is perceived to commit or, in some cases, blame all Jews for the existence of the state of Israel. This can lead to retribution or punishment in the form of discrimination, which is the second mechanism by which anti-Zionism can lead to discrimination against Jews (Topor, 2018, 2021).

The parallels to these mechanisms in general social science theory are less obvious but nevertheless present. Perhaps the clearest parallel is the concept that individuals can be blamed for actions taken by other members of their identity groups. As we discuss in more detail in Chapter 4, many consider all Muslims collectively responsible for terror attacks that are perpetrated by Muslims. Securitization theory posits that this has caused Muslims to be "securitized," which justifies actions against them that might otherwise be considered unacceptable. We argue that perceptions of Jews as disloyal agents of a foreign power may initiate a similar process. We also argue that the process used to stigmatize Muslims for alleged security reasons can also be used to stigmatize Jews even if security is not an issue.

Another literature focuses on discrimination against those seen as non-indigenous. Jewish loyalty toward Israel, combined with the perception that Jews are foreigners and perhaps linked to a foreign Israeli threat, might be another parallel mechanism from the general literature.

The empirical tests in Chapter 4 do not directly measure anti-Zionism. Rather, they test the impact of anti-Israel government behavior and anti-Israel sentiments in society on discrimination against Jews. We find a limited link between these factors and discrimination. States which vote against Israel in the United Nations engage in more GRD, but not SRD, against their Jewish minorities, but only in Christian-majority states. States in which the population holds both anti-Israel and pro-Palestine views engage in higher levels of both SRD and GRD, but the link between these attitudes and SRD is weak. Thus, whatever the mechanism, anti-Israel behavior and attitudes influence discrimination against Jews, but this link is far stronger for government-based discrimination than for societal discrimination. We posit that this implies that the many manifestations of SRD against Jews which are anecdotally attributed to anti-Zionism or anti-Israel sentiment are likely, at least in part, to be motivated by more classical forms of anti-Semitism.

It is important to remember that anti-Zionism is a complex phenomenon. Many of the anti-Zionist arguments against Israel can be seen as anti-Semitic tropes that migrated from more classical anti-Semitism. It can also be a cover for other prejudices against Jews. Yet people can legitimately criticize Israel without being either anti-Semitic or anti-Zionist. Thus, even though anti-Israel sentiments and behavior have a measurable impact on discrimination against Jews, this likely represents a more intricate relationship and is influenced by other factors, many of which we describe in this chapter and elsewhere in this book, particularly Chapter 4.

The final type of theory specific to Jews that we test in this study is conspiracy theories of Jewish control and power. Perhaps the most common is the type of conspiracy theory that posits that Jews seek or possess some form of world domination. Many of the others are subcategories of this one or are otherwise related to it. Other types include blood libels, causing wars revolutions and atrocities, well poisoning, the murder of religious figures, and controlling the media and finance.

One interesting thing about conspiracy theories and Jews is that while there are certainly many conspiracy theories whose conspiracies do not involve Jews, it is difficult to think of any people, nation, or entity which has consistently been the subject of persistent conspiracy theories for millennia across the world. While social science theory can and does address how stereotypes influence discrimination, the extent to which these stereotypes apply to Jews is arguably unique. In this case, the difference in degree is arguably a difference in kind.

We posit that there are two related mechanisms linking conspiracy theories and discrimination against the objects of these theories. Specifically, postulating a sinister and powerful group acting clandestinely behind the scenes for their own benefit to the detriment of others will be related to discrimination in two manners. First, from the perspective of those who believe in these conspiracies, the Jews pose a significant threat, and discrimination is a response to this threat. This response can be seen as a punishment or as a form of retaliation for the perceived insidious and evil behavior of the Jews, or it can be seen as a way to counter their powerful and menacing influence. Second, these conspiracy theories may simply be an indicator that prejudice and hatred toward Jews are at high levels. In this scenario, the conspiracy theories are not the cause of discrimination but, rather, are a symptom of the underlying prejudices and hate which cause the discrimination.

This study finds a strong correlation between belief in conspiracy theories about Jews and discrimination against them. Specifically, both levels of SRD and GRD are strongly predicted by the proportion of people in a country who believe that Jews have too much power or control over (1) the business world, (2) international finance markets, (3) global affairs, (4) the United States government, (5) the global media, and (6) the world's wars.

This link between belief in Jewish conspiracies and discrimination against Jews is the clearest and most consistent result found in this study. We argue that this has a number of important implications. Whether belief in conspiracy theories is itself the cause of discrimination against Jews or a symptom of the underlying causes of this discrimination, on a practical level the extent to which people believe in them is the most important and accurate indicator that societies and governments will likely discriminate against Jews.

Both the anti-Zionist and religious brands of anti-Semitism can stimulate belief in conspiracy theories about Jews. This indicates that when these types of motivations, as well as others which we do not empirically examine in this book such as populism, pass the threshold of inspiring popular belief in conspiracy theories, the negative consequences for Jews increase dramatically. Thus, every public figure who propagates these conspiracy theories or even just turns a blind eye to them is substantially contributing to a process that creates real and negative consequences for Jews not only in their own country, but also in other countries. That is, because this type of speech act tends to be reported internationally, the impact can often be international.

This result also speaks to the potential danger of conspiracy theories in general. This is important because there has been little previous research on the consequences of conspiracy theories to the objects of those conspiracy theories. We find that, at least in the case of the Jews, when conspiracy theories are widely believed, this creates a real danger for the objects of those conspiracy theories, assuming that those objects are identifiable and vulnerable. This is not always the case. For example, space aliens and the CIA are the objects of numerous conspiracy theories. The former are arguably difficult to identify and locate, and the latter have a reasonable level of insulation and protection from harm. Jews, in contrast, are easy to locate and have been demonstrated on multiple occasions to be vulnerable to acts of discrimination and violence. This is also true of many types of minorities, including those based on religion, ethnicity, immigration status, political belief, gender identity, and sexual preference. Thus, potentially, this finding has a wide applicability.

General Theories of Discrimination

The potential causes of religious discrimination against any religious minority are multiple and complex. While this study focuses on those causes of discrimination that are most associated with discrimination against Jews, levels of discrimination against Jews can also be influenced by a wide variety of other potential causes which can apply in theory to any religious minority. This is important for at least two reasons. First, as we discuss in subsequent chapters, even those causes particularly associated with discrimination against Jews are by no means wholly unique to discrimination against Jews. Second, as we discuss in Chapter 2, much of the GRD against Jews is not specific to Jews. A good part of this discrimination occurs when governments discriminate against religious minorities in general, and Jews are not the only target.

In this section we briefly list some of the causes of discrimination against religious minorities discussed in the literature which are potentially relevant to discrimination against Jews. As we note in the following, many of them overlap with the three causes of discrimination against Jews that we empirically test in this study.

While we discuss it in more detail in this chapter and in Chapter 3, it is important to note that *religious ideology* is among the most commonly discussed causes of religious discrimination and likely among the most important causes.

Anti-religious secular ideologies are also a potential source of religious discrimination. This is particularly relevant to Jews in the West. As we discuss in more detail in Chapter 2, several religious practices common to both Jews and Muslims are restricted in at least some Western countries, and these restrictions are motivated at least in part by secular ideologies. These include ritual slaughter (kosher and halal meat), head coverings for women, and infant circumcision. While infant circumcision is currently regulated only in Sweden, Denmark, and Norway, the ideology that drives these limitations is decidedly secular, and movements pushing for bans on infant circumcision are present in several European countries. Movements pressing for bans on ritual slaughter are also common in Western countries that have yet to enact such restrictions.

This overlaps with the *objectionable practices* motivation. Fox (2020) argues that sometimes religious minorities engage in activities which at least some members of the majority find objectionable and that this can be a motive for discrimination. While Jews rarely proselytize, which is the "objectionable" religious practice that most commonly attracts discrimination, the Jewish (and Muslim) practices of ritual slaughter of meat and infant circumcision are considered objectionable by many in the West.

Religious tradition: Huntington (1993, 1996), among others, argues that some religious traditions are more likely to be intolerant and to engage in conflict and discrimination. Huntington's theory is controversial.[8] Empirical support for it is mixed with some studies finding a basis for it (e.g., Grim & Finke, 2011; Toft, 2007) and others finding less support (e.g., Basedau et al., 2011; Cesari & Fox, 2016; Fox, 2004). If correct, this theory would predict more discrimination against Jews in Muslim-majority countries.

Regime: Most theoretical treatments of the topic argue that democratic regimes discriminate less than non-democratic regimes (e.g., Brathwaite & Bramsen, 2011; Rebe, 2012). However, many democracies still discriminate (Gurr, 1988). Fox (2020) finds that while there is a correlation between regime and discrimination against religious minorities, it is weaker and more complicated than many suspect. The reason for this is that while liberal democracies, when controlling for other factors, do discriminate less, these other factors are often sufficiently influential to overshadow the impact of regime on discrimination. For example, in practice, Western democracies discriminate more against religious minorities than do Christian-majority countries in the developing world, whether or not they are democracies. Fox (2020) attributes this to a number of factors which differentiate Western democracies from Christian-majority states in the developing world, including higher levels of secularism, more support for religion, and greater economic development. This is a good example of the complexity of the causes of discrimination. Accordingly, we would expect less discrimination against Jews in democracies, but only assuming all other things are equal.

Populism: In recent years many populist movements have targeted several minorities, including not only Jews, but also Muslims and often immigrants in general. As we discuss in Chapter 5, those who support populist politicians are more likely to believe in conspiracy theories, including conspiracy theories about Jews (Haynes, 2019; Wodok, 2018). Accordingly, we would expect more discrimination against Jews in countries where populist political parties are present, to the extent that they are popular or in power.

Indigenousness: Many states and cultures discriminate against minorities they consider foreign or non-indigenous. Even in countries where Jews have long histories, they are often considered foreigners, or perhaps loyal to themselves or Israel more than they are to the state. This can be a motivation for discrimination. This cause is related to all three motivations for discrimination which are the focus of this study. Jews can be considered not fully indigenous or loyal due to their religion and their perceived connections and loyalty to Israel. These themes are also common in conspiracy theories about Jews. Minorities considered non-indigenous have in particular been the targets of populist politicians and ideologies (Haynes, 2019: 88–105; Wodok, 2018). However, this motivation is present in many states where populists have little political power.

History of conflict: Most theories which address conflict between minorities and the state posit that discrimination against minorities leads to conflict. These theories tend to focus on ethnic conflict (e.g., Gurr, 1993, 2000; Horowitz, 1985), but are also applied to religious conflict (Fox, 2004; Fox et al., 2017; Akbaba & Tydas, 2011). While the causes of discrimination are addressed less often in this literature, when these causes are addressed, past conflict is posited to be a cause of discrimination (Henne & Klocek, 2017; Fox, 2020). As Jews engaging in violent conflict is rare outside of Israel, this is unlikely to have a large influence on this study.

Past discrimination: Past discrimination is among the best predictors of current discrimination. Gurr (1988) classically argues that states are more likely to use repression in the present and future if they have successfully used it in the past. Thus Jews are more likely to experience discrimination in places where anti-Semitism and anti-Jewish discrimination were more common in the past. This applies to deep institutionalized discrimination that was present over centuries, as well as more recent manifestations of discrimination. However, in some extreme cases, such as the European reaction to the Holocaust, repugnance toward past discrimination can cause a sensitivity to discrimination against Jews that may have the opposite influence.

Perceived security threats: It is not necessary for a minority to be actively engaging in conflict or violence for it to be perceived as a potential security threat. As we discuss in Chapters 4 and 5, some see Jews as agents of a foreign power or as otherwise behaving in a manner which undermines the security interests of the state. This is especially true when Jews are seen through the prism of conspiracy theories focusing on Jewish power.

Perceived political threats: When a minority is seen by leaders to be a threat to their political survival or their political agenda, this can result in discrimination (Gill, 2008). This can also occur when they are seen as competing with the majority for resources (Bohman & Hjerm, 2013: 4). Conspiracy theories of Jewish power posit that Jews pose such a political threat.

Societal discrimination: As noted earlier, SRD is theorized by Grim and Finke (2011) to be a cause of GRD. This occurs when "a dominant religion that either lacks the authority of the state or wants to go beyond the state's actions.... Religions, social movements, cultural context, and institutions beyond the state can all foster regulatory actions that lead to persecution" (Grim & Finke, 2007: 637). In addition, politicians may often share the prejudices of their constituents. Even if they do not, it may be in their interests to pander to these constituents' prejudices by discriminating against the minority in question. Fox (2020) finds empirically, using the RASM3 data, that this relationship exists for only some minorities but not others. He argues that SRD causes GRD only when there is some security or existential threat which triggers the relationship. This factor is not found to be present for Jewish minorities. This is consistent with the findings in this study that the causes of SRD and GRD against Jews are often distinct.

Overall, the general literature on the causes of discrimination takes the perspective that forms of discrimination against all types of minorities have common causes. Thus, discrimination against Jews is caused by many of the same factors that cause discrimination against other minority groups, religious and otherwise. Zick, Küpper, and Hövermann (2011), for example, make precisely this argument when they argue that anti-Semitism, homophobia, anti-immigrant attitudes, racism, anti-Muslim attitudes, and sexism all have similar patterns and origins in Europe. Our findings support this argument. In this study, particularly in Chapter 2, we demonstrate that much of the discrimination against Jews seems to be part of larger patterns of discrimination against religious minorities in general.

However, we also demonstrate in Chapter 2 that the patterns of discrimination against Jews are unique and cannot be fully explained by general causes of discrimination. A full explanation for discrimination against Jews requires an examination of a combination of both general causes and Jew-specific causes. As there have been multiple studies of the general causes of discrimination, including studies using the same data used in this study (Fox, 2016, 2020), we focus on the Jew-specific causes but take into account the known general causes. We also argue that this focus on Jew-specific causes, in particular, is the major contribution of this study.

Why Is This Study Unique?

The RASM3 data set provides an unprecedented opportunity to examine the causes of discrimination against Jews. It has a set of features which, in combination, have never previously been available. Primarily, it contains detailed data on levels of discrimination, both in society and by governments, that are specifically against Jews for all countries in which a significant number of Jews are present for the 25-year period of 1990 to 2014. The 76 Jewish minorities listed in the RASM3 data set include nearly all of the Jews in the world who do not live in Israel, where Jews are a majority. The larger data set covers 183 countries, which includes all countries with a population of at least 250,000, as well as a sampling of smaller countries. Within these countries, it includes all minorities which constitute at least 0.2% of these population. However, for Jewish, Christian, and Muslim minorities, it includes any identifiable population, even if it is smaller than 0.2% of that country's population. Arguably, minority groups that are so small as to be difficult for researchers to locate are less likely to experience discrimination. Thus, RASM3 likely includes all relevant Jewish minorities in the world. It also contains other religious minorities in all of the countries examined in this study. This allows a comparison in Chapter 2 of levels of discrimination against Jews to levels of discrimination against other religious minorities in those countries where Jewish minorities are present.

The RASM3 data are part of a process of proliferation of new data on religion in the social sciences. In 2006, Grim and Finke (2006: 3) lamented that "religion receives little attention in international quantitative studies. Including religion in cross-national studies requires data, and high-quality data are in short supply." Since then, this has changed. In addition to RASM3, many other data sets have become available. Of particular importance to this study are the World Values Survey (WVS), which provides cross-country data on religiosity which we use in Chapter 3, and the ADL 100, which includes data on anti-Semitism and views on Israel and Palestine across over 100 countries, which we use in Chapters 4 and 5. We also use data on UN General Assembly voting on resolutions concerning Israel. Thus, we now have new cross-country data that allow us to examine age-old questions in a manner not previously possible.

In the context of this study, we also address what we consider to be a significant lacuna in the existing theoretical literature. The literature on anti-Semitism has detailed and involved discussions of the causes of discrimination against Jews, though in most cases it is not framed precisely in those terms. It tends to be located within the humanities and frames the discussion as on the causes of anti-Semitism. There is a growing parallel literature in the social sciences on the causes of religious discrimination and persecution. While there is some cross-fertilization between the two literatures, mostly the sporadic use of the religion and discrimination literature within the anti-Semitism literature, we are aware of no systematic comparison of what insights each literature might provide to the other. In Chapters 3, 4, and 5 we examine central contentions within the anti-Semitism literature and what parallel literatures exist in the general social science literature on discrimination and religious discrimination. Also, in our concluding chapter, we examine what the results from this study can add to both literatures.

That being said, we are aware of no previous cross-country study that includes both data on discrimination against Jewish minorities in 76 countries and data which measure major causes of discrimination against Jews. There have been past studies of the causes of discrimination which looked at most of the world's religious minorities, including Jews (e.g., Fox, 2016, 2020; Grim & Finke, 2012) and general studies of repression of religion (e.g., Sarkissian, 2015; Koesel, 2014). However, none of these studies focused on discrimination against Jews. Also, as noted, the question of why Jews experience discrimination has been one that is present in the qualitative literature. However, there has been no previous study that has applied this methodology to focus on the question of why people discriminate against Jews.

The Book's Structure

We structure this book around this uniqueness. While we cover a wide variety of topics and some of the chapters are to some extent self-contained, they all speak to the larger question of why people discriminate against Jews. Chapter 2 establishes our baseline by examining not only the extent of discrimination against Jews, but also how this compares to discrimination against other religious minorities in the same countries. That is, in Chapter 2 we ask, what is unique about discrimination against Jews?

In Chapters 3, 4 and 5, we examine three potential causes of discrimination against Jews. As we noted earlier, we selected these three potential causes based on their centrality in the anti-Semitism literature and data availability. Chapter 3 focuses on religious causes. Chapter 4 focuses on anti-Zionism and anti-Israel sentiment. Chapter 5 focuses on belief in conspiracy theories of Jewish power and control. In focusing on these three causes, we do not seek to exclude other potential causes, but rather to illuminate those relationships we are able to address using the methodological tools available to us.

Chapter 6 provides the case study of the United Kingdom in order to provide some context and see how the findings presented in this book play out in a qualitative case study. Finally, Chapter 7 summarizes the findings in this book and examines a set of important questions. What can the anti-Semitism literature learn from our findings as well as the insights from the general discrimination literature? What do our findings as well as the anti-Semitism literature teach us about the causes of discrimination in general? Also, what do our findings tell us about the nature of anti-Semitism itself?

We'd also like to note that within the body of the book, particularly in Chapters 3, 4, and 5, we present these results in what we feel is a more user-friendly context and discuss how they relate to the central issues and theories presented in those chapters. For this reason, much of the technical statistical analysis can be found in the book's Appendix.

Conclusions

The causes of discrimination against Jews are multiple and complex. We identify belief in conspiracy theories as perhaps the most important immediate cause, or at least a predictor of this discrimination. Nevertheless, the matrix of causes includes multiple interacting factors. In this book we separate out the parts and examine them individually in order to facilitate greater understanding. We do not claim to provide the final word on the issue. However, we do apply a form of analysis to the topic of why people discriminate against Jews that is new to this topic area, and in doing so, we provide important new information and insight into the topic.

2
Patterns of Discrimination

Before we can determine the causes of discrimination against Jews, it is important to define what we mean by discrimination and, based on this definition, to establish how much discrimination is present in an objective, neutral, and transparent manner. Without this, the empirical results in Chapters 3, 4, and 5 have no context. That is, we cannot fully understand what causes discrimination against Jews until we have established three things. First, what do we mean by discrimination? Second, what are the levels of discrimination against Jews? Third, are levels of discrimination against Jews unique compared to discrimination against other religious minorities? Discrimination against any single minority rarely occurs in a vacuum. Accordingly, context is important. This chapter is intended to fulfill these tasks and answer these questions.

More specifically, this chapter examines the general patterns of discrimination in the 76 countries included in this study. This includes two types of discrimination, government-based religious discrimination (GRD) and societal-based religious discrimination (SRD). We focus on these countries because they are the 76 countries which include a Jewish minority that is coded in the Religion and State-Minorities Round 3 (RASM3) data set. However, all of these countries also have other religious minorities. This includes 122 Christian minorities, 69 Muslim minorities, and 83 minorities that are of different religions, including Hindus (15), Buddhists (22), and Bahai (17), among others.

The goal of this chapter is not to explain the causes and motivations for discrimination against Jews. That is a topic we address in subsequent chapters. In this chapter the goal is to provide a description of the extent of this discrimination and what types of discrimination are present. This is because, in order to assess the causes of discrimination, it is first important to establish the degree and nature of that discrimination. Only once this has been established is it possible to examine motivations and causes in any meaningful way.

For example, one might assume that discrimination is particularly high against Jews compared to other religious minorities. In order to test this, we compare discrimination against Jews to discrimination against other religious minorities. We confirm previous findings that discrimination against religious minorities is common worldwide against all religious minorities. (Fox, 2016, 2020) However, only SRD against Jews is higher than against other religious minorities. GRD, in contrast, is present but not particularly high compared to other religious minorities. If one were to try to explain the causes of GRD against Jews with the misunderstanding that all types of discrimination against Jews are disproportionately high, this would inhibit understanding these causes. That being said, the focus of the discussion and most examples discussed here focus on discrimination against Jews. Chapters 3, 4, and 5 examine causes and motivations.

Despite this focus on patterns of discrimination rather than motivations, some of the discussion does address motivations. Specifically, one of the major findings in this chapter is that the majority of GRD against Jews is not specifically targeted against Jews. Rather, it tends to come from policies directed at religious minorities in general. In many cases, Jews are subject to this generally applicable GRD less often than many other religious minorities. However, even so, there are still numerous cases of GRD unique to Jews in a country, and levels of GRD against Jews differ from those of other religious minorities in most states. Thus, on one hand, it is clear that there is something unique about GRD against Jews. On the other hand, some aspects of GRD against Jews take place in the context of general GRD against religious minorities. As noted earlier, mean levels of SRD against Jews are higher than against other religious minorities. Thus, the findings presented in this chapter clearly show that discrimination against Jews is sufficiently unique to justify further investigation.

This chapter also provides examples of the types of discrimination that are the basis for this study. This is important because this book's methodology looks for patterns among many cases and describes links between various theorized causes of discrimination and actual levels of discrimination. Put differently, one of the purposes of this chapter is to provide some detailed examples of the discrimination against Jews which are the basis for these aggregate numbers and findings.

The rest of this chapter examines patterns and trends in GRD and SRD. This includes a discussion of all 35 types of GRD and 27 types of SRD included in the RASM3 data set.

Government-Based Discrimination

The RASM3 definition of GRD is restrictions placed on the religious institutions or practices of minority religions that are not placed on the majority religion. This is a relatively narrow definition of discrimination since it is limited to government actions, which can include, laws, policies, actions taken by government officials, and decisions by courts. While the majority of GRD is due to national policy, RASM3 also includes actions taken by local government and officials (Fox, 2016, 2020).

This is a limited definition for at least two reasons. First, it is limited to restrictions on religious practices and institutions and does not include discrimination of other types, such as political and economic discrimination. RASM3 divides these into 35 specific types of restrictions which we discuss in more detail in the following. Each is scored on a scale of 0 to 2 based on severity, so the maximum potential GRD score is 70, though no minority reaches that score. This limitation is because the Religion and State (RAS) project, of which RASM3 is a part, focuses on government religion policy. Second, GRD constitutes only those restrictions which focus on religious minorities. If a government restricts a religious practice for all its residents, including the majority religion, this is a violation of religious freedom but not discrimination. To discriminate means to treat differently.

Both of these limitations are appropriate for this study. In most of the countries in this study, though certainly not all of them, Jews, at least in theory, have equal political rights and are often economically advantaged. Thus, restrictions on Jewish religious practices and institutions are in most countries the most significant form of discrimination by governments against Jews. The fact that these restrictions are present against Jews and other religious minorities, despite the fact that many of these states promise religious freedom in their constitutions and laws, makes this even more significant (Mataic & Finke, 2019).

The focus on differential treatment is also appropriate. This study asks whether, and if so why, Jews are singled out for different and negative treatment, not whether a country has religious freedom in general. That is, it is precisely those types of government restrictions that single out Jews and other religious minorities which are particularly relevant. Also, the motivations for restricting religion in general and for restricting only minority religions can be very different (Fox, 2015, 2020). However, we discuss motivations in more detail in later chapters. Here we simply seek to document patterns of discrimination. This is a necessary step before discussing the causes and motivations for this discrimination.

General Patterns of GRD

Patterns of GRD differ between Christian-majority and Muslim-majority states. Figure 2.1 shows the patterns of GRD against Jews, Muslims, Christians, and other religious minorities in Christian-majority states. RASM3 considers a religious group a minority if it belongs to a different religion from or a different denomination of the majority religion. Thus it is possible to have a Christian minority in a Christian-majority state if, for example, there are Protestant or Orthodox Christians in a Catholic-majority state. We use the "other" category for those groups which are not Christians, Muslim, or Jewish because there are

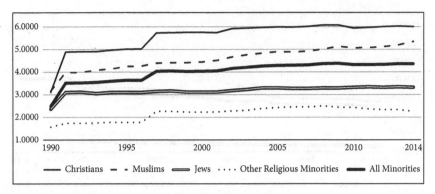

Figure 2.1 GRD in Christian-Majority Countries, 1990–2014.
Significance (t-test) of increase since 1990 for all cases <.05 in 1995, <.01 in 1996, <.001 in 1997–2014.
Significance (t-test) of increase since 1990 for Christians <.05 in 1996–2002, <.01 in 2002–2014.
Significance (t-test) of increase since 1990 for Muslims <.05 in 1997–1998, 2001–2002, <.01 in 2001, <.001 in 2001–2014.
Significance (t-test) of increase since 1990 for Jews <.05 in 2006–2011, 2013.
Significance (t-test) of increase since 1990 for Other Religious Minorities <.05 in 1996–1996, 2004–2008.
Significance (t-test) between Christians and all other minorities <.01 in 1991–2014
Significance (t-test) between Other Religious Minorities and all other minorities <.001 in 1990–2014.

too few minorities of any other individual religion for a meaningful comparison. Mean levels of GRD against Jews are lower than they are against Muslim and Christian minorities but higher than against minorities in the "other" category. While GRD against Jews increased between 1990 and 2014, this is true of religious minorities in general.

Figure 2.2 shows the patterns of GRD against Jews, Muslims, Christians, and other religious minorities in Muslim-majority states. There are only 12 states and 45 minorities in this category, as opposed to 62 Christian-majority states with 295 religious minorities. Bosnia[1] and Singapore are not included in either category since neither has a religious majority. In Muslim-majority states, Jews experience the lowest mean levels of GRD, though in absolute terms these levels are well over double those in Christian-majority states.

Thus, GRD against Jews, on average, is not particularly high as compared to other minorities, but it is still present. In 2014, 58 (77%) of the 76 Jewish minorities in this study experienced GRD. This is about the same as Christian minorities (76.3%) but less than Muslim minorities (91.3%) and more than minorities

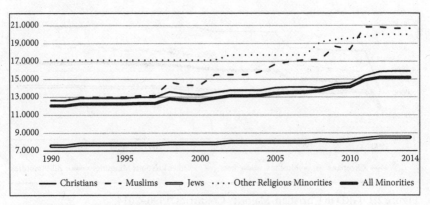

Figure 2.2 GRD in Muslim-Majority Countries, 1990–2014.
Significance (t-test) of increase since 1990 for all cases <.05 in 2005–2007, <.01 in 2002–2004, <.001 in 2008–2014.
Significance (t-test) of increase since 1990 for Christians <.05 in 2008, 2011–2014, <.01 in 2009–2010.
Significance (t-test) of increase since 1990 for Muslims <.05 in 2009–2010.
Significance (t-test) of increase since 1990 for Jews <.05 in 2011.
Significance (t-test) of increase since 1990 for Other Religious Minorities <.05 in 1996–1996, 2004–2008.
Significance (t-test) between Jews and all other minorities <.05 in 2002–2014.

in the "other" category (57.8%). However, these mean levels of GRD do not necessarily represent treatment of Jews similar to that of other religious minorities. As shown in Tables 2.1a, 2.1b, and 2.1c, which list levels of GRD against all 350 minorities discussed in this chapter, most countries treat Jews differently than they do at least some other minorities in their countries. In fact, most countries which engage in GRD treat some minorities differently from others. This suggests that motivations for discrimination are likely, at least in part, minority-specific.

There are a few exceptions. Canada, Barbados, Suriname, and Uruguay engage in no GRD against any religious minority included in RASM3; thus Jews are treated the same. Other countries with equal levels of GRD for all religious minorities include Luxembourg and Peru. For example, in Luxembourg the Catholic Church is automatically registered through a special agreement with the government, and all other religions must register. In Cyprus the two coded minorities, Jews and Muslims, have the same score in 2014 but are subject to different types of discrimination. For example, Cyprus's only Jewish cemetery does not contain a water source, which prevents mourners from performing the traditional washing after burials, while the government denies Muslims access to some but not all mosques.

Table 2.1a GRD and SRD in 2014

Country	Group	GRD	SRD	Country	Group	GRD	SRD	Country	Group	GRD	SRD
Christian Majority				France	Protestants	3	0	Norway	Buddhists	8	0
Western Democracies				Germany	Jews	1	21		Catholics	8	0
Andorra	Hindus	0	0		Muslims	17	13		Jews	10	2
	Jews	0	1		Orthodox Christians	0	0		Muslims	13	6
	Muslims	1	0		Scientologists	11	15	Portugal	Buddhists	3	1
	Protestants	0	0	Greece	Jews	13	14		Jews	3	1
Australia	Buddhists	0	0		Muslims	18	13		Muslims	3	1
	Hindus	0	0		Non-Orth. Christians	14	1		Other Christians	3	0
	Jews	0	17	Iceland	Catholics	1	0	Spain	Christians (non-Cath.)	6	0
	Muslims	1	10		Jews	3	0		Jews	3	4
Austria	Eastern Orthodox	0	0		Muslims	4	3		Muslims	4	5
	Jehovah's Wit.	0	0		Pagans	1	0	Sweden	Buddhists	8	0
	Jews	0	14	Ireland	Jews	2	1		Catholics	8	0
	Mormons	1	1		Muslims	2	3		Jews	11	11
	Muslims	3	7		Protestants	1	0		Muslims	10	11
	Protestants	1	0	Italy	Buddhists	0	0		Orthodox Christians	8	0

Continued

Table 2.1a Continued

Country	Group	GRD	SRD
Belgium	Buddhists	1	0
	Jews	1	20
	Muslims	3	12
	Other Christians	1	0
Canada	Buddhists	0	0
	Chinese Rel.	0	0
	Hindus	0	0
	Jews	0	11
	Muslims	0	8
	Protestants	0	0
	Sikhs	0	0
Cyprus, Greek	Jews	5	5
	Muslims	5	5
Denmark	Buddhists	3	0
	Catholics	3	0
	Jews	6	3
	Muslims	9	8
	Jews	0	8
	Muslims	9	3
	Orthodox Christians	0	0
	Protestants	0	0
Liechtenstein	Jews	2	2
	Muslims	3	5
	Protestants	2	0
Luxembourg	Jews	2	1
	Muslims	2	1
	Orthodox Christians	2	0
	Protestants	2	0
Malta	Jews	0	0
	Muslims	2	4
	Other Christians	0	0
Netherlands	Buddhists	1	0
	Hindus	1	1
	Jews	1	10
	Other Christians	8	0
Switzerland	Buddhists	2	0
	Hindus	2	0
	Jews	4	7
	Muslims	12	4
	Orthodox Christians	2	0
UK	Catholics	0	1
	Hindus	1	0
	Jews	1	-16
	Muslims	5	15
	Orthodox Christians	0	0
	Sikhs	2	0
USA	Bahai	0	1
	Buddhists	0	0
	Catholics	0	2
	Hindus	0	2
	Jews	0	17

Finland	Jews	2	6
	Muslims	2	7
	Orthodox	1	0
France	Buddhists	0	0
	Jehovah's Witnesses	13	6
	Jews	0	25
	Muslims	7	7
	Orthodox Christians	0	0

	Muslims	4	11
	Protestants	1	0
New Zealand	Buddhists	0	0
	Hindus	0	0
	Jews	0	3
	Muslims	1	1
	Sikhs	0	1

Mormons	0	0
Muslims	2	14
Orthodox Christians	0.	0

Table 2.1b GRD and SRD in 2014

Country	Group	GRD	SRD	Country	Group	GRD	SRD	Country	Group	GRD	SRD
Christian Majority				Colombia	Jews	1	4	Venezuela	Muslims	4	0
Latin America					Muslims	1	1		Other Christians	5	0
Argentina	Indigenous Religions	4	0		Protestants	1	0		Protestants	6	0
	Jews	5	13	Mexico	Animists	2	0		Spiritists	3	0
	Muslims	4	1		Jehovah's Witnesses	3	4	*Former Soviet*			
	Orthodox Christians	4	0		Jews	0	0	Armenia	Catholics	13	1
	Protestants	6	6		Muslims	0	0		Jews	13	5
Bahamas	Bahai	1	0		Protestants	11	12		Muslims	13	1
	Catholic	0	0	Panama	Bahai	0	0		Other Christians	31	21
	Jews	1	0		Buddhists	0	0		Protestants	14	13
	Muslims	1	0		Jews	0	0		Yedzis	13	4
	Other Christian	0	0		Muslims	1	1	Belarus	Catholics	22	0
	Spiritists	4	0		Protestants	0	0		Jews	24	10
Barbados	Catholics	0	0	Paraguay	Spiritists	0	0		Muslims	20	1
	Hindus	0	0		Animists	3	0		non-Catholic Christians	41	6
	Jews	0	0		Bahai	3	0	Bulgaria	Catholics	11	0
	Muslims	0	1		Buddhists	3	0		Jews	11	6
	Other Christians	0	0		Jews	3	0		Muslims	21	7

Country	Religion		
Belize	Bahai	1	0
	Buddhists	1	0
	Hindus	1	0
	Jews	1	0
	Muslims	1	0
	Protestants	0	0
Bolivia	Animists	3	0
	Bahai	3	0
	Jews	4	2
	Muslims	3	0
	Protestants	3	0
Brazil	Animists/Spiritists	3	10
	Buddhists	2	0
	Jews	2	8
	Muslims	1	1
	Protestants	1	0
	Other Christians	18	16
Croatia	Jews	9	7
	Muslims	8	3
	Orthodox Christians	4	19
	Other Christians	8	4
	Protestants	8	0
Czech Republic	Jews	2	13
	Muslims	8	9
Estonia	Jews	0	0
	Muslims	1	0
Georgia	Armenian Apostolic	16	7
	Jehovah's Witnesses	27	22
	Jews	14	1
	Muslims	20	3
	Other Christians	25	10
Hungary	Jews	1	12
	Protestants	1	0
Peru	Animists	6	0
	Bahai	6	0
	Buddhists	6	0
	Jews	6	1
	Muslims	6	0
	Protestants	6	0
Suriname	Bahai	0	0
	Buddhist	0	0
	Chinese Religions	0	0
	Hindus	0	0
	Jews	0	0
	Muslims	0	0
	Other Indigenous	0	0
	Spiritists	0	0
Uruguay	Bahai	0	0

Continued

Table 2.1b *Continued*

Country	Group	GRD	SRD	Country	Group	GRD	SRD	Country	Group	GRD	SRD
Chile	Bahai	6	0		Jews	0	5		Muslims	2	0
	Jehovah's Witnesses	6	0		Muslims	0	0		Orthodox Christian	2	0
	Jews	6	5		Orthodox Christians	0	0		Protestants	7	0
	Muslims	6	0		Protestants	0	0	Latvia	Jehovah's Witnesses	8	0
	Protestants	4	0		Spiritists	0	0		Jews	1	3
Colombia	Animists	1	0	Venezuela	Bahai	4	0		Muslims	8	0
	Bahai	1	0		Jews	6	9	Lithuania	Jews	1	5

Table 2.1c GRD and SRD in 2014

Country	Group	GRD	SRD	Country	Group	GRD	SRD	Country	Group	GRD	SRD
Christian Majority				Slovak Republic	Jews	1	6	Kyrgyzstan	Other Christians	24	1
Former Soviet					Muslims	12	0	Uzbekistan	Christians	32	1
Lithuania	Muslims	2	0		Orthodox Christians	0	0		Jews	9	0
	Orthodox Christians	1	0		Other Christians	7	0		Shia Muslims	26	0
	Protestants	1	0		Protestants	7	0	*Middle East & North Africa*			
Macedonia	Catholics	4	0	Slovenia	Jews	1	1	Algeria	Catholics	24	4
	Jews	3	0		Muslims	2	1		Jews	23	4
	Muslims	6	1		Orthodox Christians	0	0		Protestants	27	5
	Other Christians	11	0		Protestants	0	0	Egypt	Bahai	27	1
	Protestants	7	0	Ukraine	Catholics	0	1		Christians (Coptic)	23	47
Moldova	Jews	6	5		Jews	1	9	Iran	Jews	14	6
	Muslims	7	7		Muslims	4	1		Bahai	52	21
	Other Christians	12	13		Other Christians	4	7		Christians	35	1
	Protestants	6	0		Protestants	1	0		Jews	13	5

Continued

Table 2.1c *Continued*

Country	Group	GRD	SRD
Montenegro	Catholics	0	0
	Jews	0	0
	Muslims	3	0
	Orthodox (non Mont.)	3	4
Poland	Jews	2	13
	Muslims	1	0
	Orthodox Christian	2	0
	Other Christians	2	0
	Protestants (Lutheran)	2	0
	Spiritists	2	0
Romania	Catholics	9	10
	Jews	5	8
	Muslims	6	0
	Protestants	12	7
Russia	Animists	21	0
	Buddhists	2	0
Sub Saharan Africa			
South Africa	Animists	0	4
	Bahai	0	0
	Buddhists	0	0
	Hindus	0	0
	Jews	1	6
	Muslims	0	2
Muslim-Majority			
Former Soviet			
Azerbaijan	Jews	2	0
	Orthodox Christians	12	1
	Other Christians	16	6
	Sunni Muslims	12	2
Kazakhstan	Catholics	1	0
	Jews	1	1
Morocco	Sunni Muslims	18	2
	Christians	20	4
	Jews	3	4
	Shia Muslims	20	2
Tunisia	Bahai	19	1
	Christians	13	9
	Jews	11	12
Turkey	Alevi	12	0
	All other Christians	16	16
	Jews	8	11
Yemen	Orthodox Christians	12	10
	Christians	14	3
	Hindus	12	0
	Jews	9	13
	Shi'i Muslims	16	6

Catholics	15	4	
Hindus	17	0	
Jews	4	18	
Muslims	12	6	Kosovo
Other Christians	34	17	
Protestants	24	10	
Serbia-Yugoslav. Catholics	3	1	
Jews	3	4	Kyrgyzstan
Muslims	2	0	
Other Christians	12	5	
Protestants	9	0	

Non-Sunni Muslims	32	1	
Orthodox Christians	1	0	
Protestants	32	6	
Catholics	0	1	Kosovo
Jews	0	3	
Orthodox Christians	5	17	
Protestants	2	1	Singapore
Bahai	9	0	
Buddhists	9	0	
Jews	9	0	
Orthodox Christians	9	1	

No Majority or Other Majority			
Bosnia	Catholics	9	14
	Jews	11	3
	Muslims	11	21
	Orthodox	12	13
	Protestants	11	2
Singapore	Christians	0	0
	Hindus	0	0
	Jews	0	0
	Muslims	5	0
	Sikhs	0	0

In all but three countries—Bolivia, Sweden, and South Africa—Jews are subject to levels of GRD that are similar to or lower than other minorities. That is, at least one minority experiences levels of GRD that are similar or higher to those against Jews, but other minorities may experience lower levels. In these three countries, Jews are subject to the highest level of GRD of any religious minority in the country in question. In South Africa, no religious minority other than Jews is subject to GRD. Beginning in 2009, government officials began using openly anti-Semitic rhetoric. For example, In January 2009, Deputy Minister of Foreign Affairs Fatima Hajaig used classic anti-Semitic speech when she remarked at a public rally that "the control of America, just like the control of most Western countries, is in the hands of Jewish money. If the Jewish money controls their country, then you cannot expect anything else."[2] In Bolivia, levels and types of GRD against Jews are similar to those against other religious minorities, other than that the police refuse to investigate incidences of vandalism against Jewish property. In Sweden, levels against Jews and Muslims are similar, but the restrictions on ritual slaughter, which apply to both religions, are in practice more restrictive of kosher than halal slaughter.

Specific Types of GRD

Fox (2015, 2016, 2020) divides GRD into four categories: restrictions on religious practices, restrictions on religious institutions and clergy, restrictions on conversion and proselytizing, and other restrictions. Tables 2.2a and 2.2b show the specific types of GRD present in these 76 countries organized around this framework. While it is not possible to discuss in detail all 35 types or GRD, we address those that are particularly common against Jews and those that we deem important for other reasons.

Before addressing the specific types of GRD, it is important to note that the general patterns in these 35 types of GRD are consistent with the general analysis. In particular, no type of GRD is found more often against Jews than against other religious minorities—measured as a percentage of Jewish minorities which experience a type of discrimination compared to the percentage for other minorities. However, only four types of GRD found in these 76 countries are not present against any Jewish minority: restrictions on materials necessary for religious observance, forced renunciation of faith by recent converts to Judaism, forced conversions away from Judaism, and state surveillance. The first three of these types of GRD are rare, and the latter tends to be applied in particular to minorities considered a security threat, mostly Muslims and religions that governments consider cults. This further confirms that religious minorities in general are singled out for GRD in these countries, and Jews are no exception. However, the

Table 2.2a Restrictions on Religious Practices, Institutions, and Clergy

	Jews		Christians		Muslims		Other	
	1990	2014	1990	2014	1990	2014	1990	2014
Restrictions on religious practices								
Public observance of religion	5.3%	6.6%	15.4%	20.5%	5.8%	11.6%	8.4%	10.8%
Private observance of religion	1.3%	2.6%	9.0%	13.9%	1.4%	2.9%	2.4%	3.6%
Forced observance: religious laws of another group.	3.9%	3.9%	5.7%	5.7%	3.9%	4.3%	8.4%	8.4%
Make/obtain materials necessary for religious rites/customs/ceremonies	0.0%	0.0%	4.9%	5.7%	0.0%	0.0%	0.0%	0.0%
Circumcisions or other rite of passage ceremonies	0.0%	3.9%	0.0%	0.0%	0.0%	4.3%	0.0%	0.0%
Religious dietary laws	6.6%	8.7%	0.0%	0.0%	7.2%	8.7%	0.0%	0.0%
Write/publish/disseminate religious publications	6.6%	6.6%	10.7%	17.2%	7.2%	8.7%	4.8%	6.0%
Import religious publications	5.3%	6.6%	12.3%	14.8%	5.8%	7.2%	2.4%	7.2%
Religious publications for personal use	0.0%	2.6%	4.1%	8.2%	2.9%	2.9%	2.4%	4.8%
Religious laws concerning marriage and divorce	1.3%	1.3%	4.1%	3.3%	2.9%	4.3%	2.4%	2.4%
Religious laws concerning burial	7.9%	10.5%	7.4%	11.5%	14.5%	14.5%	4.8%	7.2%
Religious symbols or clothing	0.0%	1.3%	0.8%	0.8%	8.7%	23.2%	1.2%	1.2%
At least one type	25.0%	30.7%	31.1%	35.2%	26.2%	46.4%	19.3%	25.3%

Continued

Table 2.2a *Continued*

	Jews		Christians		Muslims		Other	
	1990	2014	1990	2014	1990	2014	1990	2014
Restrictions on religious institutions and clergy								
Building/leasing/repairing/maintaining places of worship	13.2%	18.4%	27.9%	37.7%	33.3%	46.4%	7.2%	12.0%
Access to existing places of worship	13.2%	11.8%	24.6%	28.7%	13.0%	15.9%	3.6%	1.2%
Formal religious organizations	5.3%	9.2%	11.5%	19.7%	13.0%	18.8%	4.8%	13.7%
Ordination of and/or access to clergy	3.9%	3.9%	10.7%	7.4%	8.7%	14.5%	2.4%	1.2%
Minority religions (as opposed to all religions) must register	32.9%	36.8%	45.1%	55.7%	42.0%	49.3%	39.9%	36.1%
Minority clergy access to jails	19.7%	18.4%	30.3%	29.5%	27.5%	27.5%	12.0%	14.5%
Minority clergy access to military bases	30.3%	30.3%	36.1%	36.9%	31.9%	34.8%	22.9%	26.5%
Minority clergy access to hospitals and other public facilities	15.8%	14.5%	22.1%	27.0%	24.6%	26.1%	7.2%	8.4%
At least one type	53.9%	56.6%	69.7%	71.3%	66.7%	79.7%	42.2%	44.6%

The percentages in the table represent the percentage of minorities within the given category which experience this type of GRD.

Table 2.2b Restrictions on Conversion, Proselytizing, and Other types of Restrictions

	Jews		Christians		Muslims		Other	
	1990	2014	1990	2014	1990	2014	1990	2014
Restrictions on conversion and proselytizing								
Conversion to minority religions	2.6%	2.6%	4.1%	4.1%	3.9%	1.4%	4.8%	4.8%
Forced renunciation of faith by recent converts to minority religions	0.0%	0.0%	3.3%	1.6%	0.0%	0.0%	1.2%	1.2%
Forced conversions	0.0%	0.0%	1.6%	1.6%	0.0%	1.4%	0.0%	1.2%
Efforts/campaigns to convert members of minority religion (no force)	2.6%	3.9%	4.1%	4.1%	1.4%	2.9%	3.6%	7.2%
Proselytizing by permanent residents to members of the majority religion	11.8%	14.5%	16.4%	26.2%	8.7%	14.5%	4.8%	10.8%
Proselytizing by permanent residents to members of minority religions	7.9%	9.2%	14.8%	20.5%	8.7%	13.0%	4.8%	9.6%
At least one type	17.1%	19.7%	21.3%	28.7%	23.0%	18.8%	8.4%	16.9%
Other restrictions								
Religious schools/education	11.8%	15.8%	18.9%	27.0%	14.5%	21.7%	9.6%	12.0%
Mandatory education in the majority religion	11.8%	15.8%	10.7%	17.2%	11.6%	15.9%	14.5%	14.5%
Arrest/detention/harassment other than for proselytizing	0.0%	1.3%	8.2%	15.6%	11.6%	21.7%	2.4%	2.4%

Continued

Table 2.2b *Continued*

	Jews		Christians		Muslims		Other	
	1990	2014	1990	2014	1990	2014	1990	2014
Failure to protect rel. minorities against violence or punish perpetrators	3.9%	7.6%	13.1%	15.6%	5.8%	8.7%	1.2%	2.4%
State surveillance of religious activities	0.0%	1.3%	5.7%	12.3%	5.8%	26.1%	3.6%	3.6%
Child custody granted on basis of religion	6.6%	6.6%	6.6%	7.4%	1.4%	1.4%	5.1%	5.4%
Declaration of some minority religions as dangerous or extremist sects	0.0%	0.0%	4.9%	9.8%	0.0%	2.9%	2.4%	3.6%
Anti-religious propaganda in official/semi-official government publications	10.5%	9.2%	14.8%	13.9%	7.2%	8.7%	2.4%	2.4%
Other forms of governmental religious discrimination	10.5%	11.8%	13.9%	14.8%	13.0%	18.8%	4.8%	8.4%
At least one type	32.9%	42.1%	40.2%	49.2%	37.7%	62.3%	21.7%	26.5%
At least one type for all religious discrimination	67.1%	76.3%	74.6%	77.0%	75.4%	91.3%	48.2%	57.8%

The percentages in the table represent the percentage of minorities within the given category which experience this type of GRD.

extent to which Jews are singled out for GRD is not greater than for other religious minorities.

Restrictions on Religious Practices

Restrictions on religious practices are not particularly common compared to other types, with only 23 (30.7%) Jewish minorities experiencing at least one type. Yet, when they exist, they are very significant forms of GRD. The issues of *infant circumcision* and *ritual slaughter* are important issues. Both are central practices to the Jewish faith. Both are also practices in Islam, which may explain an element of the rising restrictions on these two practices. Several Western European countries—Denmark, Germany, Iceland, Norway, Sweden, Switzerland, and as of 2019, Belgium—limit ritual slaughter. The stated justification for this type of restriction is that it is considered cruel to the animals. Accordingly, the laws of these countries require that animals be stunned before slaughter in a manner that makes ritual slaughter impossible.

Yet, ritual slaughter is a non-optional requirement for all meat that Jews and Muslims eat. It is what makes meat kosher for Jews and halal for Muslims. Many countries have this type of stunning requirement but make exceptions for ritual slaughter, recognizing that religious beliefs and the right to religious freedom are a reasonable justification for this type of exception. These include Austria, Cyprus, France, Luxembourg, the Netherlands, and Spain. Denmark, Germany, Iceland, Norway, Sweden, Switzerland, and Belgium make no such exception. However, they do allow kosher and halal meat to be imported. Incidentally, hunting, which is arguably far crueler to animals than ritual slaughter, is legal and quite popular in Sweden, with an estimated 300,000 active hunters.[3]

An event in Lower Austria, one of Austria's nine states, provides an interesting and ominous example of this growing trend. In July 2018, the cabinet minister in charge of animal welfare proposed allowing kosher slaughter but only if those allowed to buy the meat are restricted to Orthodox Jews, who would require a permit to purchase the meat. Minister Waldhäusl "claimed the proposal was 'from the point of view of animal welfare' and that religious rites slaughter should 'generally be rejected.'"[4] The proposal lost momentum when it was pointed out that registering and licensing Orthodox Jews has some negative historical connotations.

Yet this is a growing movement. At least some of its advocates genuinely believe they are pursuing a moral agenda and clearly believe that their morality should trump the religious beliefs in question. As one advocate puts it, "they want to keep living in the Middle Ages and continue to slaughter without stunning—a technique that did not exist back then—without answering to the law. . . . Well I'm sorry, in Belgium the law is above religion, and that will stay like that."[5]

There is also a similar and growing international movement against infant male circumcision. Circumcision at the age of eight days (or as soon thereafter when the child is able to medically tolerate the procedure) is a foundational ritual for Jews and represents the covenant between God and the Jews dating back to the time of Abraham. However, many consider this an unnecessary and barbaric ritual which unfairly undermines the bodily integrity of the child.

This movement is having a growing impact, thus far primarily in Nordic countries. In 2001 Sweden began regulating male circumcision. Circumcision of male infants may be performed only by a licensed doctor, or in the presence of a licensed doctor by a person certified by the National Board of Health and Welfare (NBHW). The NBHW has certified mohels (persons trained to perform the Jewish ritual of circumcision) to perform circumcisions in the presence of an anesthesiologist or other medical doctor.[6] Norway passed a similar law in 2014,[7] and in 2005 Denmark's government passed a regulation which interpreted exiting law in a manner to create a similar requirement.[8] Due to these restrictions, infant circumcisions in these countries usually take place in medical clinics rather than in synagogues or other religious settings, detracting from the solemnity of the ritual.

This issue made headlines in Germany in June 2012 when a German court ruled that the Jewish and Muslim practice of circumcision inflicts "grievous bodily harm" on young boys. The court ruled that "the fundamental right of the child to bodily integrity outweighed the fundamental rights of the parents" to perform the religious ritual of circumcision. While this ruling technically had a limited impact, as it only applied to a single Muslim boy in a single jurisdiction, it raised fears of a ban in the entire country. Doctors and hospitals across Germany suspended the procedure until Germany's Lower house passed a law allowing circumcision.[9]

Advocacy groups and politicians in Denmark, Finland, Norway, Sweden, and Iceland have called for bans on infant male circumcision. For example, in 2020 a proposed law in Denmark sought to ban all non-medically necessary male circumcisions for anyone under the age of 18. A broad spectrum of political patties supported the law, including Socialistisk Folkeparti, Enhedslisten, Nye Borgerlige, Alternativet, Liberal Alliance, and Dansk Folkeparti. The country's prime minister prevented a vote on the law. "PM Mette Frederiksen explained that Denmark made a pledge to its Jewish community after WWII to be fully inclusive of them, and that banning the ritual circumcision of boys would break that promise."[10]

While many of these advocates are likely motivated by sincere moral beliefs, a morality based primarily on modern secular values, there is also a different undercurrent. Far-right anti-immigrant groups also vocally support bans on infant circumcision. For example, "far-right groups in Norway and elsewhere in Scandinavia, . . . oppose [infant circumcision] on the grounds that they regard it as a foreign element in Nordic societies, which they say are under threat from immigration from Muslim countries."[11]

Thus the motivations for this type of restriction on Jewish rituals are complex. They are intertwined with emerging secular values and ideology, as well as anti-Muslim and anti-immigrant sentiment. However, it is likely that at least some of the advocates of these restrictions are motivated by a desire to target Jews.

The most common restriction on religious practices against Jews is *interference with Jewish burial rituals*, which is present in eight countries. It manifests in several different ways. In some cases it is an issue of control over burials by the majority religious institutions. For example, in Denmark the Evangelical Lutheran Church, the state religion, controls nearly all cemeteries, and even in non-Church cemeteries it is the official burial authority. Similarly, Church of Sweden parishes, despite the religion's disestablishment in 2000, are the principals for almost all funeral activities in the country.[12] While this type of control has a limited impact in Denmark and Sweden, it can be significant in other places. For example, in Kyrgyzstan religious funerals are under the authority of local municipalities. In some municipalities local authorities allow imams to control state-owned cemeteries, and minority religions can be denied permission to perform funerals according to their traditions. In some cases, family members were told to convert to Islam before a funeral would be conducted, or Islamic funerals were conducted without the family's permission.[13]

In some cases this involves disturbing or exhuming existing graves. For example, in Belarus there were several incidents of Jewish gravesites being disturbed by construction projects and Jewish graves being exhumed in order to make room for non-Jewish graves. In Greece all graves are exhumed after three years which is a violation of both Jewish and Muslim law. Similarly, according to Croatian law, heirless graves can be disinterred after 30 years. The Jewish community made an agreement with cemeteries in Zagreb and several smaller cities not to sell unmaintained plots in Jewish cemeteries or exhume bodies from them. Nevertheless, about 50 old Jewish graves were leveled in the Karlovac cemetery since 2000, despite an agreement with the local Jewish community not to do so.[14]

In some cases the interference is with the burial itself. In the Slovak republic the law does not allow burial until after 48 hours after death, which violates a requirement in both Judaism and Islam for early burial. As noted earlier, in Cyprus's Jewish cemetery there is no water source, which is essential to Jewish burial and mourning rituals.

While general *restrictions on the public or private observance of Judaism* are rare, where they do exist they are usually targeted against religious minorities in general, rather than just Jews. For example, in Algeria, Ordinance 06-03 which came into effect in 2008 limits worship by all non-Muslim groups to registered houses of worship. Religious services held in unapproved locations, public or private, may be shut down. Similarly, Belarus's 2002 *Law on Freedom of Conscience and Religious Organizations* prohibits public religious observance for unregistered groups, requires registered groups to obtain permission for public religious events, and limits where registered religious groups may hold religious events.

Forced observance of the religious laws or ceremonies of the majority group is even rarer and is also generally not targeted specifically at Jews. For example, in Iran all religious minorities must observe Islamic dress codes in public and may not eat in public on Ramadan. In Peru, members of the armed forces and the police, as well as relatives and civilian coworkers, are obligated to participate in Catholic services. *Restrictions on religious publications and the wearing of religious symbols or clothing*, when present against Jews, similarly apply to multiple minorities.

Restrictions on Religious Institutions and Clergy

Restrictions on religious institutions and clergy are more common against Jewish minorities than are restrictions on religious practices, with 43 (56.6%) Jewish minorities experiencing this category of restriction. Few of these restrictions are targeted specifically against Jews and tend to apply to multiple minorities. Thus, for the most part, this type of GRD is motivated by policies of preferring the majority religion or restricting all or most minority religions. Nevertheless, they can result in significant restrictions on Jewish religious institutions and clergy.

The most common form of GRD in this category against Jewish minorities is *restrictions on registration*. In most cases this is due to a general requirement to register that is not applied to the majority religion, and it is usually a bureaucratic hurdle that Jewish organizations are able to jump. Thus, it is rarely targeted specifically at Jews. For example, in Chile, under the 1999 *Religious Entities Act*, religious groups may become "juridical persons." To do so, they register with the Ministry of Justice. Registration of religious groups is optional, but necessary to obtain the benefits of the law, such as tax exemptions. While nearly all religions which sought to do so succeeded in registering, the Catholic Church was automatically registered under this law[15] (Thurston, 2000).

In other countries, such as Azerbaijan, registration is often denied and can have consequences. Unregistered groups in Azerbaijan may be fined for administrative violations or may have their activities monitored or restricted.

Individuals involved in religious activities with unregistered groups (including those which applied for registration and were denied or are in process) may be arrested and/or fined. However, this law seems to be targeted mostly at Muslim groups which the government considerers radicals and does not heavily influence Jews.[16] While Tunisia also mostly denies registration to Islamic organizations it considers unacceptable, the Association of the Jewish Community of Tunis is not officially registered, as the government never granted the group's 1999 registration request, but the group is allowed to operate for religious and charitable purposes. Nevertheless, this inability to register can be used by the government at any time to shut down or otherwise harass the organization. This use of registration denial is a common tactic by autocratic governments to restrict religious minorities while claiming to promote religious freedom (Sarkissian, 2015).

While common, *restrictions on access of clergy to jails, hospitals, and military bases* are similarly an issue not specifically targeted at Jewish minorities. In most cases it is due to preference or exclusivity being given to clergy from the majority religion. For example, in Armenia, priests from the Armenian Apostolic Church are given permanent chaplain positions in the military, hospitals, and prisons, but upon request clergy from minority religions are usually made available. This means that access is available but more limited. Georgia is a bit stricter. Georgian Orthodox priests are paid chaplains in the military, hospitals, and prisons. No other religions may have chaplaincies in state institutions, but in 2010 the minister of Correction and Legal Assistance in Georgia signed an agreement allowing prisoners and detainees affiliated with registered minority religions to meet with representatives of their religion on request. Thus in these cases chaplains are available, but Jews and other minority religions are required to jump through extra hurdles to see them. In a few countries like Latvia and Russia, Jewish chaplains are allowed access similar to those of the majority religion, while chaplains from many other religions are not.

Restrictions on building and maintaining places of worship follow a similar pattern. For example, in Tunisia, all religious minorities are rarely allowed to build new places of worship. In Belarus, permits for religious buildings for religious minorities can be delayed for many years or ignored. Refusals are common and arbitrary. Local government officials may deny, cancel, or refuse to extend leases at properties where religious groups conduct services, even for registered groups. However, there are some cases of specific targeting of synagogues. In the 1990s, all the synagogues in Algeria were closed for security reasons. In 2009, when the Jewish community was registered, it was given permission to reopen 25 synagogues, although as of 2014 none had been officially opened for use.

Restrictions on Conversion and Proselytizing

This type of GRD includes restrictions on proselytizing and conversion and is presented in Table 2.2b. While these types of GRD are technically present against a small proportion of Jewish minorities, we know of no examples of cases where it is targeted specifically against Jews. In most cases these are general laws that happen to also apply to Jews and have little impact. This is because Jews rarely seek converts. In fact, under Orthodox Jewish tradition, converts are actively discouraged, but converts are usually accepted if this discouragement fails to dissuade them. Non-Orthodox brands of Judaism are less reluctant to accept converts but are also less common outside of the United States.

Other Types of Restrictions

The "other" category for GRD, which is presented in Table 2.2b, includes those forms of GRD that do not fit into the previous three categories. While many of these types of restrictions follow the general pattern of GRD that restricts Jews in the context of restrictions on a number of religious minorities, some of these forms of GRD are more specific to Jews.

Restrictions on religious education and *mandatory education in the majority religion* fit the pattern of occurring to Jews in the context of more general discrimination. For example, in Macedonia, most religious education is restricted. While registered religious groups are permitted to organize private religious education at all levels except for primary education, the religious groups must submit the curriculum to the state for approval. Religious school instructors must be Macedonian citizens, but instruction may be conducted by foreign citizens in exceptional circumstances. In 2003, Armenia began teaching mandatory courses in the history of the Armenian Apostolic Church in public schools. The church has considerable influence over the syllabi, textbooks, and teachers for the course.

Government-sponsored anti-Jewish propaganda, while dropping during the study period, was still present in seven countries covered in this study in 2014. Most instances of this kind of GRD are specific to Jews. This category was not coded for Jews if the rhetoric and propaganda were exclusively anti-Israel; there needed to be an additional anti-Jewish element.

In an extreme example, Iran's government sanctions and propagates anti-Semitic propaganda involving official statements, media outlets, publications, and books. Similarly, Turkey's leader Erdogan and senior government officials repeatedly and publicly blame problems in the country, including anti-government protests, on "shadowy" international groups, including an "international Jewish conspiracy," the "Jewish Diaspora," and "the Rothschilds." These statements by senior political leaders are often accompanied by anti-Semitic reports and commentaries in pro-government media outlets. In 2013 pro-government TV channels aired a virulently anti-Semitic documentary, "Mastermind," which was referred to as a sequel to the *Protocols of the Elders of Zion*.[17]

In Venezuela, government-sponsored media outlets regularly publish anti-Jewish caricatures and political cartoons. For example, in 2010 the government-affiliated website Aporrea.com published an article recommending the anti-Semitic book *Protocols of the Elders of Zion*. In 2013, on a government-owned television station, National Assembly Deputy Jesus Cepeda commented on the "great Jewish tentacles that drive international economics."[18] Greece's anti-Jewish propaganda is more ecumenical. Some of the textbooks used in its public school religion classes include negative references to Catholicism, Judaism, and other minority religions.[19]

Failure to protect religious minorities: The state has an obligation to protect all its citizens. While, as is described later in this chapter, SRD is common against Jews, in five countries, authorities did not live up to this obligation in cases of significant SRD against Jews. In four of these countries this failure was not specific to Jews. In Bosnia the government generally failed to investigate claims of harassment and vandalism against most minorities. Bulgarian authorities rarely investigate a wide range of hate crimes against Jews and Muslims. The same is true for Greece in cases of hate crimes against most minority religions. Tunisian authorities rarely investigate crimes against Jews, Christians, and Sufis, and offenders who are caught are rarely prosecuted. In Bolivia, however, where multiple incidents of vandalism went uninvestigated by police, this is specific to Jews.

Overall, GRD is common against Jews, but it is present, on average, at lower levels than are present against Christian and Muslim minorities. Much of the GRD against Jews is not specific to Jewish minorities in that at least some other minorities experience the same types of GRD and much of it is targeted at religious minorities in general rather than Jews specifically. However, there are numerous instances of GRD that is targeted at Jews or that in some other fashion manifests against Jews in a manner that is unique.

Societal Religious Discrimination

The RASM3 data set defines societal religious discrimination (SRD) as societal actions taken against religious minorities by members of a country's religious majority who do not represent the government (Fox, 2020). The variable used to measure SRD includes 27 types of acts that members of the majority might take against a religious minority, including acts in the following categories: economic discrimination, speech acts, nonviolent property crimes, nonviolent harassment, violence, and other types of acts. We discuss these 27 types of SRD in detail later in this chapter. All of them are measured based on severity on a scale of 0 to 2, resulting in a composite scale that runs from 0 to 54, though SRD against no minority reaches 54.

In addition to the nature of the perpetrator, SRD is unlike GRD because nearly all of the 27 acts included in the measure could be applied to any type of minority, such as ethnic minorities or the LGBTQ community. In contrast, GRD focuses specifically on government restrictions on religious practices and institutions. Thus, while vandalism, harassment, and violent attacks against these other types of minorities occur all too often, restricting their right to practice their religion, for example, is far less likely to be targeted against them unless they also happen to constitute a religious minority. Thus what makes SRD religious is not the type of action taken, but rather the group against which the action is directed.

It is important to emphasize that SRD, as defined here, refers only to real-world actions taken against religious minorities. Most previous studies focused on societal attitudes rather than actions (e.g., Grim & Finke, 2012; Zick et al., 2011) Thus the forms of discrimination we discuss are acts, such as vandalism and violence.

As a general note, RASM3 codes violence against religious minorities but does not specifically code the motivation. Based on statements made and actions taken by the perpetrators of SRD against Jews, a significant proportion is motivated by perceived injustices perpetrated by the state of Israel. However, in most cases, there is no clear evidence of a connection between Israel and SRD. In fact, in many cases the identities of the perpetrators, much less their motivation, are unclear. Given the nature of the data, it is not possible to discern exactly what proportion of SRD against Jews is motivated by the Israel factor. However, most definitions of anti-Semitism state that holding all Jews, especially Jews living outside of Israel, responsible for actions taken by Israel, much less the commission of violence against Jews outside of Israel for this reason, is anti-Semitism. To place this in context, holding Jews living in the United States responsible for the behavior of the state of Israel is logically similar to holding an ethnic Russian living in the United States responsible for the actions of Russia.

Regardless of all of this, these 27 types of SRD are prima facie actions of discrimination, whatever the motivation. For this reason, all acts of SRD are coded based on the nature and severity of the act, not its motivation. One of the goals of this study is to determine whether and to what extent grievances against Israel can explain cross-country levels of discrimination against Jews; this issue is not directly addressed in this chapter, but rather is examined in Chapter 4.

General Patterns of SRD

Patterns of SRD differ between Christian-majority and Muslim-majority states. Figure 2.3 shows the patterns of SRD against Jews, Muslims, Christians, and other religious minorities in Christian-majority states. In these countries, Jews experience the highest average levels of SRD of any religious minority. As shown in Tables 2.1a, 2.1b, and 2.1c, this is a consistent finding. Of the 62 Christian-majority countries in this study, Jews experience the highest levels of SRD in 28 and tie for the highest levels in an additional four. Six countries have no SRD at all. This leaves 24 countries where at least one minority experiences levels of SRD higher than do Jews.

As shown in Figure 2.4, the pattern is quite different in the 12 Muslim-majority countries included in this study. In these countries, Christian minorities experience the highest levels of SRD, but Jews experience more SRD than Muslim and "other" minorities. However, Jews do experience the highest levels of SRD in Morocco, Tunisia, and Yemen. Interestingly, in absolute terms, mean

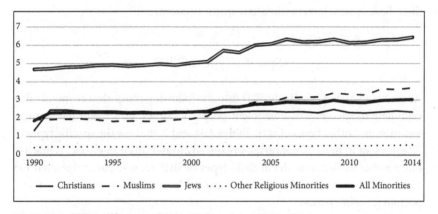

Figure 2.3 SRD in Christian-Majority Countries, 1990–2014.
Significance (t-test) of increase since 1990 for all cases <.05 in 1993–1994, <.001 in 2002–2014.
Significance (t-test) of increase since 1990 for Muslims <.01 in 2002–2003, <.001 in 2004–2014.
Significance (t-test) of increase since 1990 for Jews <.05 in 1994–1995, 1998–1999, <.01 in 2000–2003, <.001 in 2004–2014.
Significance (t-test) of increase since 1990 for "other" minorities <.05 in 2005, 2010, 2012, <.01 in 2013.
Significance (t-test) between Jews and all other minorities <.001 in 1990–2014.
Significance (t-test) between "other" minorities and all other minorities <.001 in 1990–2014.

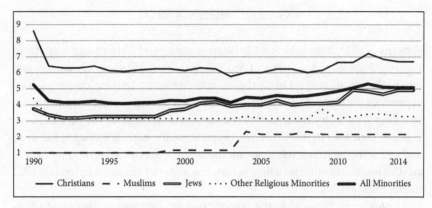

Figure 2.4 SRD in Muslim-Majority Countries, 1990–2014.
Significance (t-test) of change since 1990 for all cases <.05 in 2004, 2007–2009, <.01
in 2010–2014.
Significance (t-test) of change since 1990 for Jews <.05 in 2006, 2011, 2014.

levels of SRD against Jews in these Muslim-majority countries are slightly lower
than those against Jews in Christian-majority countries.

Specific Types of SRD

As we noted earlier, we divide SRD into the following categories: economic discrimination, speech acts, nonviolent property crimes, nonviolent harassment,
violence, and other types of acts. Tables 2.3a and 2.3b show the specific types of
SRD present in these 76 countries, organized around this framework. While it is
not possible to discuss in detail all 27 types of SRD, we give particular attention
to those that are particularly common against Jews and those that we deem important for other reasons.

Unlike the analyses up to this point, these tables show the levels of SRD present in 1990 and 2014, as well as the proportion of minorities which experienced
SRD at any point between 1990 and 2014. This is because patterns of SRD and
GRD differ in an important way. GRD is consistent over time. That is, if GRD is
present in one year, it is most likely to be present in the next one. While changes
in GRD occur often, once they do, the new status quo tends to remain consistent
over time. In contrast, SRD is often sporadic, present in some years but not
others. This is likely because SRD is the sum of a number of mostly spontaneous
but sometimes planned acts by societal actors, but GRD tends to be the result of
government policy. For this reason, this discussion and the information in these
tables show if SRD was present at any time between 1990 and 2014.

Table 2.3a Economic Discrimination, Speech Acts, Nonviolent Attacks on Property, and Nonviolent Harassment

	All Cases			Discrimination Any Time between 1990 and 2014			
				Controlling for Minority Religion			
	1990	2014	Any time 1990–2014	Jews	Christians	Muslims	Other
Economic discrimination							
In the workplace	9.7%	13.4%	16.6%	7.9%	14.8%	39.1%	8.4%
Boycott of business/denial of access to businesses, stores, etc.	1.1%	2.6%	4.3%	6.6%	4.1%	4.3%	2.4%
Other economic discrimination	1.7%	2.3%	3.7%	3.9%	3.3%	5.8%	2.4%
At least one type	11.1%	15.4%	20.3%	17.1%	18.0%	40.6%	9.6%
Speech acts							
Anti-minority propaganda/statements/articles in the media	19.7%	26.6%	31.4%	72.4%	20.5%	34.8%	7.2%
Anti-minority rhetoric by majority religion's clergy	8.6%	10.0%	12.6%	15.2%	21.3%	5.8%	2.4%
Anti-minority rhetoric in pol. campaigns or by pol. parties	10.9%	14.9%	18.6%	40.8%	9.8%	30.4%	1.2%
Dissemination of anti-minority publications	8.0%	10.0%	18.3%	47.4%	9.8%	20.3%	2.4%
At least one type	25.7%	33.7%	42.0%	77.6%	31.1%	60.9%	9.6%
Nonviolent attacks on property							
Vandalism of religious property (places of worship, community centers, schools, cemeteries)	16.6%	26.3%	37.3%	72.4%	32.0%	47.8%	6.0%

Continued

Table 2.3a *Continued*

	All Cases			Discrimination Any Time between 1990 and 2014			
				Controlling for Minority Religion			
	1990	2014	Any time 1990–2014	Jews	Christians	Muslims	Other
Vandalism of other minority property	6.3%	6.6%	14.3%	28.9%	9.0%	18.8%	4.8%
Anti-religious graffiti	12.0%	17.4%	23.4%	60.5%	12.3%	27.5%	2.4%
At least one type	20.3%	27.7%	40.6%	76.3%	34.4%	50.7%	8.4%
Nonviolent harassment							
Nonviolent harassment of clergy	2.3%	2.6%	4.9%	6.6%	6.6%	5.8%	0.0%
Nonviolent harassment of proselytizers or missionaries	2.9%	3.1%	3.7%	1.3%	9.0%	1.4%	0.0%
Nonviolent harassment of converts away from the majority religion	4.9%	4.9%	5.4%	3.9%	9.8%	4.3%	1.2%
Nonviolent harassment of other members of religious minorities	15.7%	22.0%	27.4%	57.9%	20.5%	33.3%	4.8%
Expulsion or harassment so severe that it leads to a significant number of minority members leaving a town or region	3.4%	3.7%	4.9%	7.9%	5.7%	2.9%	2.4%
Organized demonstrations and public protests against religious minorities	2.0%	3.4%	11.1%	25.0%	9.0%	11.6%	1.2%
At least one type	22.3%	27.7%	34.9%	63.2%	31.1%	43.5%	7.2%

Before addressing the specific types of SRD, it is important to note that the general patterns in these 27 types of SRD are consistent with the general analysis. In particular, 17 of these types of SRD are most common against Jews. Only one—discrimination in the workplace—is least common against Jews.

These acts against religious minorities are discriminatory for at least four reasons. First, some of them are acts of classic discrimination, as in the case of the items in the economic discrimination category, which includes denial of jobs or access to places of business. Second, "social restrictions on religion are important . . . because the enforcement of any type of legal restrictions relies on social cooperation" (Grim & Finke, 2012: 9) Third, many equate violence and harassment with discrimination (e.g., Rafferty, 2013; Sanders-Phillips, 2009). Fourth, one of the outcomes of high levels of societal discrimination is a limitation on the ability of members of the targeted minority to maintain religious institutions and practice their religion. Some of the acts cause damage to the institutions themselves. Others make it more difficult for individuals to go about their daily lives. Also, many of them intentionally cause fear, which can restrict public and even private behavior.

Economic Discrimination

Economic discrimination, as shown in Table 2.3a, is one of the few categories of SRD which is not disproportionally present against Jews. In many of the countries where *discrimination in the workplace is recorded*—such as Algeria, Iran, the Netherlands, and Portugal—this was due to general discrimination against members of minority religions. For example, in the Netherlands, employers could refuse to hire workers who do not comply with company policies, such as mandatory attire or shaking hands, for religious reasons. This, in practice, applied primarily to religious Jews and Muslims.

The *boycotting of businesses or denial of service in businesses* was rare overall, but most common against Jews. Nevertheless, these incidents are mostly isolated occurrences. In Belgium there are sporadic reports of Jews being banned from restaurants. For example, a café in Liege posted a sign which read: "Dogs are allowed in this establishment but Jews are not under any circumstances." In a similar incident in the Turkish city of Eskisehir, in 2009 some businesses posted notices to prevent "Jews, Armenians, and dogs" from entering. In a reaction to the 2014 Gaza-Israel war, British Member of Parliament George Galloway declared his city of Bradford in northern England "Israeli Free."[20] Also in the United Kingdom, in 2014 two schoolboys were refused entry to a well-known sports chain by the security guard with the words: "No Jews, no Jews."

The *other economic discrimination* category is also not very common. Against Jews, there were only three instances recorded. In Yemen, traditional attitudes among Muslims restrict where Jews may live and work. In 2009, the owner of a bike shop in Iceland's capital had a sign posted outside his door that read: "No Jews Wanted."[21] In Argentina a judge ruled that a landlord may refuse to rent to Jews because of the landlord's fear of a possible terrorist attack.

Overall, 13 Jewish minorities experienced some form of societal economic discrimination between 1990 and 2014. Proportionally this was slightly lower than Christian minorities and less than half as often as Muslim minorities.

Speech Acts

The RASM3 data set defines speech acts as anti-minority speech, propaganda, rhetoric, or statements by (1) the mainstream non-government media, (2) clergy of the majority religion, and (3) political parties (in some manner that is not directly connected to government office holders such as occurring in election campaigns), and (4) the dissemination of anti-minority publications. Thus, this includes only public speech acts. Private speech acts where individuals express their views in private are not included in these measures. These variables represent statements or publications that are consciously intended to be public and are directed at the public. For practical reasons, measuring private statements is not possible. In addition, public speech acts are qualitatively different from private ones. They demonstrate that people, particularly public figures, feel that it is appropriate and safe to publicly denigrate a minority religion.

As shown in Table 2.3a, three of the four types of speech acts—all of them other than speech acts by the majority religion's clergy—are most common against Jews. The most common, overall, against Jews is *anti-Jewish content in the media*. It is over twice as common as content against Muslims who experience the second highest levels of this type of speech act. Much of this involves conspiracy theories of Jewish power and control. For example, in August 2014 a well-known Québec media personality Gilles Proulx expressed anti-Semitic opinions in his newspaper column and on Montreal's Radio X. He accused Jewish diasporas of taking "economic control" and "manipulating governments" across the world.[22] In the Czech Republic during the 1990s, police confirmed the existence of over 20 underground magazines with small circulations propagating fascism, racism, and anti-Semitism. As is the case in most countries, these forums migrated to the internet.[23]

In Greece, anti-Semitism in the media is so endemic that a Simon Wiesenthal Center report states that the Greek media have numerous "newspaper caricatures using Holocaust imagery to Nazify the Jews," "media articles attacking Jews and Judaism as responsible for all the ills of Greece, in the language of The Protocols of the Elders of Zion," as well as content which vilifies the Jewish faith and questions "the loyalty of Greek citizens of Jewish ancestry and identity."[24]

Anti-Jewish rhetoric by the clergy, as noted earlier, is the least common form of speech act against Jews. However, public incidents of public anti-Jewish rhetoric by clergy occurred in 12 countries. In some cases the incidents were isolated. For example, Cardinal George Pell, archbishop of Sydney, in a public debate with Richard Dawkins in 2012 called Jews intellectually and morally inferior and "seemed to suggest the Germans had suffered more than the Jews during the Holocaust." He later apologized for his remarks.[25] Father Tadeusz Rydzyk runs the Radio Maryja station in Poland, where he regularly makes on-air anti-Semitic comments, including calling Jews greedy and accusing the government and various politicians of being in the Jews' pockets.[26] In other places it is more widespread. In Egypt, imams commonly used anti-Semitic rhetoric in sermons. Also, members of the Muslim Brotherhood regularly speak against Jews and Zionists. In Belarus, the Belarusian Orthodox Church distributes anti-Semitic literature through its bookstores. These publications include accusations that Christian blood is used in kosher food.

In 31 countries there are instances of *politicians and political parties engaging in anti-Jewish speech acts*. In Europe, this is particularly common in right-wing nationalist and populist parties. For example, in Hungary, the Jobbik Party, which has consistently been the second- or third-largest party in Parliament, often uses anti-Semitic rhetoric and publishes anti-Semitic articles in its official publication. In one incident in 2012, a Jobbik member of parliament called for a list of government officials of Jewish origin, stating they were a threat to the nation.[27] Bulgaria's nationalist Ataka Party, which won 7% of the vote in the 2013 national election, uses anti-Semitic rhetoric in its political campaigns, and its members wear swastikas and use Nazi salutes.[28] This type of rhetoric is particularly common in Russia. For example, in 2005, 20 nationalist and community legislators wrote a letter demanding that Jewish organizations be investigated and possibly outlawed for "fomenting ethnic hatred and stimulating anti-Semitism themselves." The letter blamed Jews for carrying out ritual killings, for collapsing the Soviet Union, and for controlling Russian and international capital.[29] While serving in Russia's Duma, Nikolay Kurianovich initiated and publicized a "list of the enemies of the Russian people," which mostly featured Jewish names. Some of his assistants were expelled from the Duma chambers for wearing swastika armbands. At the 13th Congress of the Communist Party of the Russian Federation, party leader Gennadiy Zyuganov spoke about "Jewish domination" in Russia in a public address.

This type of rhetoric is also becoming more common in left-wing political parties. In Chapter 6 we discuss the case of Britain's Labour Party under Jeremy Corbyn.

Anti-Jewish publications were distributed in 36 of the countries in this study. In the United States, protections for freedom of speech allow anti-Semitic literature of all kinds to be distributed. Some of it is distributed worldwide. For example, "the Finnish hypermarket chain Prisma, with 64 stores nationwide, promotes the book 'Jewish Domination' by American racist and anti-Semite David Duke. Its website describes the book as 'challenging,' and asks the reader to 'set aside any preconceptions they may have in order to better weigh the book's ideas and evidence.'"[30] More classic anti-Semitic literature, such as the *Protocols of the Elders of Zion*, can be found in bookstores in multiple countries.

Nonviolent Attacks on Property

Nonviolent attacks on property are the third type of SRD examined here and are shown in Table 2.3a. These include *vandalism of religious property and other property owned by a religious minority*, and *anti-minority graffiti*. This category does not include arson and bombings because they have the potential to harm and kill. Accordingly, RASM3 includes arson and bombings in the violent attacks category.

While vandalism and graffiti are public acts, they are unlike speech acts in at least three ways. First, perpetrators of these acts can remain anonymous. Because of this, the RASM3 data assumes all property attacks were perpetrated by members of the majority religion unless there is evidence to the contrary. Second, while acts like graffiti can contain words, it is nevertheless a physical act that causes physical damage and is usually intended to cause fear. While this threat is not always explicit, these acts can be perceived as a threat to engage in violence and are arguably a short step from escalating to violence. Third, hate speech is banned in many countries, but this type of law is not always enforced. In contrast, graffiti and vandalism are usually criminal acts, and most countries tend to enforce these laws. However, levels of effort and success at catching and prosecuting perpetrators of vandalism and graffiti vary.

All three categories of nonviolent attacks on property are more common against Jews than against other religious minorities. All three of them are common in the United States. There are multiple incidents per year where anti-Jewish graffiti is painted or drawn in various locations such as synagogues, Jewish schools, cemeteries, other Jewish institutions, Jewish homes, and other locations. Graffiti incidents at non-Jewish schools and universities are also common. There are also multiple incidents per year where most of these types of sites were vandalized, usually by breaking windows or turning over gravestones. The most common graffiti is swastikas or Nazi phrases such as "Heil Hitler" or "Sieg Heil." Graffiti incidents also include phrases like "Jew rats," "fuck Jews," "I hate Jews," "no Jews allowed," "kill the Jews," "you will not replace us," and "white power," among others.[31] Canada has hundreds of hate crimes against Jews each year. According to police statistics, about 85% of these anti-Jewish hate crimes are graffiti and vandalism.[32]

What is perhaps most interesting about this category is where incidents of vandalism or graffiti did not occur. The only Western or European countries where it did not occur against Jews were Andorra, Iceland, Kosovo, Luxembourg, Malta, and Montenegro, all small countries with small Jewish populations. Among these countries, only Kosovo has a population of over one million (1,823,149 in 2014). In fact, 9 of the 18 countries with no such incidents had populations of under one million. In contrast, among the countries where these incidents occurred, only Liechtenstein has a population of under one million. This indicates that it is possible that SRD against Jews may, in general, be less common in countries with smaller populations. We examine this proposition in later chapters.

Nonviolent Harassment

Nonviolent harassment, the fourth kind of SRD included in the RASM3 data set, is presented in Table 2.3b. RASM3 defines nonviolent harassment as acts of harassment and persecution taken against individuals and groups that fall short of violence and do not constitute an overt threat of violence. This includes harassment of (1) clergy, (2) proselytizers and missionaries, (3) converts away from the majority religion, and (4) other members of the minority religion, as well as (5) expulsion or harassment so severe that it causes minority members to leave the area or country and (6) mass nonviolent demonstrations and protests against religious minorities.

Four of the six types of nonviolent harassment are most common against Jews. Those that are not most common—*harassment of proselytizers, missionaries, and converts*—are likely more common against other minorities, particularly Christians, because Jews rarely proselytize, or send missionaries or seek converts. Thus, there is less opportunity for these types of harassment to occur.

Harassment of clergy is uncommon for all minorities discussed here. However, *general harassment of minorities* is more common. This is likely because unless clergy are specifically targeted for harassment, targets of opportunity are far more likely to be general members of a minority. In the United States there are multiple reports of harassment of Jewish children in non-Jewish schools across the country in any given year.[33] This is common worldwide. A particularly notorious incident in Sydney, Australia, occurred in 2014 when a gang of youths traumatized Jewish kids on a school bus, using anti-Semitic slurs and threatening to slit their throats. Six minors were arrested after the incident.[34] In many European countries, including Belgium, France, Germany, and Sweden, Jews, especially schoolchildren coming home from school, avoid wearing overt religious symbols such as kippahs or stars of David in order to avoid harassment. For example, "the Chief Rabbi of Brussels, Albert Guigui, no longer wears a kippa in public for fear of violence. In 2001 he was attacked by five North African youngsters who cursed him and spat in his face. One even kicked him in the face."[35] In 2019, Germany's government commissioner on anti-Semitism "suggested Jews should not always wear the traditional kippah cap in public, in the wake of a spike in anti-Jewish attacks."[36]

Some *mass demonstrations against Jews* began as demonstrations against the state of Israel but turned to focus on Jews in general. For example, in 2014, rallies in Paris protesting Israel's military campaign in Gaza became riots where the crowds chanted "kill the Jews" and vandalized a synagogue and Jewish-owned businesses. Similar incidents occurred in Argentina, Italy, Norway, and Uruguay. However, this is not always the case. For example, there have been multiple incidents in the Czech Republic where neo-Nazis engaged in large anti-Semitic demonstrations. In 2009, several hundred neo-Nazis marched through Pilsen shouting anti-Semitic slogans. There have been additional incidents, mostly in Pilsen and often during concerts by skinhead bands where large groups of neo-Nazis chanted anti-Semitic slogans. Protests, parades, or gatherings of neo-Nazis and extreme nationalists where anti-Semitic slogans are chanted occurred also in Germany, Hungary, Latvia, Lithuania, Poland, Sweden, Russia, and the Ukraine. In Algeria, Tunisia, and Venezuela, there were a small number of incidents of demonstrations outside synagogues. In the case of Algeria, this involved protesting the reopening of synagogues that had been closed for security reasons.

Harassment of Jews was so severe in Algeria, Belgium, France, Germany, Sweden, and Yemen that a significant number of Jews emigrated. While this harassment included other categories of SRD, including property crimes and violence, RASM3 includes it in this category. In comparison, the level of harassment of other minorities reached this level against Muslims in Bosnia and Sweden and against Christians in Bosnia, Croatia, Egypt, Mexico (Protestants and Jehovah's Witnesses), and Russia (some Protestant denominations).

Violence

Violence, the most extreme form of SRD, presented in Table 2.3b, includes eight types of violence: (1) overt threats of violence; (2) violence targeted against clergy; (3) violence targeted against proselytizers, missionaries, or converts away from the majority religion; (4) violence targeted against other members of the minority religion; (5) large-scale violence; (6) lethal violence; (7) arson, bombing, or concerted attacks against religious property; and (8) arson, bombing, or concerted attacks against other property owned or associated with the minority. While the latter two categories could be considered property crimes because they do not necessarily target people, RASM3 includes them in the violence category because they have the potential to harm or kill.

Jews experience the highest levels of five of these eight categories. As was the case with harassment, incidents involving converts and proselytizers are rare because Jews proselytize and seek converts far less often than most other religions. Levels of lethal violence were just slightly lower than those against Christians. Interestingly, large-scale violence was relatively low against Jews as compared to Muslim and Christian minorities. This indicates that most acts of violence against Jews are perpetrated by smaller groups and are less likely to be in the context of riots or pogrom-like behavior.

There were recorded overt threats of violence against exactly half of the Jewish minorities included in this study. The most common were bomb threats sent via phone or email to Jewish organizations and individuals. However, many involved other types of threats, a good portion of which involved threatening local Jews due to perceived injustices perpetrated by Israel. For example, in Australia one phone call threatened to kill 15 Jewish schoolgirls for every Palestinian killed by Israel. In the Czech Republic, a group called Narodni Odpor (National Resistance) petitioned the president in August 2006 for permission to fight with the Iranian military against Israel. The group stated that if the Czech president refused their demand to enlist in the Iranian army, they would perpetrate violence against Jews and synagogues in the country.

All of the categories of violence occurred in France, other than violence directed against proselytizers and converts. These include incidents of harassment, threats, arson, and physical attacks including murder, as well as several stabbing attacks against rabbis. Often victims were wearing symbols of Jewish identity such as a kippah or a star of David, or were near Jewish communities and religious buildings. Known perpetrators of anti-Semitic acts included Muslims and Arabs as well as members of neo-Nazi movements. Some violence against French Jews was likely linked to the Israel-Palestine conflict. For example, there was an increase in anti-Semitic acts in France following the Gaza flotilla incident in May 2010 and during Israel's 2014 campaign in Gaza.[37]

Some of the attacks have been particularly violent. On March 19, 2012, a teacher and three children were murdered at Ozar Hatorah, a private Jewish school in Toulouse, by Mohammed Merah, who had previously attacked several French soldiers.[38] Merah (who was killed by police after a stand-off) described himself as a supporter of al-Qaeda and stated that the attacks were motivated by the fate of the Palestinians, the French military presence in Afghanistan, and France's ban on the full veil.[39] Following the attack at the school, there were numerous other anti-Semitic acts across the country. In September 2012 an explosive device was thrown into a kosher supermarket, injuring a customer. [40] In December 2014 three armed youths broke into a Jewish family's apartment and raped a 19-year-old woman.[41]

These types of events are common in France. A 2013 survey of French Jews (sample of 1,192 respondents) found that 10% of the respondents said they had personally been assaulted or threatened due to being Jewish within the past five years, 35% had been harassed (in person or by email or phone) for being Jewish, and 30% had witnessed anti-Semitic attacks within the previous year. Over a third (35%) said they avoid certain areas, and half avoid wearing Jewish symbols in public for fear of anti-Semitic attacks. Further, they report an increase in anti-Semitic sentiments in the media and political speeches. Of the respondents, 52% said they have heard anti-Semitic statements at political rallies; 23% said they felt they had been personally discriminated against for their religious identity within the previous year. About half said they have considered emigrating due to anti-Semitism.[42] Jewish emigration from France, mainly to Israel or Montreal, has increased in recent years, and rising anti-Semitism is one of the stated causes for leaving France.[43] According to a 2019 study of the young Jews in 12 European countries (aged 16–34), 43% have considered emigrating (O'Flahtery, 2019: 34).

Other Types of SRD

These three types of SRD, listed in Table 2.3b, are those that do not fit into the other categories described previously. None of them was most common against Jews.

Efforts to close or prevent the opening of religious sites occurred in Algeria and Russia. As noted earlier, the civil war in Algeria resulted in the closing of many synagogues for security reasons, and there were protests when the government decided to allow them to reopen. In Russia, there are several reports of local Muslims protesting the building of new synagogues in their localities. In some cases, these efforts were successful.

The *"other"* variable covers any type of SRD which doesn't fit well into the other 26 variables. For example, in Poland, among certain sectors of the population the term "Jew" is a common slur, and at soccer games, fans routinely call each other "Jews" as a term of abuse. In Slovenia, this was coded due to general, nonspecific, complaints by the Jewish community of societal prejudice.

Conclusions

While both types of discrimination against Jews are common, SRD is far higher against Jews than against other religious minorities in Christian-majority countries. In Muslim-majority countries, most of the Jewish minorities are very small and SRD, on average, is lower than against Christians but higher than against other religious minorities. GRD against Jews, in contrast, is on average lower than the mean levels in these 76 countries, yet is still present against most Jewish minorities.

This is particularly interesting because Grim and Finke (2011) argue that SRD is a precursor to GRD. While, as we noted in Chapter 1, Fox (2020) found that this is not always the case, this pattern of relatively low GRD coupled with high SRD is unique to Jews among all religious minorities. In later chapters we uncover some of the reasons for this unique trend.

Another interesting trend uncovered in this chapter is that the majority of GRD against Jews is directed at multiple minorities in the countries in which these Jews reside, so it is not targeted specifically against Jews. Yet there are also many instances of GRD that are targeted against Jews. Also, there are some indications that SRD against Jews is less common in small countries with small Jewish populations. Finally, to the extent that it is possible to determine based on anecdotal evidence, and given that the motivation for most incidents of SRD is unclear or unknown, a portion of SRD against Jews is committed by perpetrators who claim to be at least in part motivated by anti-Israel sentiment. However, it is most likely that an even larger portion of such incidents have other motivations. As we discuss in more detail in Chapter 4, there is significant evidence that the Israel motivation is not the primary cause of most SRD against Jews.

Thus, while the goal of this chapter has been to uncover the extent and nature of discrimination against Jews, rather than to determine motivations, this exercise has revealed some information regarding motivations. The next three chapters more systematically examine the motivations for this discrimination.

3

Religious Anti-Semitism

The first potential cause of discrimination against Jews that we address in this study is religion-based anti-Semitism. This is arguably the oldest form of anti-Semitism. Also, as we discuss in detail in this chapter, it is a motivation for discrimination that is not limited to discrimination against Jews. Hatred for those who worship the incorrect Gods is a far more widespread phenomenon.

Nevertheless, it is a motivation for discrimination that has been applied to Jews for well over two millennia. Jews in the ancient world, even before Christianity, were persecuted due to their monotheistic, at the time "new," idea of worship. An early case of anti-Jewish sentiment is documented in the *Book of Esther* (3:8–9) where Haman seeks and receives the king's permission to commit genocide against the Jews of Persia, arguing that "there is a strange and separate people among the nations of your kingdom whose religion is different from every other nation who follow not the laws of the King. There is therefore no point in letting them be. If it pleases the King, let it be written to destroy them." Haman was angry that Mordechai, a leader of the Jewish community and advisor to the king, would not bow down to Haman, a privilege granted to Haman by the king (Esther 8:1–6).

While this is one of the more explicit incidents of religion-based anti-Jewish sentiment in the Jewish Bible, it is by no means the first. The enslavement of the Jews in the time of pharaoh and the story of the exodus from Egypt also contain religion-based anti-Jewish overtones. The fact that the Jewish innovation of one God was new and very uncommon led other communities and rulers to oppose Judaism and Jews. However, while the anti-Jewish attitudes in the Christian world likely began as theologically based hatred, their anti-Jewish attitudes over time also became sociological and community-based (Cohen-Sherbok, 2002: 1–18). This likely facilitated the evolution of these attitudes into other forms of anti-Semitism, some of which we discuss in subsequent chapters.

This chapter proceeds as follows. First, we discuss the evolution of theologically based anti-Semitism in the Christian world. Second, we discuss the general theory on religion as a cause of discrimination against religious minorities. Both the general and Jew-specific literatures predict that governments which support religion and societies which are more religious should engage in more discrimination.

Third, we test the impact of religiosity and government support for religion on discrimination against Jews. However, our empirical findings diverge somewhat from the predictions of the literature. On one hand, as expected, governments which more strongly support religion are more likely to discriminate against Jews. On the other hand, more religious societies engage in *less* societal religious discrimination (SRD) against Jews, and their governments are no more or less likely to discriminate against Jews than less religious societies. We argue that this counterintuitive result is a new phenomenon that is the result of secularism and modernity encroaching on religion. It is causing religious people, especially many religious Christians, to see members of other religions who are themselves religious as kindred spirits, or at least as allies against the greater threat posed to all religion by secularism. It is also a result of increased limitations placed on religious practices considered abhorrent to some manifestations of secular ideology.

Christian Anti-Semitism

Religion-based anti-Semitism is the oldest form of anti-Semitism. Ironically, it has its roots in monotheism, a concept which originated in Judaism. It evolved from the competition between Judaism and early Christianity for followers and was driven by theological intolerance for those who did not follow the correct religion. Here we briefly trace this historical process through the lens of the anti-Semitism literature in order to demonstrate that this literature ascribes religious motives to much of the historical discrimination against Jews.

Until the rise of Christianity, the non-Jewish world was polytheistic. Non-Jews generally accepted the concept of multiple gods and, while giving priority to their own pantheon, often accepted that the gods of other nations were real. The presence of a second monotheistic faith in the world changed this. As monotheistic faiths, by definition, accept no gods other than their own, this created the potential for a new form of hate against Jews. The Jewish Bible clearly is intolerant of all gods other than its one true God, and without the presence of another monotheistic religion, this type of intolerance against Jews could not exist. This potential became manifest in the explicit Christian theology that God changed his choice of the chosen people from the Jews to the Christians and his primary revelation from the Jewish Bible to the Christian New Testament. As we document in this chapter, this theologically based hatred of Jews eventually became ingrained in society and began to exist as a societal animus independent of theological justifications, though still related to them.

However, the origins of the intolerance for other gods among monotheists can be found in the Jewish Bible. The second commandment states, "Thou shall have no other gods before me." The Jewish Bible also makes multiple negative references to the worship of "strange gods" and states that God is a "jealous God." This intolerance for other religions was adopted by the other major world monotheistic religions, Christianity and Islam.

This tension between Jews and Christians was exacerbated by the accusation that the Jews were responsible for the death of Jesus. In fact, the image of the Jew as the killer of Christ is strongly built into the Christian core and story (Nicholls, 1995: 3–4, 209–210). As Frederick B. Davis (2003: 1) describes in his book *The Jew and Deicide*, the core institutionalization of Christian anti-Semitism is the conviction, the accusation. The rest is history.

The book of Matthew (27:17–25), for example, is explicit about Jewish guilt in Jesus's death. Pontius Pilate offered to free Jesus but the Jews refused, preferring that he release another. Pontius Pilate replied,

> what shall I do then with Jesus which is called Christ? They all say unto him, let him be crucified. And the governor said, why, what evil hath he done? But they cried out the more, saying, let him be crucified. When Pilate saw that he could prevail nothing, but that rather a tumult was made, he took water, and washed his hands before the multitude, saying, I am innocent of the blood of this just person: see ye to it. Then answered all the people, and said, His blood be on us, and on our children.

Thus, not only are the Jews seen as guilty of the crucifixion, they are portrayed as willingly accepting eternal guilt for the act.

Interestingly, before the crucifixion it was difficult to trace the differences and boundaries between Jews and the early Christians. Jesus was himself a Jew; along with his followers, he argued that the Jewish religion was too legally based and that the Old Testament, the Jewish Bible, should be replaced with new practices. Around 30–33 CE, Jesus was a popular teacher and healer. He traveled around the Galilee and Judea, welcomed fellowship meals, and performed healings and good deeds. He was even titled as the "king of the Jews" by some Roman rulers. During the Passover season Jesus brought some of his gospels to Jerusalem. The Roman authorities feared Jesus would cause anti-establishment demonstrations and riots. Some days before the Passover holidays, Jesus caused some protests against the widely perceived corruptions of the priestly leadership and the Roman Empire. The Roman authorities were afraid Jesus's preaching would cause massive riots and, therefore, took a preemptive action—to execute and crucify Jesus before Passover (Cunningham, 2010: 47–49).

During the early stages of Christianity, from the death of Jesus and until the death of the last of the twelve Apostles, anti-Semitism was less present as a discriminatory and racist type of social phenomena, but existed rather as a gap or divide between Judaism and Christianity. Christianity acted as a sect of Judaism.

Moreover, the first Christians were Jewish by birth or by conversion. It was only after Paul's death that Christianity emerged as a separate religion. Christianity continued to follow Jewish law, but it was of less importance (Cunningham, 2010: 47–60).

At this time, the attitudes of Christians toward Jews had little impact on Jewish life. This is because Roman authorities recognized Judaism as a legal religion and many Jews occupied positions of political and social prominence. In contrast, Christianity had no legal status and Christians were periodically persecuted. Christianity was seen as a religion of women and slaves. Because of this, many Christians would leave the religion for Judaism. To counter this, Church leaders emphasized the role of the Jews in the Crucifixion (Cunningham, 2010: 47–60). Thus, the emphasis on the Crucifixion during this period was influenced by the desire to prevent Christians from converting to Judaism.

During this time, the basic foundation for Christianity's theology of Jewish guilt for the death of Christ and that Christians are the new Jews was formed:

> God's covenant with the Jewish people always symbolized the promised coming of Christ and the Church, Jerusalem was accursed and destroyed because of the Jewish rejection and Crucifixion of Jesus, and as a result the divine covenant was transferred to Christians. Christians have been given new, universal laws and rituals that replace the temporary and preparatory Law of Moses. . . . This theological delegitimization of Judaism has been called supersessionism because it is premised on the claim that the Church has superseded the Jewish people as covenantal partners with God. (Cunningham, 2010: 59)

During the fourth century CE the social position of Christians and Jews reversed; in 313 the Emperor Constantine declared that Christianity also would be tolerated in his empire. In the Edict of Milan in the same year, he removed many disabilities that were previously placed upon Christians. In 380 Theodosius I made the Christian religion the preferred legal system of the Roman Empire. As time passed, Christian leaders promoted the passage of laws that curtailed the privileges of their Jewish rivals. This was a gradual process in which Jews were increasingly restricted over time, while at the same time facing greater social hostility based on both theological grounds and the perception of the Jews as separate and different (Cunningham, 2010: 60–61; Nicholls, 1995: 190).

Under the rule of Constantine, Judaism was gradually perceived as a threat or a rival for Christianity. Before Constantine, Jews were equal citizens, as their religion was not a threat to the pagan worshipers, even though it did cause some negative attitudes among pagans. Jews were not blamed for schism and heresy under pagan rule, but as Constantine embraced Christianity (though he was not baptized until his deathbed) Jews were gradually treated as second-class citizens.

Interestingly, the Christian clergy sought to abolish Jewish privileges and establish Christianity's priority over Judaism. This eventually led to increased discrimination against the Jews (Nicholls, 1995: 189–191).

From the time of Constantine, a series of laws, government actions, and Canon laws, as well as societal attitudes, led to increasing restrictions on Jews. These include, roughly in chronological order:

- On October 18, 315, Constantine passed a law forbidding Christians from converting to Judaism. The law was aimed at preventing Jewish proselytism and was strictly enforced. Those who broke this law were punished severely, including execution (Nicholls, 1995: 192).
- On March 7, 321, Constantine ruled that Sunday should be a day of rest for all except farm workers. The idea of a resting day was not new to Judaism, but the Sunday holiday caused indirect discrimination against the Jews. While the Christians could rest for one day only, the Jews had to observe the Sabbath on Saturday and with the new law had to lose an additional day of work on Sunday. This loss of a business day was significant socially and economically (Nicholls, 1995: 192; Seaver, 1952: 6).
- Jews were banned from circumcising their slaves; also a slave circumcised by a Jew would be granted his freedom. This caused a significant difficulty for Jews because Jewish law (Halachah) calls upon slave owners to treat them as their own home residents, which includes circumcising them. This law placed Jews in the position of either disobeying their religious laws or losing the ability to own male slaves, a significant economic hardship at that time (Nicholls, 1995: 192–194; Seaver, 1952: 27–28; Linder, 2008: 166).
- A social trend had developed by which Jews could no longer keep Christian slaves, and any pagan slaves were to be confiscated (slaves were considered as property in that era; Nicholls, 1995: 192–194). This was later formalized by an edict by Valentinian III, the emperor of the Western Roman Empire (Seaver, 1952: 63).
- Restrictions were placed on intermarriage: a Christian who married a Jew would be punished and his property confiscated. A Christian woman from the imperial arms factories who married a Jew would be returned to the factory and the Jew would be executed. This codified Canon law into Roman law. Canon law LXI states that Christians cannot marry Jews (or pagans) as there could be no communication between believers and infidels. Canon law L forbids Christians to eat with Jews (Nicholls, 1995: 192–194, 204; Hilberg, 1985: 11).
- Under Theodosius I, emperor of the Western Empire, marriage between Jews and Christians was further restricted. The authorities termed this kind of marriage as adultery, and anyone could inform such acts to the

authorities. In addition, polygamy was banned, though Jewish law did allow it (Nicholls, 1995: 196; Linder, 2008: 164).

- The building or renovation of synagogues was banned under Theodosius I. He also ordered synagogues in unpopulated places destroyed (Nicholls, 1995: 196; Linder, 2008: 156).
- In 397, Arcadius, emperor of the Eastern Empire, prohibited Jews who were in debt from being baptized. Honorius applied this rule to the Western Empire in 416 (Linder, 2008: 163).
- Honorius succeeded his father Theodosius I to rule the Western Roman Empire and passed a special tax on Jews. Honorius also prohibited the Jews from holding any public office or position, a prohibition which remained until the nineteenth century and was revived under the rule of Hitler in Nazi Germany (Nicholls, 1995: 196; Seaver, 1952: 58; Linder, 2008: 160).
- Under Theodosius II, who reigned in the Eastern Empire during the first half of the fifth century, the celebration of the Jewish holiday Purim was forbidden. Purim celebrates the deliverance of the Jews from a Persian pogrom, as described in the Book of Esther. Theodosius II likely enacted this prohibition because he saw a strong similarity between the cases of the Persian pogrom and the Christian rule, and thus prohibited the celebrations (Nicholls, 1995: 197–199; Seaver, 1952: 68–69).
- Other actions under Theodosius II included the foreclosure of synagogues to the hands of the Catholic Church and a ban on Jewish courts taking on cases between Christians or between Jews and Christians (Nicholls, 1995, 197–199; Linder, 2008: 160).
- Valentinian III, of the Western Empire, banned Jews from serving as advocates, continuing the trend of limiting the professions in which Jews were allowed to serve (Linder, 2008: 160).

During this period, the justification for restricting Jews evolved. As Parkes (1969: 238) remarks, the justification for anti-Jewish laws before Theodosius II was the need to restrain Jewish lawlessness. During and after the reign of Theodosius II, anti-Jewish laws became simple discrimination. It is also worth noting that from the time of Constantine, there are multiple reports of Christians attacking Jews, anti-Jewish riots, the destruction of synagogues, and forced conversions. So societal discrimination went hand in hand with government-based discrimination. Yet at the same time, laws protecting some minimum civic rights for Jews remained on the books (Seaver, 1952).

The religious origin of these laws and subsequent laws is clear. They began when the Roman Empire began its transition to Christianity. In addition, many of them were also explicitly applied to other groups, such as heretics, pagans, and Samaritans. Thus these laws clearly constituted restrictions placed on minorities who belonged to the incorrect religion or Christians who held incorrect beliefs (Seaver, 1952; Linder, 2008).

After Theodosius II, the situation in the Western Empire worsened.

> Even the bitterest edicts of the Middle Ages lacked the abuse showered upon the Jews by these fanatical fourth and fifth century rulers of the Roman Empire. . . . The hostile laws of the later empire did not perish with its fall, as did those insuring only the minimum civic rights to the Jewish population. . . . Many of these laws were embodied in canons by the ecclesiastical contemporaries of the imperial legislators and so passed naturally into the tradition of Western Europe by way of the Church. . . . Nothing could be clearer than the incriminating record of Christian oppression of the Jews during the fourth century both in word and deed. That the violence of this century was mostly on the Christian side is obvious not only from the literature but also from the imperial and canon laws of the fourth century. . . . On the whole, the period 315–438 is one of battle between Jews and Christians, the former clinging to the laws of their fathers, the latter eager to crush all opposition in the floodtide of new-found victory. This struggle put its stamp on the whole age, and so influenced the minds of the Christian aggressors that they were firmly convinced of the necessity of removing the Jews as a menace to Christianity. (Seaver, 1952: 81–82)

Justinian I reigned in the Byzantine Empire from 527 until 565. It is important to note that Justinian's Byzantine Empire also influenced the Turks as well as most Slavic countries, parts of Eastern Europe, and Imperial Russia. These cultural influences, including anti-Jewish attitudes, continued through modern times (Nicholls, 1995: 199; Klier, 2001: 157–172). Before Justinian's reign, Theodosius II left over fifty laws against Jews on the books. Justinian rewrote many of these laws, abolishing some and creating news ones. Under Justinian, Judaism and its legal status were not defined,[1] and the status of Jewish clergy, which once enjoyed a social status equal to that of Christian clergy, was downgraded. A new law from 547 required that Jews bear all governmental burdens such as taxes and other obligations, while not allowing the Jews to enjoy any governmental honor (Nicholls, 1995: 200).

Justinian's Novella 131 further worsened the Jewish status as it incorporated Church law, the Canon law, into state law. This meant that while Jews were mostly protected under the state law in all matters of legality, they now were highly discriminated against, based on religious Church law that naturally preferred Christians over any other religion (Nicholls, 1995: 203). Justinian banned Jews and heretics from giving evidence in court against Christians, essentially guaranteeing that Christians would have an insurmountable advantage in all court cases against Jews. He also banned the sale of property with a Church in its premises to Jews. As many properties contained chapels, this was a significant restriction (Linder, 2008: 162).

This set the pattern that would continue for over a millennium, where Church law set the basic level of restrictions on Jews, though there were often additional limitations placed on Jews by the political leadership. As is shown in Table 3.1, the Canon law restrictions became so ingrained that Nazi restrictions on Jews during the Holocaust were largely parallel to these canonical restrictions; that is, the Nazis' Jew laws and decrees based on their racial ideology were effectively mirror images of the theologically based restrictions of an earlier era.

The rhetoric recorded during the period of Theodosius II and Justinian also shows that many of the adjectives used to describe Jews were negative and foreshadowed the general stereotypes seen in later years. Linder (2008: 150–151) documents that during this period,

> one notices several religious composites with oppositional prefixes, such as "incredulity," "impiety," "the most impious," "nefarious," and "sacrilegious." Other terms, for example deformity and illness, pestilence, filth, abomination, death, infamy and madness, expressed the conviction that the Jews represented the negation of wholesomeness, health, purity, life, honor, wisdom, and sanity. While not religious in themselves, these pairs acquired a religious connotation from the context in which they were used. Further terms include "turpitude," "perversity," "contagion," "pollution," "a plague . . . that spreads by contagion," "contamination," "to defile," "to purge [from Jews]," "execrable," corrupt with filth," "deed of disgrace," "senseless," and "madness." And this collection of epithets was complemented by a smaller group of pejorative political terms, asserting that Jews are "alien and hostile to the Roman state," "enemies of the Roman laws," and motivated by the spirit of "arrogance and revolt."

Interestingly, while many modern tropes are present, including the Jews as disloyal and alien to the state, the trope of the rich greedy Jews is absent at this time. This likely developed later, as moneylending became a more common profession and Jewish monopoly in the Christian world.

As the Church gained power and influence, the anti-Jewish aspects of its Canon Law and its anti-Jewish rhetoric increased. This was a process that took centuries. At Christianity's beginning, Christian leaders acknowledged the Jewishness of Jesus and that Christianity was based upon Jewish infrastructure. In contrast, as the Church grew bigger and stronger, it neglected the Jewish Bible. In fact, most of the early fathers of the Church could not even read Hebrew (Nicholls, 1995: 208–220).

Table 3.1 Comparison between Canonical Laws and Nazi Measures against Jews

Canonical Law	Nazi Measure
Prohibition of intermarriage and sexual intercourse between Christians and Jews (Synod of Elvira, 306 CE)	Law of protection of German blood and honor (September 15, 1935)
Christians and Jews not allowed to eat together (Synod of Elvira, 306)	Jews barred from dining cars (December 30, 1939)
Jews may not hold public office (Synod of Clermont, 535)	Law for the re-establishment of the professional Civil Service (April 7, 1933)
Jews may not employ Christian servants / possess Christian slaves (3rd Synod of Orleans, 538)	Law of protection of German blood and honor (September 15, 1935)
Jews barred from the streets during passion week (3rd Synod of Orleans, 538)	Decree authorizing local authorities to bar Jews from the streets on certain days (December 3, 1938)
Burning of the Talmud and other books (12th Synod of Toledo, 681)	Book burning in Nazi Germany (such as the German Student's Union—DST in 1930s)
Christians may not patronize Jewish doctors (Trulanic Synod, 692)	Jewish doctors may treat only Jewish parents (July 25, 1938)
Christians may not live in Jewish homes (Synod of Narbonne, 1050)	Concentration of Jews in houses directive by Göring (December 28, 1938)
Jews must pay same Church tax as Christians (Synod of Gerona, 1078)	Jews must pay a special income tax in lieu of donations to the Nazi Party (December 24, 1940)
Jews may not be plaintiffs or witnesses against Christians in courts (3rd Lateran Council, 1179)	Proposal by Nazi party Chancellery that Jews may not institute civil suits (September 9, 1942)
Jews may not withhold inheritance from descendants who accepted Christianity (3rd Lateran Council, Canon 26, 1179)	Decree empowering the Justice Ministry to void wills offending the "second judgement of the people" (July 31, 1938)
The marking of Jewish clothes with a badge (4th Lateran Council, Canon 68, 1215)	Decree requiring Jews wear yellow star (September 1, 1941)
Prohibition of construction of new synagogues (Council of Oxford, 1222)	Destruction of synagogues in the entire Reich (November 11, 1938)
Christians may not attend Jewish ceremonies (Synod of Vienna, 1267)	Friendly relationships with Jews prohibited (October 24, 1941)
Compulsory ghettos (Synod of Breslau, 1267)	Compulsory ghettos ordered by Heydrich (September 21, 1939)

Table 3.1 *Continued*

Canonical Law	Nazi Measure
Christians may not sell or rent real estate to Jews (Synod of Ofen, 1279)	Decree providing for compulsory sale of Jewish real estate (December 3, 1938)
Christian conversion to Judaism or a baptized Jew returning to the Jewish religion defined as a heresy (Synod of Mainz, 1310)	Christian conversion to Judaism places the convert in jeopardy of being treated as a Jew (June 26, 1942)
Jews may not act as agents in the conclusion of contracts between Christians, especially marriage contracts (Council of Basel, Sessio XIX, 1434)	Decree liquidating Jewish real estate agencies, brokerage agencies, and marriage agencies catering to non-Jews (July 6, 1938)
Jews may not obtain academic degrees (Council of Basel, Sessio XIX, 1434)	Law against overcrowding German schools and universities (RGB 1, 225, April 25, 1933)

Source: Hilberg (1985: 11–12).

It is important to note that while, on average, the restrictions on Jews increased over time, their application was sporadic; that is, the laws restricting Jews increased in their harshness over time, but these laws were not always enforced. Nevertheless, enforcement increased on average over time in both the Eastern and Western Roman Empires. However, there were no laws banning Judaism outright. In fact, a number of laws, also sporadically enforced, protected Jews and synagogues from societal violence, including laws passed in 393 and 420. Thus, while subject to increasing discrimination, Jews also had a recognized second-class status which was similar to that placed on heretics and pagans (Seaver, 1952; Linder, 2008).

Bans and expulsions of Jews occurred only after the fall of the Western Roman Empire. Although many expulsions occurred in Europe in the high and late Middle Ages—for instance, the British expulsion in 1290 (Julius, 2005, 2010; Rose, 2015: 13–44) and the Spanish expulsion in 1492 (Roth, 2002: 271–315)—the Church often tried to protect the Jewish people from total annihilation. This protection was grounded in the traditional Christian doctrine that the Jews must be preserved until the second coming of Christ. This protection was sporadic at best. Anti-Jewish riots were common. The Crusades also resulted in considerable violence against Jews. The Crusades were intended to free Jerusalem, the holy city in which Jesus once walked, from infidels, but the Crusaders quickly found out that they could find those infidels much closer, in their hometowns in Europe (Nicholls, 1995: 229–230; Laqueur, 2006: 39–70; Wistrich, 2010).

The First Crusade of 1096 had a significant stop in Mainz. The Crusaders offered the Jewish residents the choice between baptism or death. Many Jews became martyrs (Nicholls, 1995: 229–230; Laqueur, 2006: 39–70; Wistrich, 2010). As for Jerusalem itself, the Frankish knight Godfrey of Bouillon, who was one of the leaders of the First Crusade, wrote the following to the Pope: "If you want to know what has been done with the enemy found in Jerusalem, learn that in the Porch and in the Temple of Solomon, our people had the vile blood of the Saracens up to the knees of their horses" (Hay, 1981: 27). The Second Crusade of 1146 was similarly deadly for Jews.

The next phase of this increasing anti-Semitism was not pure discrimination, but rather blood libel, false accusations, and scapegoating, which we discuss in more detail in Chapter 5.

The societal aspect of the hatred toward the Jews became more prominent in the high Middle Ages, since the year 1000. Though it was present in earlier times, this hatred became more ingrained in the culture. It manifested in multiple aspects of the culture, including philosophy, the arts, architecture, and simple common myths. In this period, this societally based hatred became more dangerous and deadly for the Jews than the original Christian theologically based hatred. Christian commoners considered Jewishness to be a permanent characteristic that could not be removed by baptism or any other form of religious or social change (Nicholls, 1995: 225–226; Keen, 2010). This was a precursor to the race-based anti-Semitism of the Nazis.

The Protestant reformation by Martin Luther rejected the monopoly of the Catholic Church and questioned many aspects of canonical law. However, it did not abolish anti-Semitism. Luther had assumed the reason the Jews did not convert was the corruption of the Catholic Church and that they'd be ready to convert to his more authentic and uncorrupted version of Christianity. When this did not occur, he reverted to what was essentially the Catholic model of anti-Jewishness. He advocated burning synagogues, Jewish houses, and books. Luther also promoted a ban on rabbis teaching Judaism to Jewish children in an attempt to annihilate the Jewish culture (Keen, 2010: 79–80; Klein, 1984; Laqueur, 2006: 39–70; Rublack, 2017: 20–56).

This combination of theologically based and societally based hatred for Jews remained the norm until the later development of racially based and anti-Zionist–based anti-Semitism, and remains present into modern times in conjunction with those other forms.

Taking a step back, while the historical literature focusing on Jews and anti-Semitism does not tend to make wide generalizations, it is fair to conclude that it argues that religious belief is a motivation for discrimination against Jews, though it by no means claims that religion is the only potential source of discrimination against Jews. More specifically, it implies that states which are more closely connected to a single religion are more likely to discriminate against Jews. It also implies that where the population is more religious, there will be more discrimination against Jews. As we will see in the following, this set of arguments is applicable to a much wider range of religious minorities and is echoed in the general literature.

Religious Ideology, Prejudice, and Discrimination in General Theory

The argument that religious ideology may motivate discrimination against religious minorities is not unique to the anti-Semitism literature, nor is it unique to discrimination against Jews. On a more general level, religions claim a monopoly on the existential truth; that is, by their very nature they tend to hold that their beliefs are a truth that is exclusively correct and valid, or in some cases the most correct and valid among all others. Even polytheistic faiths, which by their nature recognize multiple gods, can still inspire a preference for one god or set of gods over others.

With some notable exceptions, it is the ultimate goal of religious organizations to convert all of humanity to their belief system. Their short-term goals may be less ambitious, but they generally include a never-ending effort to seek converts. From this perspective, all other religions are obstacles to achieving this goal. All other religions by their very existence challenge this truth. In this context, Stark (2003: 32) argues that "those who believe in only One True God are offended by worship directed toward other Gods." This is recognized at the Passover Haggadah, which quotes Psalms 79:6–7: "Pour out Your wrath upon the nations who do not know You and upon the kingdoms that have not called Your name."

This can result in inter-religious conflict, which can take the form of religious discrimination. Furthermore, this discrimination is motivated by the belief that it is intended to save the souls of the unbelievers, or perhaps punish them for believing in the wrong god. From this perspective, the oppressors of minority religions see themselves as attempting to save these minorities from eternal punishment, rather than oppressing them.

There is no shortage of research in the social sciences which supports this argument. Sociologist Rodney Stark (2001, 2003) argues that Judaism, Christianity, and Islam are particularly intolerant of competition because they are monotheistic. Political scientists like Wald (1987) and Jelen and Wilcox (1990) argue that holding ultimate values and beliefs based on divine revelations results in intolerance of others and resistance to alternative viewpoints. Laustesen and Waever (2000: 219), in the context of international relations theory, argue that "religion deals with the constitution of being as such. Hence, one cannot be pragmatic on concerns challenging this being." Neuberg et al. (2013: 2), in the context of psychology, posit that "groups whose values are tightly woven into everyday activity—as is the case for groups with high levels of religious infusion—are thus likely to feel particularly threatened by groups holding incompatible values."

Others link religion and intolerance through other mechanisms. One of the most prominent arguments is the religious economy argument. While this approach does not deny the influence of ideology on discrimination, it focuses on the power-related interests of political and religious elites and institutions. Gill (2005, 2008) argues that religious freedom is based on elite interests, though those interests may be influenced by ideology. Essentially, leaders want to rule as efficiently as possible, and supporting the majority religious institutions can increase efficiency. This is because religions are capable of instilling morality in a population and of increasing the government's legitimacy. Both of these reduce the need for costly coercion and law enforcement.

Thus, religion can make ruling less costly and, therefore, worth the less expensive price of supporting a majority religion. However, the price for this cooperation often includes maintaining a religious monopoly, which often includes repressing religious minorities. In fact, states which support a single religion over all others are far more likely to restrict religious minorities (Fox, 2015, 2016, 2019, 2020). Sarkissian (2015) expands on Gill's arguments, noting that repression may also be targeted against religious groups seen as having the potential to engage in oppositional activities or those seen as threatening the identity or unity of a society.

Many scholars echo these arguments. Grim and Finke (2011: 46–49) argue that monopolistic religions often see other religions as competition and a threat to their privileged position. Stark and Iannaccone (1994: 232) argue that "the capacity of a single religious firm to monopolize a religious economy depends upon the degree to which a state uses coercive force to regulate the religious economy." Lucas (2004) argues that efforts by national churches to regain hegemony are responsible for the deterioration of religious freedom around the world. Barro and McCleary (2005) argue that the mere presence of other religions in a country can reduce the perceived utility of one's own religion.

Whether due to ideology or power-seeking, it is difficult to find any arguments which deny the potential of religious ideology, theology, and beliefs to cause repression, discrimination, and conflict. While there are those who argue that it is possible for religion to support reconciliation and peace (e.g., Appleby, 2000; Gopin, 2000, 2002), they essentially posit that the default influence is conflict, intolerance, and discrimination, but with some effort religion can also have a positive influence.

Religious Motivations for Discrimination
in Greece and Europe

As we note in Chapter 2, much of government-based religious discrimination (GRD) against Jews occurs in the context of GRD against multiple religious minorities. The case of Greece provides a good illustration of this phenomenon in the context of religiously motivated GRD. The Greek Orthodox Church is granted the status of the "prevailing religion" in Greece's constitution. The government is intimately connected with the Church, though as of late 2018, the government began distancing itself from the Church. This discussion focuses on the period before this distancing process.

This government support for Greek Orthodoxy, as well as its influence on the Church, is substantial. The government has the right to modify the Church charter, introduce regulations, and suspend noncompliant synods (Karagiannis, 2009). Christian religious symbols, including crucifixes and icons, are displayed in public offices, school and university classrooms, and courts, a practice which has been approved by Greece's courts.[2] Greek Orthodox religious education is mandatory in public schools, but non-Orthodox students can be exempted upon parental request. In addition, the government materially supports the Church. This includes paying salaries and pensions of clergy, paying for religious training of clergy, paying for construction and maintenance of Orthodox Church buildings, and funding of Orthodox religious instruction in primary and secondary schools. The Greek Orthodox Church is largely exempt from taxes, unlike other religious organizations in Greece. This material support has been reduced recently as part of an international bailout that saved Greece from bankruptcy.

This intimate connection between religion and state in Greece results in significant GRD. For example, while blasphemy against any religion is illegal in Greece, this is enforced only in cases of blasphemy against the Greek Orthodox Church (Mavrogordatos, 2003). One of the few cases involving incitement against Jews—a 2007 conviction against Popular Orthodox Rally (LAOS) Party candidate Kostas Plevris for inciting hatred and racial violence through his book *The Jews: The Whole Truth* was overturned on appeal. However, he was convicted of distributing anti-Semitic leaflets during the trial.[3] There has been some improvement. In September 2014 the Greek parliament passed a law making Holocaust denial a crime.[4]

Similarly, while proselytizing by any religion is illegal, this is not enforced against the Greek Orthodox Church. It is enforced sporadically against some minority religions. For example, there were several incidents of police harassing and detaining Jehovah's Witnesses, Mormons, and Evangelical Christians who were proselytizing. In most cases, the accused were acquitted.[5] In December

2011 the bishop of Piraeus Seraphim filed charges against the Catholic Church for proselytism following the blessing of the school year by a Catholic priest in the presence of Greek Orthodox students.

There were also reports that police did not intervene in cases of Greek Orthodox clergy verbally and physically harassing Mormons who were proselytizing. In fact, Amnesty International reports that the Greek police often fail to intervene in hate crimes even when present; fail to protect protestors, journalists, and bystanders; arrest victims of hate crimes rather than perpetrators; discourage the reporting of hate crimes; and fail to investigate.[6] There are also multiple reports of police harassing religious minorities. Disciplinary action is rarely taken in these cases.[7]

Jews fare better than many other minority religions because Judaism, Islam, and the Greek Orthodox Church are the only religions in Greece considered to be a "legal person in public law." All other religions must register as "legal persons of private law." Even Jewish and Muslim groups have difficulty getting permits to build houses of worship, and those unable to register (no new groups have successfully registered since 2006) cannot get such permits. These "illegal" houses of prayer regularly are closed by the authorities. The local boards which approve such permits often have Greek Orthodox priests as members. Thus, for the most part, GRD against Jews is not directed particularly at Jews but rather against any religion that is not the Greek Orthodox Church.

There are numerous reports of societal discrimination, harassment, and physical assaults against Jews and Muslims.[8] Racism in politics, while directed at Jews, is not directed at Jews exclusively, but such speech acts are common. For example, the Golden Dawn Party has repeatedly made anti-Semitic, anti-Muslim, and racist statements. Focusing on their anti-Semitic activities, members and supporters of the Golden Dawn Party, including its leader Nikos Michaloliakos, often engage in Holocaust denial, assert that a Jewish lobby is conspiring against Greece, criticize Greek citizens of Jewish heritage, and give Nazi salutes and play Nazi anthems at public events. The July 2012 issue of the newspaper *Eleftheri Ora*, associated with the Golden Dawn Party, included excerpts from the Protocols of the Elders of Zion with an introduction by Father Eustathios Kollas, honorary president of the Greek Orthodox Priests Association. During an October 2012 plenary session of parliament, a member of Golden Dawn read passages from the Protocols of the Elders of Zion. Senior clergy of the Greek Orthodox Church expressed anti-Semitic attitudes, for example that Jews control the banks. In 2010 the Greek Orthodox Church's bishop of Piraeus made anti-Semitic statements on national television. The Greek Orthodox Church's Holy Week liturgy includes anti-Semitic passages.[9]

While the extent to which the anti-Semitic activity by right-wing nationalists in Greece is motivated by religion is unclear, anti-Semitic activities by the Greek Orthodox clergy are almost certainly motivated to a great extent by their religious beliefs. This phenomenon is limited neither to actions taken against Jews nor to Greece. As noted, Orthodox clergy often directly harass religious minorities and use their political influence to harass proselytizers. It is likely due to their influence that numerous religious groups, including Scientologists, Hare Krishnas, polytheistic Hellenic groups, and Muslims outside Thrace, have been unable to register and have, accordingly, never been given a permit to build a house of prayer in Greece. Local Orthodox bishops often issue lists of minority religious groups and practices that they consider "sacrilegious" and harmful to Orthodox worshipers and ask Orthodox parishioners to shun members of these groups. These groups include Jehovah's Witnesses, Mormons, Evangelical Protestants, and the Bahai (Fox, 2020: 172).

Fox (2020) documents that this type of behavior is common among Orthodox clergy in Orthodox-majority countries, including Bulgaria, Cyprus, Macedonia, Moldova, Romania, and Russia. Outside of Orthodox-majority countries, the religious motivation for discrimination against Jews, while likely present in the West to some extent, is less obvious. In fact, a significant portion of GRD against Jews in the West is linked to secular ideologies. In particular, as discussed in Chapter 2, there have been recent movements to ban three religious practices common to Muslims and Jews because they violate Western secular values: infant circumcision, ritual slaughter, and head coverings.

What is particularly interesting about these three forms of GRD is that they are nearly exclusively present in Western democracies. Sweden, Norway, and Denmark regulate circumcisions. A German court banned them briefly, but this was overturned by a law. Denmark, Germany, Iceland, Norway, Sweden, Switzerland, and as of 2019 Belgium ban or restrict kosher and halal slaughter, but allow kosher and halal meat to be imported. On December 17, 2020, the European Union's highest court ruled that bans on ritual slaughter are legal. Religious head coverings are restricted or banned in parts of Belgium, Croatia, Denmark, France, Germany, Italy, Malta, Norway, Switzerland, and the United Kingdom. On the surface, this last type of ban seemingly only restricts Muslims. However, many Orthodox Jewish women also cover their hair after marriage. The manner in which they cover their hair is often by using wigs, bandannas, or hats, which blend better with Western fashion, but the bans in these countries could easily be applied to these Jewish Orthodox practices.

Previous Empirical Studies

Overall, the bulk of the quantitative literature supports the contention that religion can cause discrimination, intolerance, and violence. However, there is some counter-evidence.

Several studies of religion and conflict find a relationship between religion and discrimination, violence, conflict, and intractability. State support for religion and regulation of the majority religion (which are themselves correlated) are correlated with both religious discrimination against religious minorities (Finke & Martin, 2015; Grim & Finke, 2011; Fox, 2015, 2016, 2019, 2020), and other forms of discrimination, including discrimination against ethnic minorities (Fox, 2004), women (Ben-Nun Bloom, 2015; Htun & Weldon, 2015; Sweeney, 2014), and the LGBTQ community (Carlo-Gonzalez et al., 2017). However, none of these studies focuses specifically on Jewish minorities.

Several studies find that multiple religious factors increase levels of conflict, terrorism, and violence. These include state support for religion (Brown, 2019; Henne, 2012, 2019; Saiya, 2016; 2019; Zellman & Fox, 2020), commitment to religion (Alexander, 2017), religious ideology (Breslawski & Ives, 2017; Henne, 2012a), religious demands by combatants (Henne & Klocek, 2017), religion as a central issue in a conflict (Svensson & Nilsson, 2017; Toft, 2007), the use of religion to mobilize combatants (Henne & Klocek, 2017; Isaacs, 2016), religious calls for violence (Basedau et al., 2014), and elite framing of conflicts as religious (De Juan & Hasenclever, 2015).

A number of studies focus on Islam and find that a state's connection to Islam increases levels of repression (Albertson & de Soysa, 2017) and conflict (Brown, 2015) and reduces a state's willingness to use international mediation to settle conflicts (Powell, 2020). Studies which focus on whether religious conflicts are intractable tend to find they are more intractable than non-religious conflicts (Gleditsch & Rudolfsen, 2016; Johnstone & Svensson, 2013; Svensson, 2007; Svensson & Harding, 2011; Toft, 2007). Several studies also link religious discrimination and repression itself to conflict and terrorism (Fox, 2014; Basedau et al., 2019; Kim & Choi, 2017; Saiya, 2016b; Saiya & Scime, 2014).

However, a minority of cross-national empirical studies found no relationship between religion and conflict. This includes links between religion and suicide terror (Filote et al., 2016), ethnic conflict (Karkaya, 2016), and civil wars (Pearce, 2005). Similarly, some studies focusing on Islam find no link between Islam and conflict when controlling for other factors. Specifically, the percentage of Muslims in a country (Fisch et al., 2010; Karkaya, 2015) and Islamism in a country (Fisch et al., 2010) are not linked to violence and conflict.

There is also no shortage of survey-based studies which support the argument that religion can lead to intolerance, violence, and intractability. Boomgarden and Woost (2012) show that Christianity is linked to attitudes against Muslim countries joining the European Union. Cohen-Zada et al. (2016) find that as the salience of religion increases, individuals are less willing to compromise. Milligan et al. (2014) find that in a study of 23 countries, non-practicing Muslims are more tolerant than practicing Muslims. Djupe and Clafino (2012) find that when individuals are exposed during a survey to religiously exclusive statements such as "to be true to my faith, it is important to keep company with other people of my faith" they are more likely to express intolerance. Roy (2016) finds that religious cues in the United States can increase antipathy toward Muslims. Isani and Silverman (2016: 572) similarly find that among US Muslims, "Islamic cues can be quite powerful, reducing subjects' affect, trust, and support for providing aid." Gurses (2015) finds that supporters of Islamist political parties in Turkey have more negative attitudes toward women. Guth (2013) finds that in the United States, Evangelicals and fundamentalists are more likely to support militant internationalism. Hill and Matsubayashi (2008) find that conservative religious values lead to less responsiveness by politicians to policy demands by their constituents. Kunovich (2006) finds that Christian identity becomes more salient in European countries when there is a large Muslim population present. Laythe et al. (2002a, 2002b) find that Christian beliefs are correlated with prejudice against homosexuals in the United States.

However, others argue that this relationship is complex in that other factors are involved, or that this relationship holds only under certain circumstances. For example, Canetti et al. (2010: 9) argue that the explanation for support for violence among Israeli Muslims

> is to be found not in the nature of Islam, but in contextual reality and psychological stress reactions. The extent to which people suffer socio-economic inequality and perceived discrimination was pivotal in determining whether religiosity and religious affiliation induce support for political violence. . . . Religion is obviously associated somehow with support for political violence, but not in and of itself, and not necessarily in every setting.

Eisenstein (2006a, 2006b, 2008) finds similarly that increased religious commitment leads to decreased tolerance, but in some cases this is mediated by levels of religious orthodoxy. Fair and Shepard (2006), using the Global Attitudes Survey, find that Muslims are more likely to support terrorism when they believe that Islam is under threat.

A minority of survey-based studies indicate that at least some aspects of religion do not lead to violence or intolerance. Alexseev and Zhemukhov (2016) find that participation by Muslims from the North Caucasus in the Haj leads to tolerance. Cunradi et al. (2002) and Ellison and Anderson (2001) find that weekly attendance of religious services lowers violence among US couples. While Fox and Thomas (2008) show that religious people are more likely to forgive, Tsang et al. (2005) show that religion can support both forgiveness and revenge.

There is also an interesting cluster of studies on attitudes toward Muslims in Europe. Bohman and Hjerm (2013) find that "religious people emerge as being less negative towards immigration than non-religious people." Van der Noll et al. (2018) show that societal religiosity is correlated with acceptance of wearing religious symbols such as head coverings. Helbling (2014) similarly finds that religious people in Western Europe are less likely to oppose Muslim women wearing head coverings than those with "liberal values." However, those with "liberal values" are more tolerant of Muslims in general than those with religious values. This seems to indicate that while religious people may be less tolerant when asked about religious minorities in general, they tend to be more supportive of the right of these religious minorities to engage in their religious practices.

In sum, the bulk of the literature predicts that the governments which support religion and states with more religious populations will engage in more religious discrimination against religious minorities including Jews.

Testing the Influence of Religious Belief and State Support for Religion and SRD and GRD

In this section we analyze the impact of religious belief and state support for religion on societal religious discrimination (SRD) and government-based religious discrimination (GRD). The measures for SRD and GRD are those discussed in Chapter 2. The measure for state support for religion is taken from the main Religion and State (RAS) data set. It is a composite measure combining the following fifty-two ways a state might support religion:

- Marriage and divorce can only occur under religious auspices;
- Marriages performed by clergy of at least some religions are given automatic civil recognition, even in the absence of a state license;
- Restrictions on interfaith marriages;
- Restrictions on premarital sex;
- Laws which specifically make it illegal to be a homosexual or engage in homosexual sex;
- Prohibitive restrictions on abortion;
- Restrictions on access to birth control;
- Women may not go out in public unescorted;
- Women are required to wear some form of religious dress or are subject to public modesty laws other than the common restrictions on public nudity;

- Female testimony in court is given less weight than male testimony;
- Restrictions on women other than those listed elsewhere in this list.
- Dietary laws (restrictions on the production, import, selling, or consumption of specific foods);
- Restrictions or prohibitions on the sale of alcoholic beverages;
- Laws of inheritance defined by religion;
- Religious precepts used to define crimes or set punishment for crimes such as murder, theft, etc.;
- The charging of interest is illegal or significantly restricted;
- Required public dress or modesty laws for men other than common restrictions on public nudity;
- Restrictions on conversions away from the dominant religion;
- Significant restrictions on public music or dancing other than the usual zoning restrictions;
- Mandatory closing of some/all businesses during religious holidays, the Sabbath, or its equivalent;
- Other restrictions on activities during religious holidays, the Sabbath, or its equivalent;
- Blasphemy laws, or any other restriction on speech about majority religion or religious figures;
- Censorship of press or other publications on grounds of being anti-religious;
- Presence of a police force or other government agency which exists solely to enforce religious laws;
- Presence of religious courts with jurisdiction family law and inheritance;
- Presence of religious courts with jurisdiction over matters of law other than family law and inheritance;
- Government funding of religious primary/secondary schools or religious education programs in non-public schools;
- Government funding of seminary schools;
- Government funding of religious education in colleges or universities;
- Government funding of religious charitable organizations including hospitals;
- Government collects taxes on behalf of religious organizations;
- Official government positions/salaries/other funding for clergy excluding salaries of teachers;
- Direct general grants to religious organizations;
- Funding for building, maintaining, or repairing religious sites;
- Free air time on television or radio is provided to religious organizations on government channels or by government decree;
- Funding or other government support for religious pilgrimages such as the Hajj;

- Funding for religious organizations or activities other than those listed earlier;
- Some religious leaders are given diplomatic status, diplomatic passports, or immunity from prosecution by virtue of their religious office;
- Presence of an official government ministry or department dealing with religious affairs;
- Certain government officials are also given an official position in the state church by virtue of their political office;
- Certain religious officials become government officials by virtue of their religious position;
- Some or all government officials must meet certain religious requirements in order to hold office;
- Seats in legislative branch/cabinet are by law or custom granted, at least in part, along religious lines;
- Religious education is present in public schools;
- Presence of official prayer sessions in public schools;
- Public schools are segregated by religion, or separate public schools exist for members of some religions;
- The presence of religious symbols on the state's flag;
- Religion listed on state identity cards or other government documents that most citizens must possess or fill out;
- A registration process for religious organizations exists which is in some manner different from the registration process for other nonprofit organizations;
- Burial is controlled by religious organizations or clergy or otherwise subject to religious laws or oversight;
- Blasphemy laws protecting minority religions or religious figures;
- Other religious prohibitions or practices that are mandatory.[10]

In order to examine the level of religiosity in a country's population, we use the World Values Survey (WVS).[11] The WVS is a global survey of values and beliefs consisting of representative, national surveys of eighty-seven countries representing 90 percent of the world's population. Appendix A provides more details on the WVS data and a listing of cases included in this study, which are those that overlap between the WVS and RASM3 data sets, as well as the control variables used on the multivariate analysis.

We use two WVS variables to measure the religiosity of the population. The first is the percentage of respondents in a country who consider religion important in their lives.[12] The second variable represents the percentage of respondents in a country who said they attend religious services at least once a month. Thus

Table 3.2 Support for Religion, Religiosity and Discrimination

Cause of Discrimination	Influence on	
	Societal Discrimination	Government-Based Discrimination
Government support for religion	More discrimination	More discrimination
Percent of population which considers religion important in their lives	Less discrimination	No influence
Percent of population which attends religious services at least once a month	Less discrimination	No influence

The full multivariate analyses represented in this table are presented in Appendix A.

the variables represent self-identification as religious and a basic element of religious practice.

Overall, the results, as presented in Table 3.2, show that while government support for religion increases levels of both SRD[13] and GRD,[14] both religiosity variables are associated with lower levels of SRD and have no influence on GRD. We discuss these findings in more detail in the following section.

Explaining the Link between Religion and Discrimination against Jews

Both the literature on anti-Semitism and the general literature on religion and politics predict that religious beliefs and government support for religion should increase levels of discrimination against Jewish minorities. More specifically, they predict that strong religious beliefs among a country's majority will lead to discrimination against Jews and that governments more closely connected to religion are more likely to discriminate against Jewish minorities. Our findings show the latter is accurate, but the former is not.

Why Do Religious Governments Discriminate against Jews?

The results for government behavior are not particularly surprising or difficult to understand. Governments behave pretty much as most would expect; those that are more closely connected to a single religion discriminate more against Jews.

This is likely due to both theologically based intolerance and the power politics of maintaining a religious monopoly.

One reason this result is not surprising is that, as noted earlier in this chapter, all previous studies looking at GRD in general found a link between government support for religion and GRD. However, confirming that this finding applies specifically to Jewish minorities is an important contribution because previous results show that generally applicable causes of GRD sometimes do not apply to some minorities.

Government support for religion is also linked to SRD, though as described in more detail in Appendix A, this result is slightly weaker than the results for GRD. This makes sense in that one would expect government support for religion, one aspect of government religion policy, to have a stronger link to GRD, another aspect of government religion policy, than one would find with SRD, which measures societal behavior.

Many argue that societal behavior and attitudes are at least in theory linked to government religion policy. As noted in Chapters 1 and 2, Grim and Finke (2011) argue that SRD is a cause of GRD, though this study finds no such link for Jewish minorities. Helbling and Traunmuller (2015: 2) also argue for such a link in the context of explaining attitudes toward Muslim minorities in the West:

> governments play a considerable role in shaping citizens' attitudes toward the Muslim minority through the way they regulate religion. By relying on close cooperative relations between the state and the religious majority and by implementing institutions of state support for the dominant religious tradition, governments contribute to a sense of religious–cultural identity among citizens that ultimately shapes attitudes toward Muslims and their religious practices.

Thus, they in essence argue that government support for religion influences SRD. This study finds this argument to be accurate for Jewish minorities across the world.

Why Do Religious Societies Engage in Less Discrimination against Jews?

The results for religiosity's theorized influence on discrimination are more intriguing. A straightforward interpretation of the theory on the topic would lead us to expect societal religiosity to result in *higher* levels of both SRD and GRD. However, our results clearly show that this is not the case. In fact, this study not only finds no support for any causal relationship between religiosity and GRD against Jewish minorities, it also finds that increased religiosity leads to *lower* levels of SRD against Jewish minorities. This is directly counter to theory-based predictions. More specifically, religiosity, as measured by whether people consider religion important in their lives and their attendance at religious services, has no so significant influence on GRD and causes lower levels of SRD. As we discuss in Appendix A, this is not a weak or marginal result. This relationship where societal religiosity lowers SRD is substantial.

Both of these results are surprising. We might expect the influence of religiosity on GRD, a form of government policy, to be weaker than it is on societal actions. That is, since it is the members of society who are both either religious or not and who engage in SRD, the link between the two should be more direct than it is for GRD. However, it is somewhat surprising to find that the level of religiosity in society has no influence at all on GRD.

Setting that aside for the moment, that religiosity in society is associated with lower SRD is even more surprising. Those who are religious are supposed to be less tolerant of the religious other, not more tolerant. Yet there are aspects of the literature which speak to this. As noted earlier in this chapter, two studies on attitudes toward Muslims in the West by van der Noll et al. (2018) and Helbling (2014) find that religious people in Europe are more tolerant of Muslim religious practices, such as the wearing of head coverings by Muslim women, than non-religious people.

These findings, combined with the findings from this study, suggest a potential explanation. We posit that there is a difference between institutional religion and societal religion in causing discrimination. In society, religious people recognize the importance of maintaining traditional religious practices and are, therefore, more tolerant of these practices by members of other religions. That is, someone who frequents a mosque or church is more likely to respect a synagogue. Similarly, those who engage in Christian and Muslim religious practices are more likely to respect members of other religions who engage in analogous religious practices.

This is important because a good portion of SRD against Jews is against those who are visibly Jewish; that is, it focuses on those who can be identified as Jewish. Setting aside speech acts, which can occur without targeting individuals, and the targeting of individuals who are prominent in society so their Jewish identity is known, much of the SRD is against Jews whose dress and actions are religious, as well as against religious buildings or locations or those who frequent these locations. Thus, as a good portion of SRD is targeted specifically at those aspects of Judaism that religious people from other religions are most likely to recognize as religious, this can account for lower levels of SRD in societies which are more religious.

We argue that this relationship between religiosity and SRD is a modern phenomenon. In modern times, religious people feel threatened by secularity and secularism (Norris and Inglehart, 2004). This threat of modernity and secularism against religion is, at least in some contexts, becoming more important to at least some religious people than is the question of which religion is superior and dominant.

That is, there are two crosscutting influences. On one hand, many religious people desire to maintain the superiority of their religion. On the other hand, religious people are better able to understand the importance of maintaining religious rituals and practices, even those practiced by another religion. For most of history, the former has by far overshadowed the latter.

However, in modern times, many religious people across religions see secularism as a significant challenge to their religion. Due to this threat, they may feel a form of affinity or respect toward religious members of other religions. People from other religions can be seen as potential allies, or at least as kindred souls who hold similar values in a fight against a common secular enemy. Fox (2015) argues that in modern times there is an overt competition between religious and secular political actors across the globe, and we see this alliance between the religious across religions as an element of this global secular-religious competition.

This relationship is clearly contextual to situations where religious people see a common threat to all religion in secularism, and there are certainly exceptions to this relationship. Any society will likely include some religious bigots regardless of their perceptions of secularism as a threat. Also this process would likely be weaker in countries with sufficient levels of religiosity that secularism is not seen as a threat. That being said, the evidence presented here indicates that this pan-religious affinity among the religious is the dominant trend in the seventy-six countries with Jewish minorities included in this study. While the evidence suggests that this is true with regard to behavior toward Jews, further study is necessary to determine whether this also applies to other religious minorities.

Another possible element of the explanation for this phenomenon is the popularity of secular ideology. As we discuss in Chapter 2, a portion of GRD against Jews is motivated by secular ideology. These are specifically restrictions on religious practices that are considered counter to some manifestations of secular ideology. As we note, the two most relevant practices are infant circumcision and kosher slaughter, both central elements of the Jewish faith. This raises a possibility that at least some secular elements in a society resent Jews, at least in part, due to their religious practices. Thus, as the percentage of secular people in a country rises, which of course would mean a drop in the number of religious people, there would be more of this kind of SRD. Thus, at least in part, the religiosity measures used in this study may also be measuring the presence of adherents of secularism in a country.

Institutional religion, on the other hand, has the opposite effect. Supporting one religion over all others, whether or not this involves declaring an official religion, is a significant policy decision. While this does not necessarily lead to GRD, a religious monopoly is difficult to maintain without repressing religious minorities (Casanova, 2009; Froese, 2004: 36; Gill, 2005: 13; 2008: 43; Grim & Finke, 2011: 70; Stark & Bainbridge, 1985: 508; Stark & Finke, 2000: 199; Stark & Iannaccone, 1994: 232) Even without a conscious decision to repress, it indicates a bias in favor of one religion that can still influence decisions on policy toward minority religions. Thus, this institutional bias in favor of a majority religion's correlation with GRD against Jews is part of a general trend where governments more closely connected to a religion are more likely to engage in more GRD against all religious minorities (Fox, 2020).

Given the results presented here, the correlation between government support for religion and SRD against Jews can be due to either or both of two processes. First, as argued by Helbling and Traunmuller (2015: 2), the government's choice of a single religion strengthens biases against minority religions in society. Second, it is a reflection of preexisting biases against minority religions in society. While this study focuses on discrimination against Jews, this relationship hints that it may also apply to other religious minorities.

A Religious Realignment?

Overall, this finding suggests that there may be a realignment taking place in the basic dynamics of religious discrimination in modern Western societies. At the societal level, we are seeing a shift from traditional hatred of the religious other to an alliance across religions among those who still consider themselves religious against the encroachment of secularism. This realignment has not yet translated to the behavior of governments, but there are indications that it might. In recent decades, Sweden and Norway disestablished their national churches, and Greece is in the process of distancing itself from its national Church.

While none of these countries, at the time of this writing, has become fully neutral on the issue of religion, they are moving closer toward neutrality than they had been in the past. This form of neutrality is imperfect, but certainly more neutral than before. It continues to support religion, and perhaps even gives some preference to the (former) national Church. However, other religions are receiving more support from the government than they had in the past. This has two relevant implications. First, as unequal support decreases, so should GRD. Second, this may be an indication that a realignment of the relationship between government support for religion and discrimination against religious minorities, similar to the realignment that seems to be taking place at the societal level, may be in its early stages. Only time will tell.

Whether this realignment will increase or decrease discrimination against Jews is unclear. On one hand, this alliance across religions in societies where secularism is seen as a common threat will likely continue to reduce levels of this discrimination, but only if this trend continues. Historically, religions tend to be intolerant of one another, and to the extent it is present, this alliance is new and fragile. On the other hand, secularism as an ideology can be as intolerant of practices which contradict its tenets as the most intractable religious ideologies. More extreme forms of secularism can target religious practices in general. As we discuss in this chapter and in Chapter 2, secular ideologies are an important source of discrimination against Jews, among others. As this inter-religious alliance is based on the threats posed by secularism, this alliance will likely only remain in place as long as this secular threat is present and is capable of demanding restrictions on Jewish practices its advocates deem unacceptable. Thus, the very circumstances that increase religious tolerance for Jews include a newer form of secular-based intolerance. We posit that this is consistent with the Haggadah's prediction of the Jews facing a new enemy every generation.

That being said, none of this indicates that the religious motive for discrimination against Jews has disappeared or is likely to disappear. Whatever the larger trends, it is clear that in some quarters, religion remains a motivation for discrimination against Jews. For example, "the most violent American and European antisemites in the 21st century, at least all of those who murdered Jews for being Jewish, made some reference to religion in their hatred of Jews. Many explicitly justified their action in religious terms" (Jikely, 2020: 3). In addition, as noted, governments more strongly associated with a religion discriminate more. Thus, the religious motivation for discriminating against Jews is complex, with crosscutting influences.

4

Anti-Zionism and Anti-Israel Behavior and Sentiment

The second potential cause of discrimination against Jews that we address in this study is anti-Zionism and anti-Israel sentiment. On a basic level, this theory predicts a link between opposition to the state of Israel and discrimination against Jews. This relationship works concurrently along two mechanisms that are documented in the literature. First, anti-Zionism can mirror and is often a cover for more classical anti-Semitism; that is, anti-Zionism can be a "politically correct" cover for those who seek to target Jews for other reasons. Thus, when this form of anti-Zionism manifests, it is basically an indicator of levels of other forms of anti-Semitism.

Second, there is a tendency among at least some anti-Zionists to ascribe to all Jews responsibility for the perceived injustices committed by Israel or for the existence of Israel itself. Thus, the ideology can in and of itself be a motivation for discrimination against Jews.

However, in line with the vast majority of academic literature on the topic, we do not mean to imply that either of these trends can be ascribed to all anti-Zionists or to all people who hold anti-Israel views or who criticize Israel. In fact, the relationship between views on Zionism and anti-Semitism is quite complex. Views on Israel do not automatically translate into views on Jews. Also, just as many who hold anti-Zionist views do not express anti-Semitic views, there are Christian theologies that are pro-Israel but hold what can be classified as negative views on Jews. Zuckerman (1996: 25) discusses how this plays out in Armageddon theology, which

> reveals a contradictory impulse toward Jews. On the one hand, the return of Jews to Israel is to be encouraged, and Jews are to be positively supported in their endeavors to strengthen Israel as a sign of the hastening of the End of Times. On the other hand, it is anticipated that most Jews will suffer terribly during the period of Tribulation and that only those Jews who converted to Christ in the end will be redeemed.

Thus, Armageddon theology's support for Israel is combined with a belief that Jews are deserving of punishment for believing in the wrong God, a key element of the theologically based anti-Semitism discussed in the previous chapter. This set of beliefs is held only by a portion of US Christians who support Israel.

In contrast, there is a small portion of Christians who believe that Israel is a "violation of Christian teachings and as a false interpretation of the Jewish Bible" because Christians have replaced Jews as the chosen people (Jikeli, 2020: 4). Overall, Christian views on whether God's covenant with the Jews is still valid and, if valid, whether it includes a Jewish right to the state of Israel vary considerably (Jikeli, 2020).

For these reasons among others, the empirical portion of this chapter does not directly address either anti-Zionism or anti-Semitism. Rather, it focuses on anti-Israel attitudes and behavior as a potential cause for discrimination against Jews. That being said, it is difficult to discuss anti-Israel movements and attitudes without discussing anti-Zionism and its relationship to anti-Semitism. Still, we limit this discussion to the evolution and nature of the claims made by anti-Zionists and why there is a theoretical basis to believe that anti-Zionist beliefs or anti-Israel sentiment can cause discrimination against Jews outside of Israel.

This chapter proceeds as follows. First, we discuss our theoretical perspective on anti-Zionism. Second, we survey the history and content of the various manifestations of anti-Zionism. Third, we look at parallel theories in the general literature on the causes of discrimination. Finally, we examine the correlation between measures of anti-Zionism and discrimination against Jews.

Our Theoretical Perspective on Anti-Zionism

As the goal of this study is to examine the causes of discrimination against Jews, we examine the literature and theories on anti-Zionism with a view to elicit what causal predictions can be found in this literature. In doing so, we include in this discussion literatures such as those which suggest that anti-Zionism is de facto anti-Semitism and the extent to which anti-Semitic motifs and conspiracy theories about Jews are present in anti-Zionist discourse. It is not our intent to paint all who hold anti-Israel attitudes with the same brush. This group is diverse and holds a wide range of views. Rather, we seek to examine precisely those elements of the anti-Zionist movement which are most likely to cause discrimination against Jews, to demonstrate that there is a theoretical basis to believe such a causal effect might exist, and to examine the nuances of this theorized causality.

Anti-Zionism is linked to events in the Middle East. This has two manifestations. First, many anti-Zionists believe that the establishment of state of Israel is illegitimate. Second, many object to specific Israeli government policies. While these criticisms focus to a great extent on Israel's actual policies, there is also a nontrivial element that ascribes to Israel nefarious policies with little basis in fact. These fictional policies often overlap with classic conspiracy theories against Jews, the subject of Chapter 5 of this volume.

Thus, in this chapter we discuss these views when relevant to our discussion of anti-Zionism, and in Chapter 5 we discuss them in the context of conspiracy theories against Jews, a phenomenon which predates anti-Zionism by more than a millennium. We posit that the anti-Zionism and conspiracy theory literatures provide important but different perspectives on this issue, which bring up different questions and theoretical predictions. For this reason we discuss them separately.

While views which blame all Jews for Israel's behavior or existence are on the extreme end of those who hold anti-Israel or anti-Zionist views, we posit that they are particularly important to understanding the causes of discrimination against Jews. That is, it is in particular when all Jews, including those living outside of Israel, are blamed that discrimination against Jews outside of Israel becomes more likely. Thus, we place particular emphasis on this element of anti-Zionism in this discussion in order to provide a foundation for this theory. Some of this discussion necessarily focuses on the links theorized in the literature between this aspect of anti-Zionism and anti-Semitism.

In addition, we discuss the use of anti-Semitic motifs in anti-Zionist discourse. Again, we make no claim that this is representative of all anti-Zionists, and it certainly is not representative of all who criticize Israel's policies. Rather, we seek to establish that such anti-Semitic motifs are present in at least some elements of anti-Zionist discourse. We argue that the presence of anti-Semitism in at least some elements of the anti-Zionist movement may influence the link, if any, between anti-Zionism and discrimination against Jews.

In this vein, we also discuss a literature which explicitly argues that anti-Zionism often constitutes anti-Semitism. We treat this literature as a body of theory which argues that there is a link between anti-Zionism and anti-Semitism and, therefore, it predicts that anti-Israel activities and beliefs may predict discrimination against Jews. This literature also provides some predictions of the circumstances under which anti-Zionism will be more strongly linked to anti-Semitism and, therefore, to discrimination against Jews.

We do not delve into the question of the legitimacy of the existence of the state of Israel or the accuracy of the claims made by anti-Zionists about Israel, other than to sometimes note that some claims regarding Israel's activities are non-evidence-based. Nor do we take a stand on the issue of the morality, correctness, or lack thereof of any policies by the Israeli government. Our sole concern is to discuss the anti-Zionist ideology, its advocates, the movement associated with it, and the relationship between all of these and discrimination against Jewish minorities outside of the state of Israel, if any such relationship exists. That being said, both the legitimacy of the establishment of Israel and policies and actions taken by Israel's government are central issues among anti-Zionists. We accordingly address these issues in that context.

We would also like to emphasize that we do not argue that criticism of Israel's government or its policies, and even anti-Zionism, are in and of themselves anti-Semitic. No government should be immune from criticism, and Israel is no exception. However, as we note, it is not uncommon that modern anti-Zionist discourse contains classical anti-Semitic stereotypes and tropes. A very effective method of identifying anti-Semitic anti-Zionism is Sharansky's (2004) "3D" test, which posits that the presence of any of the following three phenomena indicates anti-Semitism:

- *Demonization*: When Israeli actions are brought out of their proportions and when Israeli actions are compared to Nazi actions.
- *Double standard (discrimination)*: When there is a selective criticism over Israel and not over similar cases by others; when Israel is being criticized for harming human rights, but states such as Iran, North Korea, Syria, Cuba, and China are not being criticized.
- *Delegitimization*: When Israel's right of existence is being denied, while all other states have that right.

As we argued earlier, we would add to this list manifestations of anti-Zionism that blame all Jews for the perceived bad behavior of Israel. Sharansky likely does not include the latter on his list because his list focuses on types of critiques of Israel which he argues are anti-Semitic, and this last manifestation focuses not on Israel but on world Jewry. As we discuss in detail in this chapter, in some cases anti-Zionists do explicitly hold all Jews responsible for the perceived bad behavior of Israel. We argue that it is these manifestations of anti-Zionism that are more likely to result in discrimination against Jews. This makes the line between legitimate criticism of Israel and anti-Semitic manifestations of anti-Zionism theoretically and empirically important.

We also acknowledge that previous studies have shown an empirical link between ant-Zionist attitudes and anti-Semitic attitudes. Specifically, several survey-based studies find that people who hold anti-Zionist attitudes are more likely to hold anti-Semitic attitudes and vice versa (Kaplan & Small, 2006; Frindte et al., 2005).[1] However, it is important to emphasize that these studies show probabilities; that is, anti-Zionist views are not automatically anti-Semitic, nor do they automatically mean that those who hold such views are also anti-Semites. Rather, one who holds anti-Zionist or anti-Israel attitudes is statistically more likely to also hold anti-Semitic attitudes than someone who does not hold such attitudes. Studies also show that anti-Semitic incidents in Western countries spike at times of Israeli military confrontations with Palestinians (Feinberg, 2020a, 2020b; Jacobs et al., 2011).

The empirical findings in this chapter are consistent with these studies and show that measures of anti-Israel behavior and sentiment are clearly linked to discrimination against Jews outside of Israel. This adds to previous studies which focus on anti-Israel sentiment causing anti-Jewish attitudes. Here we show that anti-Israel sentiment and behavior can also lead to actions, more specifically to discrimination against Jews.

More precisely, we find that in Christian-majority countries, states which vote more often against Israel in the United Nations General Assembly also tend to engage in more government-based religious discrimination (GRD) against Jews. Anti-Israel and pro-Palestine views within a population are linked to more GRD against Jews. However, UN voting records on Israel and Palestine do not lead to more societal religious discrimination (SRD) against Jews, and pro-Palestine views are at most weakly connected to SRD. This implies that while government actions against Jews are, at least in part, connected to anti-Israel sentiment, there is no systematic connection between anti-Israel sentiment in society and societal actions taken against Jews. This implies that anti-Jewish actions taken by members of society, ranging from graffiti on synagogues to violent attacks against Jews, likely have other motives. The "Israel" motive is likely at least in part a cover for these other motives.

This chapter proceeds as follows. First, we discuss the history and content of the various manifestations of anti-Zionism. Second, we examine the links between anti-Zionism and discrimination against Jews. Third, we look at parallel theories in the general literature on the causes of discrimination. Finally, we examine the correlation between measures of anti-Zionism and discrimination against Jews.

From National Emancipation to Delegitimization Campaigns: A Brief History of Anti-Zionism

Modern anti-Zionism can trace its roots to the success of Zionism. In the wake of the historical events surrounding World War II and the Holocaust, the Jewish people established the state of Israel in 1948. An Arab coalition declared war on the newly founded state and tried unsuccessfully to prevent Israel's establishment and independence. This coalition included Egypt, Jordan, Iraq, Syria, Saudi Arabia, the Arab Liberation Army, the Army of the Holy War, supporters from the Muslim Brotherhood movement, supporters from Pakistan, and many other countries.

Anti-Zionism as a politically relevant and important phenomenon was a re-action to Israel's establishment. That being said, it is important to emphasize two aspects of anti-Zionism. First, anti-Zionism existed before the establishment of the state of Israel. It rose concurrently with the rise of the modern Zionist movement itself in the late nineteenth century. Zionism is an idea that was never unopposed. However, this discussion focuses on anti-Zionism after the estab-lishment of the state of Israel.

Second, while it is not the focus of this book to determine what is and is not anti-Semitism, it is clear that there are some types of anti-Zionism that are not necessarily anti-Semitic, such as post-nation-state anti-Zionism, an opposition of all nation-states and not just the Jewish one.

However, as noted earlier, much of the literature on the topic is not neutral on this issue. Many explicitly argue that anti-Zionist trends are anti-Semitic. Some even call anti-Zionism the "New Antisemitism" (e.g., Sharansky, 2004; Bartov, 2005; Harrison, 2006; Wistrich, 2013; Heni, 2013; Gerstenfeld, 2015; Rosenfeld, 2015; Chesler, 2014; Johnson, 2016; Rich, 2016; Topor, 2018, 2021). They argue that anti-Zionism disguises its Jew-hatred as something else, such as left poli-tics, post-colonialism, human rights promotion, and the Enlightenment. From this perspective, the "new" anti-Semitism is not so new. This literature is not lacking in evidence that at least some anti-Zionists behave similarly to classic anti-Semites. It documents that many anti-Zionists use the exact same tropes and prejudices that classical anti-Semites use against Jews, but direct it against the state of Israel and any Jewish support for Israel. From the perspective of this literature, while pre-1948 anti-Semitism existed mostly in right-wing circles, post-1948 anti-Semitism exists in both right- and left-wing circles.

Wistrich (2013) argues that anti-Zionism is perhaps most pronounced in Arab and Muslim-majority states and, not surprisingly, among Palestinians. Some of its advocates engage in efforts to delegitimize, demonize, and dehumanize Israel, Israeli citizens, and even Jews who are not related to Israel and live in other places in the world. Extreme anti-Zionists, especially among Muslim fundamentalists, claim that the Jews created post-colonialism, post-imperialism, democracy, and the democratization process, as well as the globalization and liberalization trends, in order to suppress Muslims and Islam and to control the world. This type of argument can also be found among some left-wing political activists in the West. This is an example of anti-Zionists borrowing from older conspiracy theories about Jews controlling the world (Litvak & Webman, 2010; Rich, 2016; Topor, 2018, 2021).

There are many early links between anti-Zionism in the Muslim world and anti-Semitic motifs, conspiracy theories, and individuals. For example, after the establishment of the state of Israel, Muslim movements such as the Muslim Brotherhood promoted anti-Semitic propaganda to discredit Jewish independence. Moreover, when some Nazi officers sought shelter after the defeat of the Axis powers, Egypt embraced them as military consultants for the "Jewish problem" of the Arab world. Even the Palestinian mufti of Jerusalem, Mohammed Amin al-Husseini, supported the Nazi regime and met with Adolf Hitler himself. After the Arab defeat in 1948, Arab leaders applied common anti-Semitic prejudices to Israel and blamed the Jews for controlling the media, the global economy, and even other states. Muslim clergymen, politicians, and scholars all blamed the Jews for the failing Arab economies and societies. The alleged motivation for these nefarious activities and conspiracies was support for the state of Israel (Wistrich, 2013).

Thus, Israel was blamed for many of the ills of the Arab world. Jews in general were blamed for supporting or even spearheading the efforts to create these ills in order to support the state of Israel. The accusations against Israel and Jews mirrored closely classic anti-Semitic tropes and conspiracy theories. However, they added a new element which ascribed to the global Jewish conspiracy the goal of creating and maintaining the state of Israel. This became a common pattern for anti-Zionist inspired anti-Semitism.

Arab nationalism, which was an increasingly popular ideology in the Arab world at the time of Israel's establishment and for several decades thereafter, effectively adopted anti-Semitic motifs from the religious types and the common European types. Even before 1948, in most Arab countries classic anti-Semitic texts such as *The Protocols of the Elders of Zion*, *Ford's International Jew*, Hitler's *Mein Kampf*, and August Rohling's *Talmud Jew* were translated and widely distributed (Perry and Schweitzer, 2008; Litvak & Webman, 2010). Many in the Arab world, including governments and the media, made use of conspiracy-theory accusations. For instance, the Jews were blamed for spreading the AIDS epidemic among Arab military officers in the second half of the twentieth century in a manner similar to the case of the Black plague in medieval times (Laqueur, 2006). This is an example of the "well poisoning" trope which we discuss in more detail in Chapter 5. There were also more classic blood libels, such as a Syrian TV show broadcast widely throughout the Middle East in which Jews kill a Muslim child to get blood to bake matzah for Passover (also discussed on more detail in Chapter 5).[2]

In another example of this phenomenon, the April 1981 issue of *al-Da'wa'*, a major Muslim Brotherhood journal, was devoted to the 12 Jewish sins. These sins are almost identical to ancient Christian and Muslim anti-Semitism: opportunism, schizophrenia, racism, the desire to destroy the world, egoism, looting, sadism, lust for money, blackmail, pledge violations, lack of integrity, and spread of conflicts (Bodansky, 1999).

The 1967 war caused a transformation in anti-Zionist movement which led to the increased popularity of the movement worldwide. The Arab countries lost a significant amount of land to Israel, including the Golan Heights, the West Bank, the Sinai Peninsula, and the Gaza strip. When Israel was established in 1948, the Jewish people, previously perceived as persecuted, became the pioneers of hope and freedom. Many admired their ability to establish a state after the genocide of the Holocaust.

In contrast, in 1967 the Israelis already had a state. The 1967 military victory shifted perceptions of Israel in many quarters. It was seen as an illegitimate conqueror, occupier, and oppressor by many nations and people around the world. This created a perception of Palestinian Arabs as the new victims and as a stateless people. This view was particularly popular among the far left and in the developing world, much of which had recently gained their independence from colonial powers or had yet to gain their independence (Litvak & Webman, 2010; Topor, 2018).

This led to a rise in anti-Zionism among the global left. While much of this involved criticism of Israel's policies similar to criticism of other countries, some of it was overtly anti-Semitic. In fact, it led to new genera of anti-Semitic illustrations and caricatures of Jews in the Arab press and literature. Post-1967 caricatures depicted the Jewish people as oppressors and even as Nazis (Kotek, 2004).

Anti-Zionism also became mired in the superpower struggles of the Cold War. As the Soviet Union and the United States collided through their allies and proxies in the Middle East, the Soviets began spreading propaganda about Israel, an important American ally in the region. Internationally, this propaganda accused Israel of being an American imperial ally which tried to strengthen American control and power in the region. Domestically, some of the Soviet elite, including Stalin in the early 1950s, oppressed their Jewish citizens on the grounds that they were a fifth column that would eventually support the United States, based on the assumption of Jewish loyalty to Israel over that of their home country, a classic anti-Semitic trope (Kostychenko, 1995; Brandenberger, 2005; Brent & Naumov, 2003).

Historically, the Soviet hostility to Israel and even to Judaism was based upon the ideological foundations of Marxism and early socialism. Karl Marx was born as a Jew but quickly renounced Judaism. Though he did use anti-Semitic stereotypes in his writings, it can be argued that he criticized Judaism as an ethnocentric group that did not fall fully into his social vision. Marx wanted to free society from capitalism, Judaism, and religion in general (Blanchard, 1984). As he wrote in *The Jewish Question*: "What is the secular basis of Judaism? Practical need, *self-interest*. What is the worldly religion of the Jew? *Huckstering*. What is his worldly God? *Money*.... The *social* emancipation of the Jew is the *emancipation of society from Judaism*" (Marx, 1844).

The Socialists, the Leninists, and the revolutionary groups in Russia and elsewhere based their ideology and criticism on Marxism, and specifically on its opposition to religion in general, which included Judaism. However, since Jews were seen as money seeking and greedy, some socialists conflated Jews with capitalism and with the Western world. Thus, among these groups, opposition to the state of Israel is linked to opposition to the United States, the West, and capitalism in general (Wistrich, 1979, 1990).

After the 1967 war and during the 1970s, anti-Zionism emerged as a significant political force in Europe, as well as in the developing world. This manifestation focused on Israel's occupation of Palestinian territory, as well as arguments that Israel oppressed the Palestinians. They advocated that the Gaza strip, Sinai, the West Bank, and East Jerusalem should all be handed back to the Arabs.

Moreover, this discourse facilitated a return of anti-Semitic expressions into mainstream political discourse among the political left. The peak of this early left anti-Zionism was likely the 1975 United Nations General Assembly Resolution 3379, which regarded Zionism as racism.[3] Seventy-five nations voted in favor of characterizing Jewish nationalism (and no other form of nationalism) as racism, including the German Democratic Republic, Poland, and the Soviet Union itself, among others. Though Great Britain and France voted against the act, many of their citizens supported it (Weitzman, 2008; Litvak & Webman, 2010; Topor, 2018, 2021).

The Iranian Islamic revolution of 1979 placed into power a regime that was headed by the anti-Semitic and anti-Zionist Ayatollah Ruhollah Khomeini. The regime declared that Israel was an imperial mistake which should be corrected (Weitzman, 2008; Litvak & Webman, 2010). Since that point in time, it has repeatedly and publicly stated its desire to destroy the "Zionist entity" and has engaged in Holocaust denial and other classical forms of anti-Semitic propaganda.

In the 1990s, events contributed to a decline in the popularity of anti-Zionism. More specifically, Israel was seen as changing its behavior and seeking peace. The 1991 Madrid Conference represented an ideational shift. In Madrid, Arab states, the Palestinian delegation, and Israel had shifted from an outlook of a zero-sum game to a mutual gain outlook.[4] The conference was the first time in the history of the conflict that the Israeli and the Palestinian delegations, the latter as part of a Jordanian delegation, had negotiated with each other (Herman & Newman, 2000: 107–153). As an indirect result of the conference, Israel and Jordan signed a peace agreement in October 1994 (Barak, 2005) which complimented the 1978 peace treaty with Egypt. Moreover, just before the conference took place, the United Nations had revoked the anti-Zionist and anti-Semitic resolution 3379 and adopted the General Assembly's resolution 46/86. Now, while 72 nations voted in favor of resolution 3379, 111 nations voted in favor of its revocation. Interestingly, Israel's Arab and Muslim neighbors voted against it, including

Jordan, Lebanon, Syria, Saudi Arabia, Iraq, and Iran, among others. Egypt abstained.[5]

What became known as the Oslo peace process began shortly thereafter. Yasser Arafat, chairman of the Palestine Liberation Organization (PLO), sent a letter to the late Israeli prime minister, Yitzhak Rabin, on September 9, 1993. Arafat promised to recognize Israel's right of existence, to accept UN Security Council Resolutions 242[6] and 338,[7] and to negotiate a peace settlement with Israel. Israel, in response, recognized the PLO as the Palestinians' representative. On September 13 of that year, the Declaration of Principles between Israel and the PLO, concerning the former's existence and the latter's sovereignty, was signed in Washington, DC—the First Oslo Accord (Oslo A). This was followed by the second Oslo agreement (Oslo B) on September 28, 1995. This agreement was meant to strengthen what was now the Palestinian Authority and to give it responsibility over all Palestinian internal affairs (Herman & Newman, 2000: 107–153).

As a result of this, anti-Zionism declined in the 1990s with the belief that Israel would give up land and some regional interests, allowing a Palestinian independent state to be established. This decline continued until the failure of the 2000 Camp David Summit. Israeli prime minister Ehud Barak offered Yasser Arafat more than 90% of the West Bank, but Arafat rejected the offer. This led to the second Palestinian Intifada (Swisher, 2004: 312–334). These events revived the negative and critical stance within the European and global left which depicted Israel as an illegal and illegitimate occupier and oppressor (Topor, 2018).

This coincided with another shift in global trends in anti-Zionism. From 1948 until the early 2000s, anti-Zionism was mostly initiated by Arab and Muslim nations, opposing Israel's right of existence. This opposition was also supported and promoted by the Palestinians and the global post-colonial left ideology (Topor, 2018). The element of critiques of Israel's behavior was present, but it was not dominant.

At the beginning of the twenty-first century, critiques of Israel's behavior, real and imagined, increased. Some nongovernmental actors started promoting anti-Zionism. In some cases they blamed Israel and its Jewish supporters worldwide for most of the problems in the Middle East. However, most of them focused on Israel's policies toward the Palestinians.

Nongovernmental organizations (NGOs) and civil society organizations (CSOs) intensified their criticism over Israel, specifically regarding its policies toward the Palestinians. NGOs such as Human Rights Watch, the United Nations Human Rights Council, Amnesty International, and the International Federation of Human Rights began to devote more resources toward highlighting Israel's policies toward the Palestinians. While these organizations engage in a wide variety of other projects of promoting human rights and anti-racist acts, many argue that the resources they devoted to the rights of the Palestinians were highly disproportional. That is, they posit that, even if one accepts that all allegations made by these organizations are fully accurate, Israel is given a wildly disproportionate level of attention. Some go so far as to argue that this constitutes a double standard and discrimination against Israel (Steinberg, 2011).

The Durban conference against racism in 2001 serves as a good example. At this conference, despite the unfortunate abundance of human rights violators in the world, Israel was given a much higher level of attention. At the entrance of the conference, flyers were distributed widely among the visitors. The flyers contained anti-Semitic stereotypes applied to the state of Israel, including copies of the *Protocols of the Elders of Zion* and Nazi-like caricatures of Jews. The Durban conference and, later, the United Nations Human Rights Council called for an immediate weapons embargo and economic sanctions on Israel. Moreover, Israel was compared to the South African apartheid regime. Other countries that have objectively poor human rights records and that arguably behave worse in this respect than Israel, such as Iran, Venezuela, and North Korea, were largely ignored. Many consider this a manifestation of anti-Zionism (Steinberg, 2011; Schoenberg, 2008; Bayefsky, 2002; Topor, 2021).[8]

On a more general level, this double standard argument holds that, while it is legitimate to discuss and even focus on Israel's treatment of the Palestinians, the level of disproportionality of this criticism of Israel as compared to other states is unjustifiably high. This literature attributes this criticism to anti-Semitism. While the literature tends to consider the disproportionality sufficient proof for this charge, it also argues that the anti-Semitic motifs that are present in at least some of this criticism support this argument.

This literature also argues that many of the critiques essentially posit that Israel behaves illegitimately based on actions that objectively are common behaviors among states. Kontorovich argues that this is true of the international law literature. For example, many critics argue that Israel is a discriminating state, apartheid, since it passed the Jewish Nation State law in its Knesset in July 2018, which describes Israel as a Jewish nation. Yet multiple countries, including several European countries, have similar laws, often in their constitutions. As of 2014, other than Israel, at least 42 countries, including nearly all Middle Eastern countries, declare an official religion. None of them is religiously homogeneous (Fox, 2015, 2019, 2020). Kontrovich similarly argues that Israel is often criticized for violating international law for other acts, such as the siege of Gaza, despite that these acts technically do not violate international laws and that countries engaging in similar acts elsewhere are rarely similarly criticized.[9]

However, anti-Semitism is not the only potential motive. This criticism of Israel may also be a diversionary tactic. Henne (2018), for example, in a study that does not focus on Israel, demonstrates that many countries are active in human rights efforts precisely to deflect criticism away from their own poor human rights records.

While this discussion has emphasized the elements of anti-Zionism which overlap with anti-Semitism, again, it is not our intention to argue that all anti-Zionists and all who criticize Israel are anti-Semitic. Rather, our purpose is to establish that such trends are present in anti-Zionist and anti-Israel discourse and movements. In the next section we discuss how these elements can potentially cause discrimination against Jews.

From Anti-Zionism to Discrimination

We argue here that a key link between anti-Zionism and discrimination against Jews is that in many cases, Jews outside of Israel are blamed and sometimes targeted for the perceived bad behavior of Israel. In some cases, those who criticize Israel's behavior consider all Jews to be part of the "evils" committed by Israel. Among those who oppose Israel's existence, some blame Jews for supporting the state of Israel. Thus they consider Jews complicit in and responsible for Israel's illegitimate existence. This, we argue, potentially provides a motivation to discriminate against Jews. This is a proposition we test empirically later in this chapter.

One manifestation of this phenomenon is the belief that Jews in countries like Britain, Germany, or the United States cannot be true citizens because of their loyalty to Israel. That some Jews actively oppose Israel's policies does not seem to undermine this in the eyes of at least some who hold this type of view; that is, even Jews who denounce Israel can still be suspect. This is analogous to the trend within Christianity described in Chapter 2 where even Jews who convert to Christianity are suspect due to an inherent imperfection that cannot be erased though conversion.

Another manifestation focuses on racism. If Zionism is racism, as enshrined by the UNGA 3379 resolution, and if Israel and the Jewish people are a whole, then all Jews are racists. This belief has led to some odd occurrences. On several occasions, anti-racist leftist groups in the United States and the United Kingdom blocked Jews and Israelis from attending and supporting other anti-racist and anti-fascist rallies. An awkward situation has evolved in which some anti-racist groups discriminate against Jews based on claims that all Jews, who are also Israel supporters, are racist and that all Jews are suspected of supporting Israel unless proven otherwise (Fine & Spencer, 2017; Topor, 2021).

A third manifestation excuses anti-Semitism and even violence toward Jews as the fault of Israel and Jewish support for Israel. Norman Geras argues that while not all who criticize Israel are anti-Semitic, a "substantial section" of the left uses Israel as an "alibi for a new climate of anti-Semitism on the left." This alibi phenomenon has multiple manifestations. First, it posits that anti-Semitism is caused solely by Israel. For example, according to this perspective, Arabs would not engage in Holocaust denial if it were not for their anger over the issue of Israel. Thus Israel's behavior or even existence is the reason for all anti-Semitism and, therefore, excuses it. Those who make this claim do not address why anti-Semitism existed before the founding of the state of Israel.[10]

A second manifestation of this phenomenon has it that expressing anti-Semitic tropes is not anti-Semitic unless the speaker intends them to be anti-Semitic. Geras (2013, n.p.) points out that this is an odd argument since "for no other kind of racism would such a narrowly-conceived" definition, which ignores "a language that embodies negative stereotypes, or of unconscious prejudicial assumptions, or of discriminatory practices, and so forth . . . be taken seriously even for a moment." Third, many simply ignore, dismiss as unimportant, or turn a blind eye to anti-Semitism. This can include the overtly anti-Semitic language used by groups like Hamas and Hezbollah in which anti-Semitism is ignored while the focus is shifted to their anti-Israel programs as criticism against Israel is indeed legitimate. It can also involve referring to terror attacks against Jews in the West as motivated by Israel, rather than anti-Semitism, despite abundant evidence of anti-Semitic ideas expressed by the terrorists.[11]

Finally, the intersectionality movement, which originated in feminist theory and has become "the dominant paradigm in many fields of study in the humanities and softer social sciences, [and] advocates treating oppressions as integrally linked" (Elman & Romirowsky, 2019: 228), has become increasingly anti-Zionist. Within this movement there is a developing "trend toward wiping the category 'liberal Zionist' off the map . . . even to the point of denying that Zionists of any kind can be feminists at all" (Brahm, 2019: 163). This has developed into a mandatory ideology in which disagreement is not permitted. "If you hold to one 'progressive' position, you've got to hold to everything else the leading progressives deem worthy of inclusion in their society. There is no room for disagreement among intersectional feminists" (Brahm, 2019: 163). There is also a trend within the movement which associates all Jews with "white privilege" and "oppression" (Brahm, 2019). Elman and Romirowsky (2019: 229) argue that this constitutes "anti-Jewish animus under the guise of anti-Zionism."[12]

This has led to a situation where Jews who identify with most aspects of the progressive movement but support Israel are ostracized. For example, in 2017 and 2018 at Chicago's "Dyke March," Jewish marchers were ejected for displaying a rainbow flag with a Jewish star, a Jewish symbol dating back to at least the twelfth century, which is also present on Israel's flag.

March organizers said last year in a statement that the women were ejected because they were pro-Israel while the march was explicitly anti-Zionist, and because of the Jewish star flag's "similarity to the Israeli flag and the flag's long history of use in pinkwashing efforts." Pinkwashing is a term used by critics of Israel alleging that the Israeli government touts its pro-LGBT policies in order to distract from its treatment of the Palestinians.[13]

The 2019 Washington, DC, Dyke March enacted a similar policy.[14] To place this in context, this would be akin to banning the cross because one is upset with Denmark, Finland, or Iceland, among many other countries, which have crosses on their flags.

Anti-Zionist ideologies can have practical consequences. That is, when Jews are blamed for Israel's policies, this can lead to overt discriminatory acts against Jews. This type of targeting is common on US college campuses. For example, in 2014 a pro-Palestinian organization marked the doors of many Jewish students and put paper notes on their dormitory room doors, blaming these Jewish students for Israeli policies in the conflict with the Palestinians.[15] A similar incident occurred in the dorms at Emory University in 2019, where activists posted eviction notices on the doors of Jewish students in protest against Israel's policies toward Palestinians.[16] To be clear, had these forms of protest been posted on all the doors in a dorm, this would not be singling out Jews for blame. That in both of these cases the notices were placed only on the doors of Jews signals that Jews outside of Israel are being blamed for Israel's perceived injustices. It is also a form of societal harassment and involves an implied threat in that it implicitly states, "we know who you are and where you live."

Another incident occurred at the University of California, Los Angeles, which focused on the dual loyalty trope. Rachel Beyda, a Jewish student who ran for student council, was asked by several student members whether she can be objective and not biased toward the state of Israel, simply because she is a Jew and belonged to a Jewish religious organization; that is, Rachel was asked whether she has dual loyalties. At first, the council voted against Rachel's attempt to be elected, and only after a university counselor intervened was she allowed to run for student council.[17]

In a similar incident at the University of Illinois at Champaign, the university's vice chancellor removed a Jewish student from the Campus Student Elections Commission during a discussion about divesting from Israeli companies and a debate over an Illinois Student Government resolution condemning the conflation of anti-Zionism with anti-Semitism, in which some students held up signs labeled "Free Palestine," "F— Zionists," and "F— Nazis, support Palestinians."[18] Other incidents at the university's campus between 2015 and 2020 include other incidents of Jews elected to student government being prevented from participating in the student legislation process, multiple incidents of vandalism of the university's Chabad house, anti-Semitic graffiti on campus including swastikas, rocks thrown through Jewish students' windows, and calling pro-Israel students "Nazis" and "white supremacists."[19]

These types of incidents are common. There have been anti-Semitic incidents at the majority of US college campuses with large Jewish populations. While the majority of these incidents take the form of classic anti-Semitism, about one-quarter of them are directly anti-Israel. However, anti-Israel incidents are more likely to show intent to harm Jewish students and staff. A study also found that the presence of anti-Israel activities and organizations on US college campuses is a strong predictor of anti-Semitic incidents on those campuses.[20]

This phenomenon is not limited to the United States. A 2019 study of young Jews (ages 16–34) in 12 European countries found that 46% had been subject to at least one anti-Semitic incident in the past 12 months. The report notes:

> Existing evidence shows that Jewish university students—especially those involved in some way in student politics—are known to be particularly susceptible to anti-Semitic harassment from their fellow students, often expressed in the form of anti-Israel discourse . . . over half of the young Jewish Europeans in this sample are students. . . . Such highly politicized university environments, often fueled by staunchly leftist political agendas, can feel acutely uncomfortable, and indeed anti-Semitic, for many of them. (O'Flahtery, 2019: 26)

In sum, several manifestations of anti-Zionism are very similar to classic anti-Semitism. The demonization of Israel is similar to the demonization of Jews in past (and current) ages (Sicher, 2011). As Johnson (2016) claimed in a report over allegations of anti-Semitism in the British Labour Party, anti-Semitism was once explained by religious, cosmopolitan, pseudo-scientific, communist, and capitalist explanations. Now, it is explained by the opposition to the right of existence of Israel. From this perspective, once, Jews were persecuted and discriminated against because of their religion. Then they were persecuted for their race. Now they are persecuted and discriminated against because of a Jewish state (Sacks, 2015: 3–44; Bergman, 2013). The empirical analysis in this chapter is intended to see whether the evidence supports this contention.

Anti-Zionism and General Social Science Theory?

It is difficult to find any academic theories or literature on the causes of anti-Zionism that fail to focus also on anti-Semitism in the time after the establishment of the state of Israel.[21] While there have been attempts to link the issue to larger issues such as racism (e.g., Marcus, 2007), the word "anti-Semitism" generally appears prominently in those discussions.

Be that as it may, if one wants to discuss the question of whether there is any general social science theory which can lend understanding to the more specific case of anti-Zionism, there are two pertinent questions. First, is there any analogous situation where an entire identity group, whether that identity is based on religion, ethnicity, nationality, race, or some other basis for identity, is held responsible across a large number of countries for the behavior or perceived behavior of a state associated with that identity group? Second, if yes, is there any social science theory which addresses this situation that can be applied to understand the link between anti-Zionism and discrimination against Jews? It is not the purpose of this discussion to arrive at a definitive answer on the uniqueness of anti-Zionism, but rather to evaluate how anti-Zionism as a potential cause of discrimination against Jews fits into the larger social science literature.

It is certainly possible to find examples of individuals being sanctioned or attacked due to the behavior of other members of their perceived identity group. For example, across Western countries, societal discrimination against Muslims tends to spike after terror-related activity by Muslims. This certainly happened in the United States after September 11, 2001. In another interesting example, in Australia in September 2014, hundreds of police raided dozens of locations and arrested two Muslims on terrorism charges. This led to a wave of societal discrimination against Muslims in Australia. This occurred despite the fact that no terrorist acts had been committed in this case. These acts against Muslims included vandalism, verbal abuse in public, and anti-Muslim social media comments. There were some reports of low-level physical attacks, such as a coffee cup thrown at one Muslim, and another where a baby's stroller was kicked.[22]

There is a considerable social science discussion of this phenomenon in the context of Muslims in the West. There are several theories that are applied to explain this phenomenon. The relevance of these theories toward explaining the potential link between anti-Zionism and discrimination against Jews varies.

The first such argument is that discrimination occurs because Muslims pose a perceived security threat. This argument is most often framed in the context of securitization theory. Securitization theory was developed at least in part to explain how liberal democratic states are able to justify actions taken against Muslims and other immigrants that on their face violate liberal norms. It was also developed to explain how leaders use scapegoating in order to enhance their political power, though the focus of this discussion is on how the theory might help explain discrimination against Jews.

Securitization theory posits that when a minority is perceived as a security threat, this can attract discrimination. Specifically, when a group or minority is perceived as an "existential threat," a process of "securitization" may occur. This process is driven by "speech acts" by leaders that "securitize" the group. This process removes policy toward the group from normal policy and transforms it into the realm of extraordinary politics (Buzan et al., 1998; Mabee, 2007; Waever, 1995, 2011). "The theory suggests that a state representative can 'securitize' an issue by invoking 'security.' 'Securitized' issues are lifted above normal ordinary politics and moved from normal to emergency politics. They are assigned an urgency that requires extraordinary measures to eliminate the threat" (Fox & Akbaba, 2015: 176). This legitimizes discriminatory actions that would be illegitimate under normal circumstances. Many argue that this is what drives policy toward Muslims in the West (Cesari, 2013; Donnelly, 2007; Gearty, 2007; Razack, 2008).

Cesari (2013) takes this a step further, arguing that discriminatory acts that have little or no connection to security are often justified when a minority is hyper-securitized. This explains some types of common forms of discrimination against Muslims in the West which in no way address security concerns. These include restrictions on halal slaughter of meat, Muslim women wearing their traditional head coverings, and the building of new mosques.

While it is difficult to argue that Jews pose a security threat in the West, it is possible to apply the classic anti-Semitic trope of accusing Jews of dual loyalties. More specifically, securitization theory posits that speech acts are used to securitize a minority and depict them as an existential threat. In this case, painting Jews as loyal to a foreign government is an analogous type of speech act which portrays Jews as a threat. Though the danger Jews are said to pose is not strictly a security threat, these alleged foreign loyalties can be presented as a form of existential threat. As is the case with the securitization of Muslims, the truth of this accusation is less relevant than whether leaders are willing to engage in speech acts which make the accusation and whether these accusations find fertile ground; that is, securitization is about perceptions, which need not have a basis in reality. In both cases, the accusations create a perceived threat which justifies discrimination. Also, it is worth noting that based on core securitization theory, these speech acts are often made by opportunistic politicians, including but not limited to populists, seeking to amass power, who do not necessarily believe the accusations they are making.

Another branch of securitization theory applies it more broadly to immigrants in the West. For example, Chebel d'Appollonia (2015: 2) argues that

> since the 1990s, the categories of "new comers," "illegal immigrants," "bogus" asylum seekers, and "suspicious minorities" have been increasingly conflated in the media and general public discourse. Western governments have responded to concerns raised by the so-called new immigration (itself a euphemism for "non-European") by linking immigration policy to other high profile issues.

While these issues include security issues like terrorism, they also include others, such as job security, drug trafficking, and other types of crime. Thus, it is arguable that all immigrants can be securitized under this rubric. If Jews are portrayed as foreign or as having dual loyalties, this can be seen as similar to the threat posed by "alien" immigrants.

This "speech act" and "securitization" process can also explain how leaders deal with Israel directly. Many leaders posit that Israel is a security threat or a threat to world peace. Multiple polls on the topic show that large numbers of people consider Israel the greatest threat to world security and world peace.[23] Setting aside how this may justify actions against Israel, to the extent that Jews are held responsible for Israel's actions, it can also securitize Jews living outside Israel.

The securitization framework, as a description of the process of how elites stigmatize Jews, is also useful to understand anti-Semitism throughout history. For example, as described in more detail in Chapter 3, in the early days of the Christian church, church leaders actively portrayed Jews as Christ killers. Their motivation at that time was at least in part to create a distinct Christian identity and to prevent Christians from leaving the church for Judaism. In time this became less of a concern, but the pattern of religious and secular elites across religions using speech acts to accuse Jews of various crimes in order to spark hatred and stigmatize Jews in order to justify discrimination against them has become a time-worn pattern.

It is clear that in both the Jewish and Muslim cases, speech acts are used to undermine the legitimacy of a minority and to justify discriminatory acts. In both cases, the minority is painted as somehow dangerous, alien, and deserving of punishment. However, the nature of the transgressions attributed to Muslims and Jews are qualitatively different. We discuss this in the context of conspiracy theories about Jews in Chapter 5. In Chapter 7 we propose expanding securitization theory beyond the issues of security and immigrants; that is, we propose using the securitization framework to address a wider array of reasons that a minority might be stigmatized using an elite-driven speech act process.

The second literature that seeks to explain discrimination against Muslims in the West focuses on threats to national culture. This type of argument focuses on protecting a national culture from perceived foreign encroachment. Muslims are seen as adhering to their foreign culture and refusing to assimilate, thereby undermining the national culture. Religion is generally recognized as a potential element of national identity (Breakwell, 1986; Little, 1995; Gurr, 1993, 2000; Horowitz, 1985; Smith, 2000). It is also linked to multiple national ideologies (Friedland, 2001: 129–130; Smith, 1999, 2000). In addition, some studies link individual religiosity and nationalism (Sorek & Cebanu, 2009; Voicu, 2011). Studies of ethnic conflict show that perceived cultural differences can result in discrimination against minority groups (Gurr, 1993, 2000; Horowitz, 1985). In fact, many compare nationalism and religion because they are both ideologies that confer exclusive identity and inspire high levels of commitment (Beit-Hallahmi, 2003: 20; Green, 2000: 70–71; Juergensmeyer, 1993).

This body of theory both applies and does not apply to anti-Zionism. On one hand, in most Western and European countries, Jews are considered part of the national culture and history, at least among the mainstream. For example, numerous Western and European states, including but not limited to Austria, Belgium, Germany, Hungary, Latvia, Lithuania, Poland, and Russia, have laws recognizing religions considered indigenous or traditional, or otherwise list those religions considered legal and legitimate. These lists include Judaism.

On the other hand, to an increasing extent, Jews are being depicted as foreign in Western countries in both far right- and left-wing circles. For example, UK Labour Party leader Jeremy Corbyn stated that Zionists "don't understand English irony." In a more blatant example, French philosopher Alain Finkielkraut, who is Jewish, was verbally assaulted by yellow vest protesters. The verbal attacks included "dirty Zionist [expletive deleted]" "go back to Tel Aviv" and "we are the French people, France is ours."[24] Incidentally, the hypocrisy of, on one hand, questioning the legitimacy of Jews having a state while in the same breath telling a Jew who has lived in France all of his life to go "back" to that state is inescapable.

Be that as it may, as discussed earlier, the anti-Zionist motivation for discrimination against Jews outside of Israel works through the mechanism of depicting Jews as foreign or somehow illegitimately loyal to Israel, or otherwise responsible or complicit in its behavior. From this perspective, all Jews are linked to this foreign power and, with perhaps the exception of those Jews who publicly denounce that foreign power, are complicit (though, as noted previously, there are some who would still consider these Jewish Israel-denouncers complicit). Thus, they pose a threat to the nation, though not the culture because there is no hint of a refusal to accept cultural norms, unless one considers anti-Zionism a cultural norm. In contrast, Muslims are perceived to pose a cultural threat precisely because they are seen as not subscribing to the cultural norms of the West.

Consequently, when applied to anti-Zionism, the securitization and the protection of national culture explanations merge. In both cases, Jews are stigmatized as loyal to a foreign power that is seen as illegitimate and even evil through elite speech acts. From both of these perspectives, Jews are seen as a threat, and the threat is not precisely a security threat, nor is it precisely due to cultural differences between Jews and other Westerners. Rather, from these perspectives, the threat is based on foreign-ness and having dual loyalties, a classic anti-Semitic trope.

A third potentially analogous phenomenon is also related to perceived foreign threats. There are numerous specific incidents where states involved in a conflict mistreat those perceived as being associated with the enemy state. A classic example of this phenomenon was the internment of US Japanese citizens during World War II. However, these cases are rarely persistent over long periods of time and tend to be limited to a single country or a small number of countries involved in a conflict; that is, they tend to be local responses to specific and usually local events during limited periods of time. While resentments can persist after the conflict, they tend to fade over time unless the conflict itself persists or reignites. Thus, this type of case does not provide a good basis for understanding the dynamics of anti-Zionism and discrimination.

A fourth body of theory used to explain discrimination against Muslims in the West is Samuel Huntington's "clash of civilizations" theory. Huntington (1993a, 1996) predicted that after the end of the Cold War most conflict would be between different civilizations. He divided the world into the Western, Slavic-Orthodox, Sino-Confucian, Islamic, Hindu, Japanese, Latin American, Buddhist, and African civilizations. He also predicted that conflict between the Islamic and Western civilizations would be particularly intense and violent. Huntington (1996: 252–254; 2000) specifically applies this theory to domestic conflict.[25] In fact, he argues that international conflicts are "a small, and possibly quite unrepresentative, sample of the violent conflicts in the world" (Huntington, 2000: 609). Thus his theory is easily applied as an explanation for discrimination against Muslim minorities in the West.[26]

It is difficult to apply this body of theory to Jews in the West for two reasons. First, Huntington (1996: 48) states, "Judaism clearly is not a major civilization.... It is historically affiliated with both Christianity and Islam, and for several centuries Jews maintained their cultural identity within Western, Orthodox, and Islamic civilizations." Second, most studies on Huntington's theory which assign Israel a civilization consider it part of the West. While Israel may be associated with the West, especially in the perceptions of many Muslims, Jewish minorities in Muslim-majority countries are generally considered indigenous.

Finally, there are at least two other examples of states considered illegitimate in world politics. Taiwan is considered by China to be part of China and therefore illegitimate. Many states do not recognize Taiwan, though this seems to be largely due to a desire to maintain good relations with China, a country that is a major world power. The Turkish government in Cyprus is recognized only by Turkey and is not recognized by any other country. Yet in neither of these cases does this illegitimacy lead to worldwide discrimination against either Taiwanese or Turks.

There is also no shortage of countries across the world that objectively violate human rights and other accepted international norms. Yet, it is difficult to think of any other case where an entire identity group is consistently, across dozens of countries, held responsible for the actions or perceived actions, much less the perceived illegitimacy, of a single state. For example, the concept of holding any random ethnic Russian responsible for the policies of Vladimir Putin's Russia seems ludicrous. Holding all ethnic Chinese responsible for the actions taken by China in Tibet or more recently against the Uyghur Muslims seems similarly farfetched. Yet synagogues across the world are regularly attacked and defaced by perpetrators who specifically state that their motivation is Israel's behavior. This is particularly interesting because most synagogues have no formal association with Israel, and most who attend synagogues outside of Israel are not Israeli. In the eyes of the perpetrators, being Jewish is enough. That being said, as we will see from the following evidence, it is likely that many of these societal attacks on Jews have motivations other than or in addition to anti-Zionism.

In sum, some of the social science literature which explains discrimination can be applied to map the dynamics or mechanism that links anti-Zionism to discrimination against Jews, particularly securitization theory and theories which focus on associating minorities with foreign threats. Yet, the anti-Zionist motivation for discrimination is distinct from how these theories apply to other minorities in both cases due to the exact nature of the perceived threat, and in that a single identity group is tied globally to the perceived injustices perpetrated by the actions taken by a single state, and even to that state's existence.

Testing the Influence of Anti-Zionist Behavior and Sentiment on SRD and GRD

This study does not strictly measure anti-Zionism. Anti-Zionism is a multi-faceted and complex phenomenon that would be difficult to properly capture without a multi-country data-collection effort using a large battery of variables.

However, this study can measure anti-Israel government behavior and anti-Israel attitudes in society, which we argue provide good surrogate variables for the phenomenon we'd prefer to measure. More specifically, it measures societal attitudes toward Israel and Palestine, as well as how the government voted on Israel-related resolutions in the UN General Assembly between 1990 and 2014. Because many states abstain or fail to vote, we measure both the percentage of times a state votes in favor of Israel and the percentage of times it voted against Israel.[27] We also use polling data from the ADL Global 100 survey on what percentage of a country's population holds both anti-Israel and pro-Palestine views. For more details on these variables and the multivariate tests, see Appendix A.

As shown in Table 4.1, the results are mixed. Anti-Israel UN voting causes higher levels of GRD, but only in Christian majority countries.[28] This is logical because Muslim-majority countries nearly uniformly vote against Israel in the UN General Assembly. It is a known statistical reality that if a variable shows no

Table 4.1 UN Voting on Israel and Views on Israel and Palestine as Causes of SRD and GRD

Cause of Discrimination	Societal Discrimination	Government-Based Discrimination
UN voting		
Anti-Israel	Less discrimination	More discrimination in Christian-majority countries; no influence in Muslim-majority countries
Pro-Israel	No influence	No influence
Views of country's population		
% Israel unfavorable	No influence	More discrimination
% Palestine favorable	More discrimination (weak result)	More discrimination

The full multivariate analyses represented in this table are presented in Appendix A.

variation (that is, it is basically the same for all cases) it will not correlate with another variable. It is sort of like predicting that only people who breathe oxygen will be anti-Semites. As all humans need to breathe oxygen to live, this prediction is technically true, but it does not in practice discern who is and who is not an anti-Semite.

The results for SRD are perplexing. Anti-Israel UN General Assembly voting predicts less SRD.[29] We would expect the opposite. This is likely because a small number of countries which vote most often in favor of Israel in the United Nations—Australia, Canada, and the United States—also have relatively high levels of SRD against Jews.

An interesting aspect of these results is that while anti-Israel UN General Assembly voting influences both types of discrimination, pro-Israel voting does not. This means that supporting Israel is not necessarily a sign of favoritism toward Jews, but siding against it in the international political arena does have an influence, albeit a mixed one where SRD decreases but GRD increases.

The results for the ADL global 100 polling data are more straightforward. Higher levels of anti-Israel[30] and pro-Palestine[31] views in a country lead to more GRD. However, the results only weakly predict SRD and only on the Palestine-favorable variable.[32] This result is sufficiently weak that many would not consider it a statistically significant result.

We discuss the implications of these results in the following.

Conclusions

It is unlikely that anti-Zionism is the primary motivation for SRD. The ADL Global 100 variables which measure societal views on Israel show a weak, at best, connection between anti-Israel views and with SRD. UN voting by a country shows that anti-Israel government behavior is associated with lower SRD. This implies that even when those engaging in SRD against Jews in some manner communicate that they are doing so for anti-Zionist or anti-Israel reasons, other motivations are likely involved. Thus, at least in the case of SRD, saying that activities are motivated by Israel's behavior is likely a cover for other motivations for discriminating against Jews.

However, anti-Israel views are more strongly associated with GRD, as is anti-Israel UN voting, but only among Christian-majority countries for the latter. This is likely through two mechanisms. First, politicians respond to attitudes in society, and one of their responses to anti-Israel attitudes is GRD against Jews. Second, the attitudes of the politicians themselves may reflect those of their constituents.

We posit that both of these mechanisms influence GRD and that, at least during the study period of 1990–2014, anti-Zionist motivations for GRD are mostly an elite phenomenon. This is not to say that there is no anti-Zionism among non-elites, but rather it only translates to discrimination when elites are involved. If non-elite societal actors motivated by anti-Zionism were commonly directly involved in discrimination against Jews, we would see a stronger link between societal anti-Israel attitudes and SRD against Jews. However, when these attitudes are present, policymakers seem to be more willing to translate societal sentiments into government policy discriminating against Jews. Thus, while societal anti-Zionism does have an influence on GRD, it is likely mediated through elites.

If we rely on the concept that speech acts by elites are used to stigmatize Jews as complicit in Israel's perceived sins, as is posited by the modified version of securitization theory we discuss in this chapter, this brings anti-Zionist motivations for discrimination against Jews even further into the realm of elites. If this theory is accurate, societal anti-Zionist attitudes are to a great extent a result of the same process that causes GRD. That is, elite speech acts both mobilize anti-Zionist attitudes and justify the discriminatory policies of the government. Thus, the link between the two, to the extent that it exists, is that both anti-Israel attitudes and discrimination against Jews are at least in part a consequence of elite actions and decisions.

This complex relationship between anti-Zionism and discrimination against Jews is not surprising. This is because anti-Zionism is itself complex. It can involve criticism of Israel's behavior, as well as opposition to the state's existence.

It can overlap with a wide range of political ideologies of both the left and the right. It often involves the use of anti-Semitic tropes that migrated from more classical anti-Semitism, a topic we discuss in more detail in Chapter 5. It can also be a cover for other types of anti-Semitism. Thus, while the measures used in this chapter are intended to measure the extent of anti-Israel sentiment and government policy in a country, in practice this involves tapping into a far more complex phenomenon.

It is also important to reiterate that the empirical portion of this chapter does not measure anti-Zionism directly. Rather, it measures attitudes in a society toward Israel and Palestine and how a country's government votes in the United Nations. This means that, irrespective of whether anti-Israel attitudes, pro-Palestine attitudes, or a country's UN voting record constitutes or is somehow influenced by anti-Zionism, these phenomena are strongly correlated with GRD—government-based discrimination against Jews. These results also remain valid whether or not there is any link between anti-Israel sentiment and anti-Israel UN voting, on one hand, and anti-Zionism or anti-Semitism, on the other. As we discuss in more detail in Chapter 7, this has considerable implications for our understanding of both anti-Semitism and anti-Zionism and their influence on the treatment of Jews worldwide.

5

Conspiracy Theories

Conspiracy theories and religion have at least one thing in common. Both have it that unseen forces deeply influence the workings of politics, economics, and society. However, religion focuses on the influence of supernatural forces, and conspiracy theories, with the possible exception of those that focus on space aliens, focus on forces that are very much of this world.

Sunstein and Vermeule (2009: 205) define a conspiracy theory as "an effort to explain some event or practice by reference to the machinations of powerful people, who attempt to conceal their role (at least until their aims are accomplished)." Douglas et al. (2019: 4) elaborate that conspiracy theories typically postulate attempts "to usurp political or economic power, violate rights, infringe upon established agreements, withhold vital secrets, or alter bedrock institutions." While not all conspiracy theories are about Jews, few would dispute that conspiracy theories with Jews as the conspirators are common. In this chapter, we examine the proposition that to the extent to which conspiracy theories about Jews are popular in a country, discrimination against Jews will also be more common.

It is important to note that this chapter is not meant to be a comprehensive discussion of all conspiracy theories about Jews. Rather, we provide an overview of these conspiracy theories in order to demonstrate that they are common and are not limited to the political and societal fringes. This is an important prerequisite to establishing that conspiracy theories can be related to discrimination against Jews. We also discuss the general literature on conspiracy theories and some relevant social science studies on the causes of discrimination to help put the specific case of conspiracy theories about Jews into the appropriate wider context.

Clearly, the ideologies and beliefs which we discussed in previous chapters, such as religious ideologies and anti-Zionism, can contribute to the belief in conspiracy theories about Jews. In fact, as we discussed in Chapters 3 and 4, conspiracy theories are integral elements of religion-based and anti-Zionist-based hatred of Jews. However, we believe that conspiracy theories warrant consideration separately for three interrelated reasons.

First, a focused discussion of conspiracy theories, both in the context of conspiracy theories specific to Jews and the general dynamics of conspiracy theories, provides additional insight into the causes of discrimination against Jews. Second, as we argue in detail in this chapter, whatever the underlying cause for the belief in conspiracy theories about Jews, when these conspiracy theories manifest, discrimination against Jews will increase. That is, even if conspiracy theories are nothing but extensions of the religious and anti-Zionist motivations for discrimination against Jews, when these motivations reach the level that they inspire conspiracy theories, discrimination will increase. This makes conspiracy theories a critical element of the dynamics that trigger discrimination against Jews. Our empirical findings presented at the end of this chapter strongly support this proposition. Third, we do not believe that conspiracy theories about Jews are simply manifestations of other motivations for discrimination. Rather, conspiracy theories have a dynamic of their own which creates new avenues that lead to a more persistent, pernicious, and intractable pattern of discrimination.

One of the reasons conspiracy theories are popular is that they simplify the world. The causes of people's problems can be complex and hard to understand. It is far easier to comprehend and accept that a sinister group is the cause of all of one's problems. Most people lack sufficient knowledge or information to understand and explain traumatic and difficult events such as terror, war, crime, or economic woes, among many others. It is simpler to find a scapegoat such as the Jews and to develop conspiracy theories which explain the lack of obvious evidence that assigns the blame in the intended direction. Theoretical and anecdotal treatments of the topic argue that these false conspiracy theories and scapegoating techniques create genuine and serious risks for their targets, including persecution and discrimination (Sunstein & Vermeule, 2009).

However, this proposition that there is a connection between conspiracy theories and consequences for the objects of those conspiracy theories has not been previously tested in a systematic cross-national study. Thus, this study provides important evidence that belief in conspiracy theories about a group can have negative real-world consequences for that group. While we show here that this is true of conspiracy theories about Jews, this finding implies that a similar relationship may exist when conspiracy theories target other vulnerable groups.

As we discuss in more detail in the following, there are two likely mechanisms for this correlation. First, conspiracy theories directly cause discrimination. That is, these conspiracy theories depict Jews as a significant and insidious threat, which stimulates discrimination. This discrimination can be a punishment or retaliation for the perceived bad behavior of Jews, or it can be intended as a counter to the perceived threat the Jews are posited to pose in these conspiracy theories. Second, the presence of these beliefs is an indicator of high levels of hostility and prejudice toward Jews, and it is this hostility and prejudice which causes both discrimination and the conspiracy theories. In either case, the evidence shows that levels of anti-Jewish conspiracy theories in society are strong predictors of discrimination against Jews.

This chapter proceeds as follows. First, we discuss the nature and history of anti-Jewish conspiracy theories and how they have historically caused negative behavior toward Jews. Second, we examine general theories regarding conspiracy theories, with an eye toward how these theories can help us better understand the Jewish case. Finally, we examine the empirical link between belief in conspiracy theories about Jews and discrimination against Jews, and we find that belief in Jewish conspiracy theories predicts discrimination against Jews.

Anti-Jewish Conspiracy Theories

In this section we discuss the nature and evolution of conspiracy theories about Jews. This includes how these conspiracy theories are linked to both religion and anti-Zionism. This discussion is not intended to be a comprehensive discussion of all conspiracy theories about Jews. Rather, we seek to achieve three goals. First, we describe and categorize the different type of conspiracy theories and show how they can move from mediums such as religious anti-Semitism to other mediums such as anti-Zionism and populism. Second, we show that these conspiracy theories are common and are not limited to just the political fringes. In fact, we demonstrate that these theories are persistent over time, are common, and are believed and propagated by a significant proportion of the populations of many countries, including agents that are not outside the mainstream. Third, we demonstrate that belief in conspiracy theories has historically contributed to concrete actions taken against Jews. All of this helps to establish that the proposition that conspiracy theories about Jews are a potential cause of discrimination against Jews merits consideration and empirical testing.

Throughout history, anti-Jewish attitudes involved belief in conspiracy theories about Jews. These conspiracy theories were the fuel, explanation, and justification for hating Jews and discriminating against them. Jews were blamed for killing religious figures, including Jesus and Muhammed. This gave Christians and Muslims alike a plausible cause for acting against Jews. Later, Jews were accused of various blood libels with a common theme—Jews were accused of murdering children for religious ceremonies in a manner not dissimilar to beliefs regarding vampires or witches. In fact, as discussed in Chapter 6, Bram Stoker's character and novel *Dracula* were created as a reflection of the typical perception of the "wandering Jew" stereotype.

Many of these conspiracy theories center on Jewish control and power in the world. Politicians and public influencers argue that wars and disasters serve Jewish interests. They also posit that Jews control the media and global finance which these Jews use to support their sinister plans. Essentially, these conspiracy theories portray Jews as the bogeymen who are responsible for all bad things that happen in the world. For example, Jews or Israel are accused of developing terror groups or plots, such as the 9/11 attacks in the United States and the 7/7 London terror attack, as "false flag" operations. Israel is similarly accused of creating ISIS (Sunstein & Vermeule, 2009).

Jews were even accused of creating and spreading the COVID-19 (coronavirus) global pandemic in early 2020. White supremacists blamed Jews for spreading the virus to further their global dominance and financial gains. Anti-Zionist countries like Iran and Turkey blamed Israel and the United States for purposely creating a biological weapon to control the world and the Middle East, and even blamed Jews of population dilution.[1]

Historically, there is a long list of anti-Semitic conspiracy theories. In this chapter we discuss the larger themes of the more common conspiracy theories and provide some illustrative examples. These themes include the following:[2]

> *World domination*: This category of conspiracy theory has it that Jews in some manner are pulling strings behind the scenes with the goal of controlling the world or a particular locale. The purpose of this control generally is to advance Jewish interests at the expense of others. This trope overlaps with many of the others on this list, perhaps all of them. It is also the most common of the conspiracy theories about Jews.
>
> *Controlling the media*: This is related to the world denomination theme. This aspect of it focuses on how Jews manipulate the media behind the scenes to control information and world events.
>
> *Controlling world finance and the economy* includes similar themes but focuses on economic power and control. It also plays into the trope of the greedy rich Jew.
>
> *Causing wars, revolutions, or calamities*: This is also related to the world domination theme, but focuses on Jews as the cause of various negative events which suit their own sinister purposes. Some specific examples in this category include causing terror attacks, founding ISIS, playing a role in the slave trade (historically), and that the Israeli defense Forces (IDF) train US police to kill ethnic minorities.
>
> *Blood libels*: This category originally manifested as the belief that Jews use the blood of gentiles, usually children's blood, in religious rituals, such as using it to bake matzahs for Passover. This can also manifest as other forms of ritual murder, torture, or organ harvesting. While this conspiracy is mostly religious, the organ harvesting manifestation involves financial gain. One of the first documented religious blood libels and conspiracy theories occurred in Norwich, England, in 1144 when English Jews were blamed for murdering a young Christian boy to bake their Passover matzah bread

(Laqueur, 2006: 191–206; Bodansky, 1999; Bostom, 2008: 31–262). We discuss this case in more detail in Chapter 6.

Well poisoning: This trope originated during Europe's Black Death period, when Jews were blamed for causing the bubonic plague by poisoning the wells. When it became clear that the Jews were not poisoning the wells, they were accused of placing curses on the wells. This can be seen as a subset of the previous category and involves Jews causing diseases as part of their conspiracy to achieve world domination. Modern manifestations of this include blaming the Jews or Israel for creating and spreading AIDS (Nattrass, 2012) or the COVID-19 global pandemic.[3] For instance, Steven Cokley, an aide to 1980s Chicago mayor Eugene Sawyer, "asserted among other things that Jewish doctors were infecting black babies with the AIDS virus, and he warned of an international Jewish conspiracy 'to rule the world.'" While Cokley was dismissed after the remarks were made public, several black politicians rallied to his defense.[4]

The murder of religious figures: The Jews are accused of directly murdering or being otherwise responsible for the death of important religious figures. This can overlap with the world domination theme if one assumes these alleged murders were intended to maintain political control. It can also overlap with the causing of calamities trope. This conspiracy theory began with accusations that the Jews killed Jesus or caused him to be killed. We have discussed this in more detail in Chapter 3. Later, some Muslims adopted this trope and accused Jews of being responsible for the death of their prophet, Muhammad (Laqueur, 2006: 191–206; Bodansky, 1999; Bostom, 2008: 31–262). The Muslim Hadith depicts Jews as traitorous, evil cowards. It also depicts the Jews as those who rejected the prophet while attempting to murder him. According to this religious text, as the Jewish leaders negotiated with Muhammad, after the conquest of Khaybar in the seventh century, a Jewish woman named Zaynab bint Al-Harith attempted to murder the prophet. She cooked sheep (or lamb) and put poison in it, and later, she gave the dish to the prophet as a gesture. The dish did not kill the prophet, and Zaynab bint Al-Harith was executed later for a different murder she allegedly committed (Najeebabadi, 2000: 208; Watt, 1970; Bostom, 2008).[5]

We discuss examples of these themes in detail in the following.

Perhaps the most famous example of these conspiracy theories are *The Protocols of the Elders of Zion*, which were fabricated by the Russian tsar's secret police, Okhrana (Russian: Охрана). The texts, or protocols, were divided into several subjects, including alleged Jewish conspiracies and plots to dominate the world (see Jacobs & Weitzman, 2003). These alleged conspiracies included:

- "Economic War and Disorganization Lead to International Government" (Protocol 2);
- "Abolition of the Constitution; Rise of the Autocracy" (Protocol 10);
- "The Kingdom of the Press and Control" (Protocol 12);
- "The Financial Program and Construction" (Protocol 20).

Despite being among the most famous of forged documents, the Protocols remain widely circulated today. This is particularly true in Muslim-majority states where, in Saudi Arabia for example, excerpts are included in school textbooks and are presented as fact.[6]

Most common modern conspiracy theories are also based on the example of *The Protocols of the Elders of Zion* and focus on Jewish control and world domination. This, of course, includes the themes of Jewish control of finance and the media, as well as accusations that the Jews are responsible for wars and terrorism. It also blends with other anti-Semitic tropes, including that Jews are non-indigenous immigrants who are a social burden and a fifth column.

For example, the British journalist Arnold Henry White described the Jews as a social burden and as aliens to native British men, during the South African Second Boer war:

> The English armies in Normandy and Gascony contained no Jewish archers or javelin men; no Jew was found in the train of knight or baron; they grew rich and prospered at home while the blood of Norman nobles and English men-at-arms was fertilizing the plains of France. (White, 1899: 118)

Similarly, Sir Oswald Mosely, the founder of the British Union of Fascists, claimed that Jews were responsible for World War I and that they promoted wars for financial benefit (Wistrich, 2011).

The views of the former mayor of Vienna, Dr. Karl Lueger, concerning the Jews in 1897 provide another example. Jewish immigration to Austria was high during the 1890s, fueled by Jews escaping pogroms in tsarist Russia. Local Viennese politicians exploited anti-immigration rhetoric, and many spoke against the economic and social burden of the new immigrants, the Jews (Pulzer 1988: 138–142). Karl Lueger claimed that the large Jewish influx came to Vienna to tear down and take over the local economy; he also argued that the Jews are not similar or equal to the Viennese, but a separate people. He utilized his racism and discrimination against the Jews with the famous sentence, "I decide who is a Jew" (Geehr, 1982: 188), to determine who is wealthy or poor enough to be considered a social burden or a threat (Boyer 1981; Geehr 1982; Pulzer 1988: 156–164).

Stalin's "Doctor's Plot" is another well-known manifestation of this type of conspiracy theory, which also draws on the well poisoning trope. In January

1953, the Soviet propaganda newspapers *Izvestiya* and *Pravda* published that nine Jewish medical doctors were arrested and blamed for poisoning Soviet senior officials. Only six of the nine doctors arrested were Jewish. Nevertheless, they all were treated as Jews and were blamed for plotting against the Soviet Union and for acting on behalf of the US and British foreign intelligence services. Moreover, they were blamed for being a part of a worldwide Jewish plot to undermine the Soviet Union. Stalin blamed the Jews for being a fifth column and planned to exile all Russian Jews to Siberia. His sudden death in March 1953 prevented the expulsion. Interestingly, Nikita Khrushchev, the first secretary of the Communist Party of the Soviet Union, gave a secret speech in February 1956, stating that Stalin himself plotted against Russian Jews in order to exile them to Siberia (Kostyrchenko, 1995; Brandenberg, 2005; Brent & Naumov, 2003).

Jews are also alleged to have undue influence on world leaders. In May 7, 2019, Andrew Anglin, the founder and editor of the neo-Nazi anti-Semitic site *The Daily Stormer* posted an article titled, "Donald Trump Should Be Prosecuted for Failing to Register as an Agent of a Foreign Government," with a picture of the US president alongside Jewish rabbis. Anglin blamed Trump for being an agent of Israel and of the Jews.[7] This theme also appears in the more mainstream media. On April 25, 2019, the international version of the *New York Times* published a syndicated political cartoon which depicted US president Trump wearing a kippah, holding a dog on a leash; the dog had the face of the Israeli prime minister and a collar with a Jewish star on it. Setting aside the obvious anti-Semitic tropes in the cartoon, for which the *New York Times* apologized, the message of this cartoon was little different from the conspiracy theory posted shortly thereafter by Andrew Anglin.

Another recent example of claims of sinister, illegitimate, and perhaps unnatural Jewish power and influence can be found with Ilhan Abdullahi Omar, who is a Somali-American politician serving as the US representative for Minnesota's fifth congressional district since 2019. In 2012, during a conflict between Israel and Hamas in the Gaza strip, she tweeted the following: "Israel has hypnotized the world, may Allah awaken the people and help them see the evil doings of Israel. #Gaza #Palestine #Israel."[8] In February 2019, Ms. Omar was criticized by both Republicans and Democrats in the US Congress after she tweeted that the US support for Israel was paid for with money from a pro-Israel lobbying group, referring to the American Israel Public Affairs Committee (AIPAC), which incidentally endorses no political candidates nor contributes to their campaigns.[9]

This theme of Jewish greed and sinister financial control often centers on the Rothschild family, whose fortune began with the rise of its banking empire in the eighteenth century. This Jewish family has been blamed for "controlling the world economy, bankrolling Adolf Hitler, plotting to kill Presidents Abraham Lincoln and John F. Kennedy, founding Israel, funding the Islamic State, inflicting financial distress on Asians and, most recently, controlling the weather."[10] The latter conspiracy theory is based on their purchase of a controlling interest in the *Weather Channel* in 2011. Based on this, a member of Washington, DC's elected city council blamed them for the bad weather in that city.

Other wealthy Jews are also the topic of conspiracy theories. For example, Hungary's populist Prime Minister Viktor Orbán regularly blames the Jewish billionaire of Hungarian descent George Soros for causing many of Hungary's problems for the purpose of financial gain. This includes, in particular, causing Europe's refugee crisis (Kalmar, 2020).[11] In fact, he named a 2018 anti-immigrant law the "Stop Soros" law.[12] His obsession with George Soros has real-world consequences. In 2018 he forced Central European University, which had been located in Budapest, to relocate to Vienna, because the university is supported by George Soros's philanthropy.[13]

George Soros is also a common target of right-wing conspiracy theorists. His large donations to the US Democratic Party and his philanthropy in support of democracy worldwide, as well as other liberal causes, have made him the object of conspiracy theories accusing him of being the mastermind behind numerous nefarious acts.

On both sides of the Atlantic, a loose network of activists and political figures on the right have spent years seeking to cast Mr. Soros not just as a well-heeled political opponent but also as the personification of all they detest. Employing barely coded anti-Semitism, they have built a warped portrayal of him as the mastermind of a "globalist" movement, a left-wing radical who would under-mine the established order and a proponent of diluting the white, Christian na-ture of their societies through immigration.[14]

Some of these conspiracy theories about him go beyond classic tropes of Jewish power and control and enter into the realm of the bizarre. For example, some even call him a "Nazi sympathizer" and allege that he aided the Nazis during World War II. In fact, he used a fake name to hide from them as a child.[15]

These conspiracy theories have moved from the fringes to the mainstream and have been invoked in prominent right-wing media outlets, such as *Fox News*, and mainstream politicians, such as US president Donald Trump.[16] For ex-ample, in 2010, *Fox* talk show host Glen Beck devoted three hour-long episodes to describing Soros as a "puppet master." More recently, in 2019, *Fox News* host Tucker Carlson accused Soros of "hijacking" US democracy. In this discourse, Soros is often called a "globalist," which has become "an anti-Semitic slur, embraced in alt-right circles before spreading into broader political discourse."[17] It "is a reference to Jewish people who are seen as having allegiances not to their countries of origin like the United States, but to some global conspiracy."[18] As this resulted in an unsuccessful pipe bomb attack against Soros, these conspiracy theories have had potentially lethal real-world consequences.[19]

A typical manifestation of this phenomenon occurred when a broad array of conspiracy theorists and right-wing politicians blamed George Soros for funding the nationwide protests in the United States in May and June 2020 in the wake of the killing of George Floyd by the police in Minneapolis, Minnesota.

> Over 90 videos in five languages mentioning Soros conspiracies were . . . posted to YouTube over the past seven days, according to an analysis by *The New York Times*. On Facebook, 72,000 posts mentioned Mr. Soros in the past week, up from 12,600 the week before, according to *The Times*'s analysis. Of the 10 most engaged posts about Mr. Soros on the social network, nine featured false conspiracies linking him to the unrest. They were collectively shared over 110,000 times. Two of the top Facebook posts sharing Soros conspiracies were from Texas' agriculture commissioner, Sid Miller, an outspoken supporter of Mr. Trump. "I have no doubt in my mind that George Soros is funding these so-called 'spontaneous' protests,'" Mr. Miller wrote in one of the posts. "Soros is pure evil and is hell-bent on destroying our country!"[20]

On Twitter, anti-Soros posts increased from 20,000 a day to 500,000 a day during the protests. According to these conspiracy theories, his motive is to cause the downfall of the United States, cause the confiscation of all guns in the United States, or further some "globalist" agenda.[21] This narrative was expressed by former US House of Representatives Speaker Newt Gingrich, speaking on *Fox News* on September 16, 2020: "Progressive district attorneys are anti-police, pro-criminal, and overwhelmingly elected with George Soros's money. And they're a major cause of the violence we're seeing because they keep putting the violent criminals back on the street."[22] Gingrich, also on *Fox News*, later accused Soros of orchestrating election fraud in the 2020 US elections.[23] This demonstrates that this type of conspiracy theory is sufficiently widespread and mainstream in the United States to have significant consequences for both George Soros as an individual and Jews in general.

This fits into a larger pattern where Jews who are particularly wealthy and powerful become the personification of Jewish world domination conspiracy theories. In this sense, George Soros is today's Rothschild.

Modern versions of Jews being responsible for all bad things that happen in the world manifest in multiple ways. A common one connects Jews, Israel, and terrorism. Many such conspiracies assert that Israel or Jews are responsible for terror attacks which according to all known evidence were perpetrated by non-Jews. Jews and Israel have often been blamed for the September 11, 2001, attacks on the United States. These conspiracy theories are often spread by people holding respectable positions, such as clergy and academics. For instance, in 2015, the English Reverend Stephen Sizer posted a link on social media that accused Israel of plotting and executing the September 11 terror attack.[24]

In a particularly detailed version, the Reverend Louis Farrakhan in a public sermon stated that "Zionist Jews" and Israel perpetrated the September 11 attacks. He said more specifically:

> We now know that the crime they say is at the root of terrorism was not committed by Arabs or Muslims at all. . . . It is now becoming apparent that there were many Israelis and Zionist Jews in key roles in the 9/11 attacks. . . . We know that many Israelis were arrested immediately after the attacks, but quickly released and sent to Israel. . . . We know that the World Trade Center was insured by its owner Larry Silverstein right before the attack. . . . We know that an Israeli film crew dressed as Arabs were filming the Twin Towers before the first plane went in. In other words, these Israelis had full knowledge of the attacks. . . . We know that many Jews received a text message not to come to work on September 11th. Who sent that message that kept them from showing up? Within minutes of the attacks, Ehud Barak, the founder and master of the Israeli military's covert operation force, was in a London studio of the BBC blaming Osama bin Laden and calling for a war on terror. And we know that Benjamin Netanyahu told an audience in Israel, we are benefitting from one thing and that is the attack on the Twin Towers and Pentagon and the American struggle in Iraq. He added that these catastrophes and wars would swing the American public opinion in the favor of Israel. . . . It now appears that 9/11 was a false flag operation, which is an attack by one country but made to appear like that attack came from another in order to start a war between them.[25]

In making this statement, Farrakhan managed to include the world domination, well poisoning, causing of wars and catastrophes, and control of finance conspiracies into a single conspiracy theory which involved both Israelis and US Jews.

Many other terror incidents have been blamed on Israel. In fact, in recent times it is difficult to find a terror incident in the West where no attempt is made to blame Israel. For example, in March 2019, the chairman of the Mt. Roskill Masjid E. Umar Mosque, Ahmed Bhamji, blamed the Israeli Mossad for plotting the New Zealand Christchurch mosque shooting spree that left 49 Muslim worshipers dead, even though authorities arrested the alleged shooter behind the attack, Brenton Tarrant, a neo-Nazi who opposes both Jews and Muslims alike.[26]

Jews and Israel are also blamed for supporting and creating terror organizations which themselves are openly hostile to Israel. For, example, Zeid Truscott, a student running for the British National Union of Students (NUS), was disqualified from the election following anti-Semitic social media posts which argued that Israel had trained the ISIS terrorist organization's leader.[27] Similarly, Joy Karega, a professor at Oberlin College, in 2016 made repeated social media posts asserting that the Jews and Israel were behind the September 11 attacks, the Charlie Hebdo terror attacks in France in 2015, and the creation of ISIS.[28]

The terror theme has at least two other manifestations which are not quite conspiracy theories but are nevertheless related to them. The first is that Israel is compared to terrorist organizations. For example, Member of Parliament Hussein al-Taee, of the Social Democratic Party of Finland (SDP), compared Israel to ISIS and faced parliamentary investigation over his allegations (Weinthal, 2019).[29] The second is that Israel's actions cause terror attacks. Specifically, terrorists attack targets around the world in response to Israel's policies. This is true even of terror incidents not targeted specifically at Jews. For example, British Labour leader Jeremy Corbyn hinted that the 7/7 terror attack in London in 2015 was linked to British support for Israel—days after the tragedy took the lives of 52 people.[30]

Israel is blamed not only for terror, but also for police violence in the United States against blacks. In 2017, Charlotte Greensit, who later became the managing editor of the *New York Times* opinion page, tweeted, "Israel security forces are training American cops despite history of rights abuses." This was likely based on Amnesty International's 2016 claim on its website that thousands of US police officers received training by the Israeli police in "crowd control, use of force and surveillance" and linked this to the inappropriate use of violence by US police departments. This was clear from the post's title, "With Whom Are Many U.S. Police Departments Training? With a Chronic Human Rights Violator—Israel."[31] Amnesty International later admitted that this was inaccurate.

> The programs that took American officers to Israel were for "police chiefs, assistant chiefs, and captains." Amnesty's report contained no evidence that American officers received any information, let alone "training," from their Israeli peers on relevant matters such as the militarizing of the American police, targeting minorities for traffic stops and minor violations, or using deadly force in routine encounters.[32]

While Israel has provided training for some US police officers, it is generally focused on counter-terror tactics, rather than other aspects of policing.

Nevertheless, this conspiracy theory has been cited as fact in diverse mainstream outlets, such as the *Washington Post* and the webpage of the *New York Review of Books*. These claims have morphed into claims that Israel trains US police to kill blacks.[33] For instance, in 2020, UK Labour Party shadow education secretary Rebecca Long-Bailey was fired for retweeting an article claiming that the tactics used by the police in the United States, such as kneeling on George

Floyd's neck, were learned from the Israeli secret service.[34,35] Thus, as the right wing blamed Gorge Soros for inciting the George Floyd protests, many on the left blamed Israel for training the police to commit the act that started the protests.

The blood libel theme also remains present in modern times. Blood libels accusing Jews of using Christian blood to bake the Passover matzahs originated in the Christian world. They are now more common in the Muslim world. For example, in 2003, a Syrian produced Hezbollah TV series, which was at the time viewed in over 30 countries, produced an episode in which Jews killed a Christian child in order to use his blood to bake the Passover matzahs.[36] It is also often advanced by Arab academics and Muslim clergy in the media.[37]

However, the specific manifestations of blood libels can evolve. For example, recently, Israel has been accused of harvesting organs. This manifestation of blood libel began with a 2009 article in the Swedish tabloid *Aftonbladet*, one of the largest daily newspapers in the Nordic countries. It accused the Israeli army of harvesting the organs of Palestinians who died in their custody. Afterward, this theme spread. For example, the *Palestine Telegraph* reported that Israel, specifically the IDF medical humanitarian aid unit sent to Haiti to help with disaster relief, was harvesting Haitians for their organs. The British baroness Jenny Tonge also cited this report as the former health spokeswoman in the House of Lords for Nick Clegg, who later removed her from the position.[38] This accusation was repeated in other outlets, including the Iranian news, and by Iranian Ayatollah Ahmad Kahatami.[39]

More recently, in early 2020, the coronavirus crisis attracted conspiracy theories blaming Jews and Israel for the spread of the virus, following the well poisoning theme as well as several other conspiracy theory types. The "world domination" type is common. This version has Israel creating or spreading the disease to target its enemies. For example, Fatih Erbakan, head of Turkey's Refah Party, said, "though we do not have certain evidence, this virus serves Zionism's goals of decreasing the number of people and preventing it from increasing."[40] There are also accusations that Jews are making money off the virus through plans to sell a vaccine or other machinations. Many of these involve Jewish billionaire George Soros. Others spread these conspiracy theories without specifying the motives. For example, former Ku Klux Klan wizard David Duke tweeted on March 12, 2020, "Does President Donald Trump have coronavirus? Are Israel and the Global Zionist elite up to their old tricks?"[41]

These conspiracy theories have real-world consequences for Jews. As noted in Chapter 3, Jews were collectively punished by Christians for the betrayal of Jesus by Judas Iscariot (Ruether, 1974: 184–194). Jews were also collectively punished for alleged child murder–blood libels. For example, in 1144 in Norwich, England, Jews were blamed for murdering a young Christian boy to bake their Passover matzah bread with his blood and body. This accusation resulted in considerable retaliation (Rose, 2015: 13–44). In a much later example from 1911, in Russia, a little boy was found murdered. The authorities found the killer quickly (a woman named Vera), but instead chose to blame a Jew, Menachem Mendel Beillis, as an attempt to stop the proposed future cancellation of the pale of settlement (a policy where Jews were allowed to reside only in certain areas) (Weinberg, 2013: 18–63).

A more recent example of dangerous real-world consequences pertains to the coronavirus. In 2020, some white supremacists encouraged their members to spread COVID-19 to "cops" (the authorities) and Jews, if infected themselves. One user on the dark web even pleaded, "Please, dear god, let it hit Europe as hard as possible, and destroy the whole fucking (((system))) there."[42]

A recent psychological study, focused on scapegoating and anti-Semitism in Poland and Ukraine in 2010, found that economic deprivation led to increased discriminatory intentions toward Jews. This was because people perceived Jews as dominant in financial matters (Bilewicz & Krzeminski, 2010).

While most of the archetypes of these conspiracy theories originated in the Christian world, they have spread beyond it. For example, Webman (2019: 5) argues that "despite the intensified exploitation of Islam in the incitement against Israel, Zionism, and the Jews, the most popular recurring anti-Semitic themes were derived from classical Christian and Western vocabulary, especially conspiracy theories, the blood libel, Nazi imagery, and Holocaust denial."

While this has been a brief and incomplete discussion of conspiracy theories about Jews, it is sufficient to support several points. First, such conspiracy theories are common, widespread, and can be found not just in the fringes of society, politics, and the media, but also in the mainstream. Second, it is likely that belief in these conspiracy theories varies over time and place. Third, it is plausible to argue that the presence of these conspiracy theories either causes or is otherwise linked to discrimination against Jews. We discuss the likely mechanisms for this link in the following section, which focuses on how conspiracy theories are linked to discrimination.

It is also worth noting that the anti-Semitism literature tends to focus on conspiracy theories against Jews with limited comparison to other objects of conspiracy theories.

Conspiracy Theories and Discrimination in General Theory

In this section we look at two aspects of the literature. The first is the conspiracy theory literature. This literature is informative on how conspiracy theories shape individual and perhaps group attitudes. In doing so, it certainly shows that there is reason to assert that belief in conspiracy theories about Jews can cause discrimination against them, but few within this literature directly address this issue. Nor could we find any empirical test of whether any kind of conspiracy theory leads to real-world discrimination or violence against the object of these conspiracy theories. Second, we examine the more general social science literature on the causes of discrimination as it relates to conspiracy theories. In this literature we also find arguments and evidence which suggest that conspiracy theories can lead to discrimination against the objects of those conspiracy theories.

A good portion of the general literature on conspiracy theories addresses conspiracy theories about Jews, though the majority of this literature does not focus on Jewish conspiracies and, rather, addresses Jews as part of a broader discussion. Most of these studies of conspiracy theories outside the anti-Semitism literature tend to focus on what type of individuals are more likely to believe in conspiracy theories or the content of these conspiracy theories. They find that belief in conspiracy theories is more common among people with high levels of anomie, feelings of powerlessness, political cynicism, paranormal beliefs, and authoritarianism, as well as low levels of trust, self-esteem, and agreeableness (Abalakina-Paap et al., 2002; Lantain, 2013).

The interplay between conspiracy theories and religion is not limited to conspiracy theories about Jews. Dyrendal et al. (2018: 3) argue that "both religion and conspiracy theory are typically seen as involving specific patterns of thought and ideas, and that both relate in complicated ways to social power . . . the interplay between religion and conspiracy theories, then, will vary with shifting relations of power." In fact, conspiracy theories can be seen a serving social functions similar to religion, including explaining a complex world using unseen forces as an explanation and providing a guide for how to deal with one's problems. In addition, both can inspire a tendency among believers to dismiss facts that contradict their belief systems (Dyrendal et al., 2018)

It is clear that conspiracy theories can have real-world consequences. For example, Brotherton et al. (2013) argue that

> some conspiracy theories are associated with negative outcomes; conspiracist beliefs about the origin and treatment of HIV/AIDS have been found to detrimentally affect attitudes toward preventative measures and adherence to treatment programs, and conspiracist fears concerning the safety of childhood vaccinations have played a role in declining vaccination rates. Other conspiracy theories can lead to social and political disengagement and may help to foster political extremism.

Douglas et al. (2019), in a thorough review of the literature, similarly argue that there are a number of consequences to conspiracy theories. These include negative attitudes and prejudice toward specific groups, poor health-related choices, violent intentions, and science denial. In addition, in different contexts, conspiracy theories can both lower and increase the likelihood of political participation. Thus, there is a clear consensus that conspiracy theories can influence both attitudes and behavior.

There is considerably less attention given in empirical studies to how belief in these conspiracy theories influences real-world treatment of the objects of these conspiracy theories. That is, they show that belief in conspiracy theory can lead to discriminatory attitudes, but do not directly address the question of whether belief in a conspiracy theory involving group X will influence actual behavior toward that group. However, the assumption that it will is inherent in the literature.

There is, as noted, some research which focuses on attitudes. That is, they focus on how conspiracy theories influence how people feel about the object of these conspiracy theories. Several of these studies look at the impact of conspiracy theories on attitudes toward Jews and find that they predict anti-Israel (Swami, 2012) and anti-Semitic attitudes and beliefs (de Zavala & Cichocka, 2012; Bilewicz et al., 2013). Van Prooijen et al. (2015) found that members of both left-wing and right-wing extremist groups tend to believe in the trope that Jews control the economy, banks, and finance. This is part of a larger trend where members of extremist groups are more likely to believe in conspiracy theories in general (Douglas et al., 2019). On a more general level, belief in conspiracy makes support for violence or violent thoughts more likely (Sunstein & Vermeule, 2009). This likely applies specifically to Jews because Bilewicz et al. (2013) find that respondents who believe in conspiracy theories about Jews are more likely to be in favor of discrimination against Jews.

All of this, along with abundant anecdotal evidence of conspiracy theories being used to incite violence, implies that conspiracy theories ought to result in negative actions, such as discrimination, taken against the objects of those discrimination theories. Yet, nearly all of these studies are based solely on links between different types of attitudes in surveys and do not attempt to connect belief in conspiracy theories to actions taken against minority groups in the real world. While these studies may look at whether belief in conspiracy theories may lead to violent thoughts or support for violence or discrimination, they do not test whether these thoughts get translated into action. This is important, because attitudes are often a poor predictor of actions. In addition, most empirical research on conspiracy theories "is largely focused on processes occurring at the level of the individual. However, conspiracy theories are also important intergroup phenomena" (Douglas & Sutton, 2019: 290).

There is likely no religious group in the world today more subject to conspiracy theories than Jews. In fact, conspiracy theories about Jews have a broad appeal, even in numerous countries where few if any Jews are to be found (Swami, 2012).

Nevertheless, the stereotype of the unfairly and perhaps sinisterly powerful minority is not unique to Jews. More specifically, minorities perceived as relatively advantaged, wealthy, and powerful often attract similar negative stereotypes, and these stereotypes can lead to discrimination.

This is a common theme in the literature on ethnic conflict. While this literature focuses on minorities that are disadvantaged, when it addresses advantaged minorities who are not ruling minorities, the description parallels stereotypes of Jews and argues that these stereotypes are a potential motivation for discrimination. However, this literature rarely makes an explicit comparison between these advantaged minorities and Jews. In fact, much of this literature addresses countries where few, if any, Jews live. It also makes few references to conspiracy theories and, rather, focuses on power relationships in society and politics. Nevertheless, these studies show some interesting parallels to conspiracy theories about Jews.

Perhaps one of the most interesting such parallel analyses is an examination by Donald Horowitz (1985) in his book *Ethnic Groups in Conflict*. This is a broad study of ethnic conflict in the developing world that examines many dimensions and causes of ethnic conflict. This is not a book about Jews. In the text of the nearly 700-page tome, the words "Jew" or "Jewish" appear only four times. Horowitz's observations focus almost exclusively on other minorities in countries with a Jewish population of close to zero.

In this study, Horowitz (1985: 169) discusses how "backward" and "advanced" ethnic groups often view each other. While Horowitz derived a list of stereotypical traits assigned to "advanced" groups from ethnic conflicts that involved no Jews, his list of traits ascribed to advantaged groups could easily have been taken from the stereotype of the illegitimately powerful and influential Jew:

> enterprising, aggressive, ruthless, money-hungry, industrious, shrewd, successful, stingy, arrogant, cunning, intelligent, energetic, resourceful, serious, clannish, nepotistic, tribalistic, progressive, crafty, frugal, avaricious, pushy, efficient, thrifty, ambitious, coarse, miserly, [and] clever. (Horowitz, 1985: 169)

Horowitz (1985: 169–171) goes on to describe how these stereotypes are present for ethnic minorities such as the Tamils in Sri Lanka, East Indians in Guyana, Biharis in East Bengal, and South Indians in Bombay, among others. The common theme, according to Horowitz, is the unity, industriousness, and education of these immigrant minority groups which give them an economic advantage over the majority. This, combined with their perceived non-indigenousness, leads to resentment and discrimination.

Gurr (1993, 2000) similarly discusses financially advantaged ethnic minorities. When dividing ethnic minorities into categories, Gurr includes the concept of "ethnoclasses," groups who are ethnic minorities but also occupy a distinct economic strata. While most such groups tend to be disadvantaged, some are advantaged. One interesting example of such an advantaged minority are the Chinese in Indonesia. This minority originally immigrated during Dutch colonial rule. During this period, the Dutch encouraged the Chinese to play an economic middleman role between the colonial government and the indigenous population. While offered citizenship upon Indonesia's independence, many refused for personal reasons. In addition, many Chinese converted to Christianity rather than adopt the country's majority religion, Islam. This has led to a legacy where they are perceived as foreign but wealthy and advantaged. This, in turn, contributes to significant political and societal persecution of the country's ethnic Chinese. The Chinese minorities in Malaysia, Thailand, and Vietnam have similar histories.[43]

Both Horowitz (1985) and Gurr (1993, 2000) emphasize that not all members of advantaged minorities are equally advantaged. Most of these minorities include members whose economic status is below the mean level for the society in which they live. Yet the stereotypes associated with advantage are still often associated with even the poorest members of these minorities. This is consistent with the nature of stereotypes, which tend to paint all members of a group with the same brush.

Despite the many parallels, the circumstances of these ethnic minorities differ from that of Jews in at least one significant way. These prejudices and stereotypes are mostly local. They exist in certain places, at certain points in time, due to historical circumstances. In temporal terms, Horowitz (1985: 171–175) discusses how these stereotypes can dissipate as economic differences are eliminated. In spatial terms, the only international component of these stereotypes toward non-Jewish ethnic minorities is that in many cases, such as the Chinese in Indonesia, Malaysia, Thailand, and Vietnam, they have ethnic kin who are a majority in another country, which is often their country of origin. These countries may seek to intervene in cases where their ethnic kin are persecuted. However, this literature identifies no perception of wide-ranging international conspiracies concerning these ethnic groups, though localized conspiracy theories do exist.

On a more general level, conspiracy theories are by no means limited to those about Jews. In fact, many are not even about minorities, but are rather about other nefarious groups and individuals who seek to control the government or engage in other despicable acts, and are sometimes about the government itself. In a widely cited study, Goertzel (1994) conducted a survey in 1992 in New Jersey and found that a majority of residents believed in at least one conspiracy theory. The conspiracy theories included conspiracies surrounding the Kennedy assassination, that the US government spread AIDS and delivers drugs to certain communities, and a Japanese conspiracy to undermine the US economy, among others. None of them focused on Jews or any particular minority as the source of the conspiracy.

This finding that a majority of people believe in conspiracies of some kind is important because it demonstrates they can be sufficiently widespread to have a measurable impact on collective behavior. This finding is replicated multiple times in the literature. For example, a 2016 survey found that over 80% of respondents in Saudi Arabia and Egypt endorsed at least two anti-Western and anti-Jewish conspiracy theories, such as that Jews carried out the 9/11 attacks (Nyhan & Zeitoff, 2018).

> Over 50 percent of people—regardless of age, educational level, or political preference—believe the JFK assassination was the work of more than one person, according to a 2017 poll. A 2019 survey indicated 45 percent of American adults have doubts about the safety of vaccinations, while Gallup reports 68 percent of Americans believe the government is hiding information regarding UFOs. (Pease, 2019)

A 2016 survey similarly shows that many Americans believe in conspiracies about the 9/11 attacks (54.3%), the JFK assassination (49.6%), alien encounters (42.6%), global warming (42.1%), plans for a one-world government (32.9%), US president Barack Obama's birth certificate (30.2%), the origin of the AIDS virus (30.1%), the death of US Supreme Court justice Antonin Scalia (27.8%), and the moon landing (24.2%); 74.0% of Americans believe in at least one of these conspiracy theories, and a majority of 52.4% believed in at least three of them. The survey also found that 33% believed in a tenth conspiracy based on a train crash in North Dakota, an event that the researchers made up.[44] The survey did not directly address conspiracy theories about Israel or Jews.

Yet, in a way, even these conspiracy theories are related to Jews because conspiracy theories tend to be interrelated in that those who believe in one conspiracy theory are more likely to believe in others. For example, Swami et al. (2011) examined belief among Austrians in a conspiracy theory made up by the researchers involving Red Bull, an energy drink. That is, the researchers fabricated a conspiracy theory which involved events that never occurred and asked respondents if they agreed with that fabricated conspiracy theory. They found that those who felt the made-up conspiracy was true were more likely to believe in "real world" conspiracies. These "real world" conspiracies, those that involve the causes of an event which actually occurred, focused on the bombings in the United Kingdom on July 7, 2005.

This applies specifically to conspiracy theories about Jews. Swami (2012) examined the relationship between conspiracy theories about Jews and other conspiracy theories in Malaysia, a country which has no Jewish population.

He found that "belief in the Jewish conspiracy theory was associated with anti-Israeli attitudes, [and] modern racism directed at the Chinese." Swami (2012) and Reid (2010) argue that anti-Jewish conspiracy theories in Malaysia about Jews may be surrogates for resentment against the country's Chinese minority, which, as noted earlier, fills the same middleman role as Jews classically filled in Europe. While anti-Chinese rhetoric is banned by the government, anti-Jewish rhetoric is not.

Another study shows that "populists across the world are significantly more likely to believe in conspiracy theories about vaccinations, global warming and the 9/11 terrorist attacks.... Analysis of the survey found the clearest tendency among people with strongly held populist attitudes was a belief in conspiracy theories that were contradicted by science or factual evidence." According to this survey, populists are also more likely to believe that "there is a single group of people who secretly control events and rule the world together."[45]

This is not surprising, as anti-Semitic rhetoric which propagates conspiracy theories about Jews is common among populists, especially right-wing populists. Wodak (2018) documents that this incudes Holocaust denial and that Jews are foreign, untrustworthy, anti-nationalists, and as well as conspiracy theories of Jewish political and financial power. Wodak (2018: 9) argues that "it is not possible to establish any clear causal connection between the rise of the right and anti-Semitic hate crimes, but the aggressiveness of right-wing and extreme-right propaganda certainly contributes to a more general climate that supports hate crimes against all 'others,' thus also against Jews." The relationship is also complicated by the fact that some Western right-wing populists have sought to ally themselves with right-wing Jewish and Israeli organizations against Muslims. Hungary's populist prime minister Viktor Orbán, whom we discussed earlier, is a good example of this phenomenon.

Wodak (2018: 9) argues that

> in countries with a fascist and National Socialist past, anti-Semitism seems to be an inherent part of right-wing populist and extreme-right parties (hence in Greece, Austria, Germany, Hungary, Portugal, Spain, Romania, and Ukraine). Meanwhile, in other countries, mostly in Western Europe, rising anti-Muslim sentiments have caused right-wing parties to align with respective Jewish populations in their aim to instrumentalize such anti-Muslim attitudes in their election campaigns (Denmark, France, Belgium, Sweden, and the Netherlands).

However, Sutton and Douglas (2020: 119) caution that while conspiracy theories can be found across the ideological spectrum, "general belief in conspiracy theories is strongest at either extreme of the political spectrum, though it may be stronger at the right-hand extreme. In other words, conspiracy beliefs appear to be associated with ideological polarization, rather than with liberalism or con-servatism in particular."

There is also a growing literature on conspiracy theories regarding Muslims. The more popular current conspiracy theories in the West regarding Muslims likely date back to at least the 1990s, but have only recently been gaining aca-demic attention. In fact, one recent article on the topic states that "Islamophobic conspiracy theories are a relatively new phenomenon, so little research is cur-rently available" (Uenal, 2016: 94). One anti-Muslim conspiracy theory is based on a narrative of growing popularity among the far right in Europe and North America that there is a secret plan to Islamize the West. The premises for this conspiracy theory are different from those regarding Jews; they focus on asym-metrical population growth in the Muslim world, which is driving masses of un-employed Muslims coming to the West. Yet like conspiracy theories about Jews, it involves an ascribed secret control over governments and a desire to domi-nate. For example, Uenal (2016: 95) argues that this conspiracy theory has it that this Islamization process is "supported by certain leftist politicians, yet concealed from the masses by deliberate media disinformation . . . with the ultimate goal of enforcing Islamic laws . . . and eventually dominating the entire Western world."

This is part of a larger conspiracy theory known as "white genocide," or "re-placement theology." Among far-right nationalist and white supremacist groups, it can be Muslims, Jews, or both, who are trying to replace whites. This use of Muslims and Jews as the co-villains in this conspiracy is also another example of how those who believe in one conspiracy are likely to believe in others. Yet even here there is a distinction. Muslims are feared to be a conspiring underclass which seeks to rise up and overthrow the white majority, and Jews are seen as an already entrenched, powerful, and sinister minority that seeks to use that power to dominate whites. White genocide is also viewed by some as a result of the mul-ticultural policies of Western governments in general. Others, blame Jews for bringing Muslim migrants to the West, for example, in 2018 US Congresswoman Marjorie Taylor Greene, of "Jewish space laser" fame, shared a video claiming that "Zionists supremicists" are conspiring to bring migrants into the West in order to replace the white population.[46]

Interestingly, replacement theology can be said to echo a theme of replacement in religious theology among Abrahamic religions. Christian theology has it that Christians are the new Jews, with the New Testament replacing the Jewish Bible. Similarly, Muslims believe that the divine revelation to Muhammed supersedes the revelations which are the basis of Christianity and Judaism (Jiley, 2020: 3–4). The Jewish Bible also has a theme of replacement, where Isaac replaced his older brother Ishmael as Abraham's heir, and Jacob replaced his older brother Esau as Isaac's heir.

Conspiracy theories tend to be pernicious and difficult to eradicate. They are "extremely resistant to correction," and believers are often able to twist clear evidence that no conspiracy exists into proof of the conspiracy itself (Sunstein & Vermeule, 2009, 2010). Once one believes in the existence of powerful and sinister actors who work clandestinely, it follows that they use their power to hide their conspiracy, including through fabricating evidence. Thus, facts and proof which contradict conspiracy theories are often seen as fabrications by the conspirators. In addition, conspiracy theories often become historical narratives that spread through cultural transmission (Van Prooijen & Douglas, 2017). The ability of conspiracy theories about Jews to survive for centuries is an example of these phenomena.

In addition, it is quite common for believers in conspiracy theories to believe in contradictory facts. For example, those who believe Princess Diana's death in the United Kingdom was a murder are more likely to believe that she faked her own death. Thus they simultaneously believe she is both dead and alive (Wood et al., 2012). Similarly, Jews can be both communists and capitalists, both wealthy exploiters and a poor underclass which leeches off of society, as well as both white and not white.

While it is difficult to think of a minority of any kind that has been as subject to conspiracy theories of control, power, and domination, as broadly geographically and over time as the Jews, whether or not Jews are the most common subject of conspiracy theories is a question that need not be answered for the purposes of this study. What is important is that belief in these conspiracy theories and the stereotype of Jewish power are widespread but not evenly spread across the world. Based on this, we posit that, to the extent that the population of a country hold negative stereotypes about Jews, many of which involve Jewish power and control, Jews will be more subject to discrimination. As the extent of these beliefs across the world can and have been measured, this is a testable proposition.

There are two potential mechanisms for this connection between conspiracy theories about Jews and discrimination against Jews. First, they are a direct cause of discrimination. These conspiracy theories about Jews portray them as a threat. This threat can be against a body politic, a nation, a religion, or another identity-defined group. It can take the form of an economic threat, as well as a physical or security threat. Whether these perceived threats are real or imagined is not important. What is important is that, especially where threat is concerned, people act based on their perceptions. A common way in which majority groups respond to perceived threats by minority groups is discrimination against the minority groups that pose this perceived threat. As these conspiracy theories nearly always portray some form of threat posed by Jews, the connection between them and discrimination is straightforward.

Sunstein and Vermeule (2009: 220) argue similarly that

in the racial context, a belief in conspiracies has often played a significant role in producing violence; conspiracy theories have had large effects on behavior. And even if only a small fraction of adherents to a particular conspiracy theory act on the basis of their beliefs, that small fraction may be enough to cause serious harms.

Second, the presence of conspiracy theories can be seen as an indicator of high hostility and prejudice toward Jews. Based on this mechanism, both discrimination against Jews and the belief in conspiracy theories are caused by this hostility. Nevertheless, this would still result in a correlation between belief in conspiracy theories about Jews and discrimination. Likely the correlation between conspiracy and discrimination is explained by a combination of these two mechanisms.

Testing the Influence of Stereotypes and Belief in Conspiracy on Discrimination

The ADL 100 data, which we described in the previous chapter, includes 11 statements intended to measure anti-Semitism and asks respondents whether they agree or disagree:

1. Jews are more loyal to Israel than to this country.
2. Jews have too much power in the business world.
3. Jews have too much power in international finance markets.
4. Jews still talk too much about what happened to them in the Holocaust.
5. Jews don't care about what happens to anyone but their own kind.
6. Jews have too much control over global affairs.
7. Jews have too much control over the United States government.
8. Jews think they are better than other people.
9. Jews have too much control over the global media.
10. Jews are responsible for most of the world's wars.
11. People hate Jews because of the way they behave.[47]

The survey's creators consider a respondent anti-Semitic if they respond "true" or "probably true" to a majority of these statements. This study examines the impact of the percentage of a country's population which agrees with each of these statements on discrimination.

While, other than perhaps item 10, these measures do not directly measure belief in conspiracies, items 2, 3, 6, 7, and 9 measure stereotypes of Jewish power and control. Thus, while all of these represent common anti-Semitic tropes, if conspiracy theories and stereotypes of Jewish power and control drive discrimination, these six items from the ADL 100 list should be significantly correlated with discrimination. We examine the other five for purposes of comparison.

Table 5.1 summarizes the results predicting government-based religious discrimination (GRD) and societal religious discrimination (SRD), respectively, using the same controls as in previous chapters. The full multivariate tests are presented in Appendix A. Overall they demonstrate a strong and consistent correlation between negative attitudes about Jews and both GRD and SRD.

Table 5.1 Views on ADL 100 Significantly Correlated with Discrimination against Jews

ADL Survey Question	Societal Discrimination	Government-Based Discrimination
Global ADL Score	✔	✔
Jews are more loyal to Israel than to this country.		✔
Jews have too much power in the business world.	✔	✔
Jews have too much power in international finance markets.	✔	✔
Jews still talk too much about what happened to them in the Holocaust.		
Jews don't care about what happens to anyone but their own kind.	✔	✔
Jews have too much control over global affairs.	✔	✔
Jews have too much control over the United States government.	✔	✔
Jews think they are better than other people.	✔	✔
Jews have too much control over the global media.	✔	✔
Jews are responsible for most of the world's wars.	✔	✔
People hate Jews because of the way they behave.	✔	✔

The full multivariate analyses represented in this table are presented in Appendix A.

✔ = Significant at 0.5 level.

✔ = Significant at .1 level.

The global ADL score, which measures the percentage of respondents who thought at least six of the statements were at least probably true, is strongly and significantly correlated with both SRD[48] and GRD.[49] Items 2, 3, 6, 7, and 9, which measure stereotypes of Jewish power and control, are also correlated significantly with both SRD and GRD, as is item 10, "Jews are responsible for most of the world's wars," which is the most conspiracy theory-like measure in the study. Two items which focus on Jewish selfishness—"Jews don't care about what happens to anyone but their own kind" and "Jews think they are better than other people"—are significant for GRD but only marginally significant for SRD. The dual loyalty trope—"Jews are more loyal to Israel than to this country"— significantly predicts only GRD.

Interestingly, the Holocaust question is not significantly correlated with either variable. We conjecture that this may be because the Holocaust is perhaps the historical event that most strongly disproves the belief that Jews control the world. In a world where Jews have the level of power and control ascribed to them in many conspiracy theories, an event such as the Holocaust could never happen.

It is important to note that government support for religion, which is an important and significant predictor of both SRD and GRD against Jews in all other tests in this study, loses its significance in predicting SRD when tropes of Jewish power are taken into account. This means that conspiracy theories are a particularly important predictor of SRD against Jews.

Conclusions

In this chapter we ask whether belief in conspiracy theories about Jews is related to discrimination against Jews. The results show that all six measures of belief in Jewish power, control, and conspiracies predict higher levels of discrimination against Jews both by governments and society. In addition, four of five other measures of anti-Semitism are also predictors of government-based discrimination against Jews, as is the global indicator which combines all 11 of these indicators.

These results have at least six important implications. First, belief in conspiracy theories of Jewish power consistently and significantly predict both SRD and GRD against Jews. Other than that discrimination is higher in countries with Orthodox Christian majorities, no other factor in these tests consistently predicts both GRD and SRD. This indicates that discrimination against Jews is most likely when a population holds negative stereotypes about Jews, particularly stereotypes about Jewish power and control over business, finance, global affairs, media, government, and wars. This trigger for discrimination is a more consistent predictor of discrimination against Jews than those involving religious ideology and anti-Zionism. It is also the only factor tested in this entire study that consistently predicts higher SRD against Jews with statistical significance.[50]

However, this is not unrelated to the other two theories on the causes of discrimination against Jews tested in this study in Chapters 3 and 4. Both those with religious motives to discriminate against Jews and those with anti-Zionist motivations often express these types of tropes about Jews. Again, it is not our claim that all religious people and all of those who criticize Israel also express these tropes or support discrimination against Jews. Rather, we claim that when these potential motivations do lead to belief in these tropes, this catalyzes the relationship between these two potential motivations and discrimination against Jews. Thus, while the presence of anti-Jewish stereotypes and conspiracy theories is a better indicator for predicting discrimination against Jews, religious ideology and anti-Zionism likely influence levels of belief in these stereotypes and conspiracy theories.

Based on this, belief in conspiracy theories about Jews, including beliefs in Jewish control of governments, the media, and finance, are both causes of discrimination and indicators of hostility toward Jews, which, in turn, can cause discrimination. These two mechanisms are related but distinct. In the first, these beliefs directly cause discrimination. In the second, both these beliefs and discrimination against Jews are the result of hostility and prejudice toward Jews. While the evidence in this study is not structured in a manner that allows us to sort out which mechanism is in play, we posit that it is likely a complex combination of both.

In either case, on a practical level, this means that as conspiracy theories about Jews become more popular and more mainstream, the lot of Jews in a country becomes more precarious. This is true irrespective of whether these conspiracy theories focus on Jewish power in general or focus on Israel. Public figures engaging in speech acts which propagate and legitimize these tropes and bring them into the mainstream are taking part in a process that increases discrimination against Jews. In fact, studies show that mere exposure to conspiracy theories make belief in them more likely (Lantain, 2013). Jolley et al. (2019) show that this applies specifically to conspiracy theories about Jews. In an experimental survey they found that exposing respondents to conspiracy theories about Jews made them more likely to express "anti-Jewish" attitudes and less likely to be willing to vote for a Jewish political candidate. Thus, the mainstreaming of conspiracy theories of Jewish power is both dangerous and infectious.

This combines well with the adaptation of securitization theory that we discuss in Chapter 4. It demonstrates that speech acts emphasizing conspiracy theories are particularly effective at "securitizing" or stigmatizing a minority. This is arguably an integral element of the process that leads to discrimination against Jews.

Second, it is also important to remember that in many ways these tropes have a life of their own. Anti-Semitism, as noted elsewhere in this study, can be like a virus that mutates over time but still has the same core. Thus, when religion is a popular ideology it manifests religiously, and when nationalism is a popular ideology it manifests as opposition to the Jewish nation-state. We posit that these tropes of Jewish power are closely associated with the core of anti-Semitism, either as a basic element of that core, a symptom of its presence, or the means through which anti-Semitism is transmitted. Likely all three of these associations are present simultaneously.

That being said, it is clear that the presence of these beliefs among a country's population is strongly associated with discrimination against Jews. Thus, they are likely the most important indicator of whether a country is likely to discriminate against Jews. This implies that fighting and countering these tropes can be a particularly effective means to lowering discrimination against Jews. Of course, fighting these tropes is no small task because they are resistant to change and evidence which contradicts them (Sunstein & Vermeule, 2009). Also, fighting them publicly gives them more exposure, which, as noted, can catalyze their growth in popularity.

Third, while these tropes strongly influence both SRD and GRD, their influence on GRD is stronger. That is, levels of discrimination against Jews by governments are more sensitive to societal attitudes toward Jews than is societal discrimination. At the same time, as we discussed in more detail in Chapter 2, average levels of SRD against Jews are disproportionally high, while average levels of GRD against Jews are below the mean for the countries included on this study. Thus, while GRD is more sensitive to belief in conspiracy theories, the impact of these beliefs is felt more in levels of SRD.

More specifically, while those tropes which cause SRD are mostly those of Jewish power and conspiracy, a wider array of negative stereotypes influence levels of GRD. In particular, GRD is more influenced by stereotypes of Jewish selfishness and dual loyalty. In retrospect, it seems logical that governments would be particularly concerned by fears that a domestic population is loyal to a foreign government. This is the only one of the 11 items on the ADL 100 list which has no significant relationship with SRD but is a significant cause of GRD.

Fourth, on a positive note, the belief that Jews talk too much about the Holocaust has no statistically significant influence on either form of discrimination tested in this study. This likely means that while an average 39% of respondents across countries would prefer that Jews talk less about the Holocaust, doing so does not precipitate discrimination against Jews. However, it is likely that if a variable measuring Holocaust denial were available, it would be significantly correlated with discrimination.

Fifth, conspiracy theories alter the dynamics of discrimination. The literature on conspiracy theories demonstrates that they are persistent and difficult to eradicate, even with objective evidence and irrefutable facts. Mere exposure to conspiracy theories makes belief in them more likely. Also, those who believe in one conspiracy are more likely to believe in others. Thus, if anti-Semitism is a virus, conspiracy theories about Jews are a super-virus. These conspiracy theories are likely among the most powerful and efficient means through which negative stereotypes of Jews spread, take hold, and move from one generation to the next. In doing so, they both motivate and catalyze discrimination against Jews.

Finally, while our theoretical focus in this chapter is on conspiracy theories about Jews, we can also look at these results from another perspective. Our independent variables can be seen as measures of resentment against Jews in society. For example, belief in Jewish control of the business world and international finance markets can be seen as resentment over perceived Jewish wealth. From this perspective, the link between these variables and discrimination against Jews is straightforward. Higher resentment leads to higher discrimination. This is fully consistent with our argument that an element of the mechanism that connects belief in conspiracy theories about Jews is at least in part a measure of anti-Jewish sentiment in society, and it is this sentiment that increases both belief in these conspiracy theories and discrimination against Jews. However, we argue that when this resentment reaches the level of belief in conspiracy theories, discrimination becomes far more likely.

In sum, while conspiracy theories about Jews are intimately connected to discrimination against Jews, this relationship is complex and is linked to the other potential causes of discrimination discussed in this book. Both religious ideology and anti-Zionism can fuel belief in conspiracy theories about Jews. The evidence presented in this chapter, combined with the evidence from the previous chapters, suggests that discrimination is most likely precisely when this occurs.

6

The British Example

The British case provides a good case study of the historical evolution and ramifications of discrimination against Jews, illustrating the findings presented in this book. It begins with one of the earliest recorded cases and examples of anti-Jewish attitudes and anti-Jewish discrimination in Europe. Some British cases of discrimination against Jews even preceded the German and Austrian cases. This includes the Norwich blood libels and the discovery of the earliest anti-Jewish caricature to date (Julius, 2005; Topor, 2018). The British anti-Jewish attitudes can be divided into four key types: the radical anti-Semitism of blood libels and scapegoating, cultural and literary anti-Semitism, daily scorn and contempt, and newer anti-Zionism. Currently, the daily expression of anti-Jewish attitudes combines these types, though not all individual expressions of anti-Semitism include all four. We argue that these types of anti-Semitism are responsible for instigating or justifying discrimination against Jews (Julius, 2005).

In this chapter we focus on the three causes of discrimination against Jews that we discussed in previous chapters: religious causes, anti-Zionism, and conspiracy theories. However, it is difficult to separate out the conspiracy theories from the first two causes because they are part and parcel of memes and tropes used to spread these types of anti-Jewish attitudes. Accordingly, we discuss religious anti-Semitism and anti-Zionism in separate sections and include most of the discussion of conspiracy theories in those discussions.

We also examine the case of Jeremy Corbyn's Labour Party. It is not our goal to determine whether Corbyn or the Labour Party under his leadership are anti-Semitic. Rather, we seek to understand the influence, if any, of Corbyn's behavior and the behavior of the Labour Party under his leadership on discrimination against Jews. We argue that Corbyn's behavior as party leader was, at the very least, taken as license by some Labour Party members to engage in acts of harassment against Jews.

Religious Anti-Semitism

The first known record of a Jewish settlement in England was in 1070. At that time and for much of the history of England, the most common motivation for discrimination against Jews in Britain was widespread religious anti-Semitism.

However, this religious anti-Semitism existed in parallel with a societal animus toward Jews. As we discussed in Chapter 3, this societal animus is related to and likely originates from the religious anti-Semitism, but exists independently. Throughout this history, conspiracy theories of Jewish power and control, as well as others such as blood libels, were persistently present.

During the initial period of Jewish habitation in England until their expulsion in 1290, the small Jewish minority in England required the king's special permission and support to live and act in England. Thus, on one hand, the government made special allowances for Jews through legislative acts but, on the other hand, it was necessary to do so in order for Jews to be allowed to live in a Christian country. This characterized a relationship where the Jews were given special dispensations but were also despised and persecuted.

The Christian church traditionally ruled that usury was illegal for Christians, so only Jews could lend money. This was an important contribution to the economy, and taxing the Jewish moneylending businesses was an important source of income for the Crown. In fact, it was also a form of indirect taxation on the nobility. Members of the nobility often needed loans. It was difficult for the king to increase taxes on the nobility, but it was simple to tax the Jews who profited from loaning money to the nobility. Thus, to a large extent the Crown used the Jews as a means to transfer wealth from the nobility to the Crown, but most of the animosity over this transfer was directed against the Jews rather than the king.

Many acts, or royal statutes, placed significant limitations on Jews. This included the types of occupations they could hold and where they could live. Between 1070 and 1290, the kings' attitudes toward the Jews deteriorated. Initially it was a positive attitude, along with greater benefits and protections than the rest of the community. It then worsened over time until the Jews were expelled in 1290 (Brand, 2000).

Religion-based blood libels were historically common and dangerous because they usually led to violence against Jews. One of the earliest documented blood libels occurred in Norwich, in the eastern part of England, in 1144. English Jews were blamed for murdering a young Christian boy in order to use his blood and body to bake their Passover matzahs. Interestingly, these allegations against Jewish people living in England happened after the death of Henry I in 1135 and during the Anarchy, the early civil war in England and Normandy until 1153. In March 1144 the dead body of a young apprentice, William, was discovered under a tree on the outskirts of Norwich. Since handling and reporting the finding of a dead body was very disturbing, both emotionally and bureaucratically because it involved detailed and complicated Norman laws, the first ones to discover the body just ignored it and walked away, hoping somebody else or even an animal would handle the body. Even Lady Legarda, an aristocratic nun who came across the body, said a prayer along with her fellow nuns and walked away, alerting no one (Rose, 2015: 13–44).

As Easter came close at the end of March and through the beginning of April, the authorities were unable to solve what was believed to be the homicide. The local clergymen and the representatives of the ruler decided the best way to solve the unsolved case was to blame the Jews. Specifically, Thomas of Monmouth, a Benedictine monk, arrived at Norwich and began investigating the case. The proximity to Easter gave him the idea to blame the Jews and accuse them of using William's body for their magic and spells. Thomas and his colleagues even claimed that the Jews tried to crucify William in mockery of the crucifixion of Jesus. The Jews in Norwich were particularly easy targets because they came from France and were associated with the aristocracy but belonged to a different, unwanted religion and had lesser civil rights, even less than Christian peasants. They were also resented due to their perceived wealth. Those who blamed the Jews correctly believed that no common men would defend the wealthier Jews (Rose, 2015: 13–44). This incident contributed to growing anti-Jewish senti-ment. It also benefited Thomas of Monmouth, who unsuccessfully sought to use the incident to get William declared a saint. However, he did succeed in creating a cult centered on the martyrdom of William.

Over time, the situation deteriorated. Jewish moneylenders were important to both the aristocracy and kings, including Richard I, John, Henry III, and his son Edward I. However, they were generally disliked and resented. As their tenure in England continued, persecution and oppression against them increased to the point where murderous pogroms became more common. These pogroms be-came especially acute in 1189 and 1190.

Two incidents during these two years stand out. First, in 1189 in London, a number of Jews attended a banquet after King Richard I's coronation but were expelled due to a long-standing custom against Jews being admitted to corona-tion ceremonies. Those expelled were attacked, and the rumor spread through London and Westminster that the king had ordered the murder of Jews. This led to widespread attacks and arson of Jewish homes and property. Richard I was re-portedly incensed at these events which occurred in his name, but was unable to punish many offenders because of widespread participation and the high social standing of some of the participants.

Second, in 1190 in York on the Sabbath before Passover, known to Jews as Shabbat Hagadol (The Great Sabbath), Crusaders about to leave on their Crusade killed a large number of Jews. The Jews fled to York Castle, where they were surrounded by the Crusaders, who demanded that the Jews convert to Christianity. Many of the Jews chose to kill their families and commit suicide rather than convert. Many of those who did not die in this manner were killed when the Crusaders set fire to the castle, or were murdered by rioters. This is the best documented of several similar incidents involving the Crusades during this period (Julius, 2010).

In 1263 the second Baron's war broke out in England between the Crown—Henry III and later his son Edward I—and Simon de Montfort, the Earl of Leicester. Jews were blamed for the war, as some were extremely wealthy and worked along with the kings and the royalty. It is believed that Aaron of Lincoln, the wealthiest moneylender in England, was almost as wealthy as King Henry III himself, if not wealthier. Jewish moneylenders had a Jewry exchequer and paid the king a special fee just to avoid prosecutions (Julius, 2005, 2010; Rose, 2015: 13–44). This is one example of a general trend where Jews were blamed for financing the wars of the kings and barons.

All of this contributed to significant anti-Jewish attitudes. The mixing of the tropes of Jewish power and religious anti-Semitism can be seen in the first known anti-Jewish caricature, which is dated to 1233. This caricature is an interesting and valuable display of the perceptions of Jews by England's thirteenth-century population. The caricature in Figure 6.1 depicts some Jewish moneylenders and their families as influencing King Henry III, along with the devils Colbif and Dagon. The devils are visually linked to the Jewish moneylenders, creating a conceptual connection between Jews and devils. This scene contains several common Jewish conspiracy themes. These include illegitimate Jewish power behind the scenes and Jewish financial power and greed. These themes are quite similar to those found in many contemporary anti-Semitic cartoons.

Before the 1290 expulsion, King Edward I engaged in several acts that clearly reflected the deteriorating status of Jews in England. In 1275 he issued the statute of Jewry, which forbade Jews from working in usury and allowed them to make a living through commerce. Since previously Jews in England rarely dealt in

Figure 6.1 A cartoon from 1233, during the reign of King Henry III (The National Archives, n.d.).

146 WHY DO PEOPLE DISCRIMINATE AGAINST JEWS?

commerce, it led to a significant downgrade in their financial status. While the exact motives and outcome of this law are unclear, all possible interpretations show a high level of discrimination against Jews. Brand (2000: 1153) documents that

> the 1275 statute was an attempt at radical social engineering. It sought to turn Jewish owners of capital from money lenders into merchants not just by depriving them as money lenders of the royal assistance they had hitherto enjoyed in enforcing repayment of their loans but also by making the lending of money for profit itself illegal. Scholars have generally doubted whether this attempt was successful and have held that it was its very lack of success that explains (either in part or in whole) the Expulsion of 1290.

However, others argue that the new trade activities were in fact a disguised form of moneylending. In either case, it was clear that by the 1280s the Crown considered the attempt to end usury by Jews unsuccessful (Brand, 2000).

In another incident, known as the "Coin Clipping Scandal," which occurred in 1278–1279, the Crown accused the Jews of clipping some precious metal from coins. Coin clipping is a widespread practice in societies which use precious metal coins. The coins are valued based on their weight in a precious metal such as copper, silver, or gold. "Clippers" scrape or clip some of the metal off the coin and then can spend the coin as if it had its original value, but still retain some of the precious metal.

In this scandal, Jews were blamed for the coin clipping which had occurred in the country and of using the clipped metal to create counterfeit coins. The phenomenon, also known as coin debasement, was practiced by Christians, Jews, and others in Britain and in the rest of Europe. Thus, the Jews accused of this crime were likely guilty, but were selectively targeted for a crime that was far more widespread. This type of selective enforcement of laws is a classic tool of repressive states in general and those that target religious minorities for repression specifically (Sarkissian, 2015).

In fact, there is considerable evidence that this was a "sting" operation, where a Jew who converted to Christianity but still did business with Jews was sent by the king to collect information on them. Almost 600 Jews and some Christians were arrested. Some were executed and others paid for royal pardons. There is some evidence that, unlike Christians, the Jews were denied the right to defend themselves at trials, which might explain why so many Jews and so few Christians were convicted. Regardless of the reasons for focusing the blame almost entirely on Jews, the king made an estimated 10 percent of his annual profits from these allegations and collective punishment, which later led to the expulsion of the Jews. Thus there was likely a financial motive for this incident (Brand, 2000; Rokéah, 1988, 1990).

As noted, in 1290 King Edward I expelled every Jew from England, the first European expulsion. Jews were not officially allowed to live in Britain again until 1655 (Julius, 2005, 2010; Rose, 2015: 13–44). Many factors contributed to the 1290 expulsion, including church influence, church-based anti-Jewish religious prejudices, popular prejudices against Jews, financial problems, and even pressure from the royal families on King Edward I. About 16,000 Jews were expelled from the mainland; some sought asylum in Calais, Savoy, Germany, Italy, Spain, and Venice (Singer, 1964). From then until 1656, England was virtually free of Jews.

Nevertheless, anti-Jewish attitudes and cultural motifs not only survived during this period, but developed and evolved (see Glassman, 2017). These attitudes and motifs thrived in the works of many English writers and playwrights. These literary works made use of classic anti-Jewish tropes and conspiracy theories. Perhaps the best-known example from this period is Shakespeare's *The Merchant of Venice*. It was written between 1596 and 1599 and depicted the Jewish character of Shylock as a stereotypical greedy moneylending Jew. Charles Dickens's *Oliver Twist* from 1839 depicted the character of Fagin in a similar manner. Fagin's Jewish heritage is unambiguous in the novel, which refers to him as "the Jew" 257 times in the first 38 chapters.[1] Another well-known and artistically admired character is the blood-lusting creature *Dracula* by the Irish author Bram Stoker from 1879. Stoker created the character of *Dracula* as a reflection of the typical "wandering Jew" stereotype, which was widespread at his time. That is, *Dracula*, the wandering evil bloodthirsty creature, was influenced by the image of Jews, who were seen as creatures who murdered children for their blood and were bound to a life of eternal wandering on the earth (Davidson, 2004: 87–157).

In 1656 Jews were allowed to return to England as "non-Protestant citizens." This meant they could not serve in public administration positions or in the Parliament. Moreover, the Parliament tried, but failed, to pass a special tax on the Jewish community in 1689, intended to fund the Anglo-French war of 1689–1697, a part of the Nine-Years War. The sum of this tax would have been 100,000 pounds, a tremendous amount at that time, as some English officials had perceived the Jews to be very wealthy (Lebzelter, 1978: 1–11; Julius, 2010: 148–200).

Beginning in the mid-nineteenth century, Jews could serve in Parliament. Lionel Nathan Freiherr de Rothschild, a British banker, was elected as the first Jewish member of Parliament for the city of London in 1847, but could not take the required oath because the oath was a Christian oath. The House of Lords rejected two proposed "Jewish disabilities bills" before finally approving the proposed bill in 1858 which allowed Lionel Rothschild to take a non-Christian oath and become the first Jewish MP (Julius, 2010: 242–347).

As the number of Jewish immigrants in Britain grew, the British public service tried to stop the large migration influx. There were approximately 65,000 Jews living in Britain in 1880 and 300,000 in 1914. The government passed the 1905 "Aliens Act" to give the British immigration officers the power to exclude "undesirable aliens." While the word "Jew" did not appear in the document itself, it was intended to stop the Jewish community from growing and to prevent Jewish immigrants from entering the Kingdom (Julius, 2010: 280–285).

The following poem provides a good example of the types of anti-Semitic tropes popular in England at that time. "In Excelsis" was published in 1924, between the two world wars, by Lord Alfred Bruce Douglas, who is now known to have been Oscar Wilde's lover:

> *The leprous spawn of scattered Israel*
> *Spreads its contagion in your English blood;*
> *Teeming corruption rises like a flood*
> *Whose fountain swelters in the womb of hell.*
> *Your Jew-kept politicians buy and sell*
> *In markets redolent Jewish mud,*
> *And While the "Learned Elders" chew the cud*
> *Of liquidation's fruits, they weave their spell.*
> *They weave the spell that blinds the heart's desire*
> *To gold and gluttony and sweating lust:*
> *In hidden holds they stew the mandrake mess*
> *That kills the soul and turns the blood to fire,*
> *They weave the spell that turns desire to dust*
> *And postulates the abyss of nothingness.* (Lebzelter: 1978, 26)

As shown in Table 6.1, each of the poem's 14 lines contains an anti-Semitic trope.

The trope of Jews causing wars became common in the United Kingdom during World War II and was combined with other tropes of Jewish power. During the war years, anti-Jewish posters were widespread across public places in Britain, with arguments such as:

> *JEWS*
> *they plan it*
> *make it*
> *finance it*
> *and you fight it*
> *WAR.*

(Lebzelter, 1978, 46)

Table 6.1 Common Anti-Semitic Tropes and Prejudices in "In Excelsis"

Line #	"In Excelsis"	Trope / Prejudice
1	*The leprous spawn of scattered Israel*	Jews are *leprous*/dangerous.
2	*Spreads its contagion in your English blood*	Jews are manipulative.
3	*Teeming corruption rises like a flood*	Jews are corrupt.
4	*Whose fountain swelters in the womb of hell*	Jews from or come belong to hell.
5	*Your Jew-kept politicians buy and sell*	Jews control politics.
6	*In markets redolent Jewish mud*	Jews control the markets.
7	*And While the "Learned Elders" chew the cud*	Jews engage in conspiracy.
8	*Of liquidation's fruits, they weave their spell*	Jews do sorcery.
9	*They weave the spell that blinds the heart's desire*	Jews do sorcery, manipulate.
10	*To gold and gluttony and sweating lust*	Jews are greedy.
11	*In hidden holds they stew the mandrake mess*	Jews engage in conspiracy.
12	*That kills the soul and turns the blood to fire*	Jews from or come belong to hell/devil.
13	*They weave the spell that turns desire to dust*	Jews do sorcery.
14	*And postulates the abyss of nothingness*	Jews engage in conspiracy.

Many British fascists, including Oswald Mosely, the founder of the British Union of Fascists, blamed the Jews for dragging Britain into war with Nazi Germany and conspiring to control the British media and financial systems (Wistrich, 2011; Goodwin, 2011: 19–25).

Overall, the anti-Semitism against the Jews in Britain until after World War II was largely a combination of religious sentiment and an independent societal animus that likely originated from the religious motive but became independent of it over time. Jews were seen as alien and the cause of all ills and evils. Governments over time saw Jews as a potential source of income that could be exploited, often cynically and cruelly.

Anti-Zionism

While it is difficult to argue that anti-Zionism in its current manifestation existed before the establishment of the state of Israel, some elements of this ideology can be seen during the period of the British mandate where the United Kingdom was granted stewardship over Palestine after World War I until Israel's independence. From 1938 until 1948, Britain closed the borders of mandatory Palestine to Jews, following the large numbers of Jewish immigrants who fled Nazi Germany and its allies. Some fled to other countries in Europe, some fled to the United States, and some to mandatory Palestine. Ernest Bevin, who served as the secretary of state at the time while representing the Labour Party, had negative attitudes toward the Jews, the Israeli residents, and even the Israeli government at the time of its establishment in 1948. Richard Crossman, a young Labour MP who knew Bevin, concluded in 1947 that British policy in mandatory Palestine was excessively influenced by "one man's determination to teach the Jews a lesson." Only about 5,000 Jews entered mandatory Palestine at Bevin's time of service (Wistrich, 2011).

After the establishment of the state of Israel, many of the anti-Jewish trends transformed into anti-Zionism. As occurred worldwide, this trend became more common and intense after Israel's victory in the 1967 war. Many British people who held leftist worldviews argued that Israel is a part of Western and American imperialism. After 1967, they could even argue that Israel is an offensive occupying state that hurts the basic human rights of the Palestinians. Anti-Jewish attitudes started to rise in post-colonial leftist circles and even in the Labour Party (Topor, 2018).

For example, in 1970, the *Soviet Weekly*, an English-language Soviet outlet published in the United Kingdom, reprinted, in four consecutive issues, an article which targets Israel and Zionism as a part of international and American imperialism. "Zionism today is not so much the Jewish nationalist movement it used to be as an organic part of the international—primarily American—imperialist machinery for the carrying out of neocolonialist policies and ideological subversion" (Hazan, 2017: 150).

Johnson (2019: 31–32) calls this the "anti-imperialism of idiots." He argues that it is characterized by two traits: first, blaming Israel's "imperialism" for all ills in the world, essentially applying all of the stereotypical anti-Jewish conspiracy theories to Israel; and second, associating all Jews with these conspiracies.

> The Stalinist states (often in alliance with authoritarian Arab states and far left groups in Europe) ran well-funded, state-sponsored anti-Semitic campaigns— vile Judeaphobic propaganda "dressed up" . . . as "anti-Zionism" . . . Because the Soviet Union could not officially use the language of anti-Semitism, they began to use the word "Zionist" to mean exactly what anti-Semites mean when they speak of Jews. (Johnson, 2019: 31)

The Soviet propaganda against the West, and Israel alongside it, had an impact on genuine British leftists as well. While many of them did not associate Israel and Jews with imperialism, they did consider Zionism illegitimate for various reasons. For example, the October 1979 issue of the London-based *Social Leader* journal included an article titled "Zionism—Religious Fascism." The main argument of the article was that Zionism is in fact a product of Judaism.

> It was primarily in pursuance of, and for the eventual fulfillment of, such prophecies that Zionism was founded at the turn of the century, with the express purpose of restoring the "Chosen Race" to Israel. . . . The real paradox inherent hitherto in the current state of Israel is that it was actually founded for a different purpose from which its present leaders advocate. Currently, we have the still further paradox of a Zionist radical state claiming the sympathy and support as a "National Home" for the Jews. (Cesarani, 2007: 130)

When a right-wing government led by Menachem Begin took power in Israel in 1977, British leftists such as the Marxists, Trotskyites, Maoists, and Revolutionary Groups denounced Israel even further. Their student supporters claimed "no platform for racists" and banned Jewish student societies from their platforms (Cesarani, 2007: 130). In doing so, they effectively held all British Jews responsible for the behavior and even existence of the state of Israel.

During the 1970s and 1980s, and specifically after the acceptance of the United Nations General Assembly (UNGA) Resolution 3379 in 1975, which "determine[d] that Zionism is a form of racism and racial discrimination," many Brits, including many socialist students, openly agreed with the UNGA Resolution's assertion that "Zionism is Racism." This led to discrimination against any Israel supporters on British campuses. Many anti-racism student activists who also supported Israel's right to exist were banned from British student clubs, demonstrations, and even anti-racist demonstrations. This was true even of those who criticized Israel's policies but supported its right to exist (Topor, 2018; Cesarani, 2006; Rich, 2016: 170–180). This perception was very significant on university campuses, in student clubs, and in leftist circles.

For example, the British *International Socialism* journal published in 2008 that "from the standpoint of Marxism and international socialism an illiterate, conservative, superstitious Muslim Palestinian peasant who supports Hamas is more progressive than an educated liberal atheist Israeli who supports Zionism (even critically)" (Rich, 2016: 179). This set the tone for subsequent anti-Zionism in the United Kingdom and elsewhere. For many of these anti-Zionists, supporting the state of Israel's right to exist, even among those who criticize its policies, was considered beyond the pale. Jews who do not openly reject the state of Israel's right to exist are suspected of and are even assumed to be supporters of Israel and, thus, racists and deserving of exclusion.

Increasing Violence against Jews

In recent years, many British Jews have either left the United Kingdom or have been considering migrating from the Kingdom. Many feel insecure due to an increasing trend of anti-Semitism among extreme Muslim immigrants, post-colonial leftists, and alt-right-wingers. They feel a growing gap in personal and cultural security. British Jews claim that British police do not make sufficient effort to stop these hate crimes and provide insufficient protection[2] (Topor, 2018). For this reason, the Jewish community in Britain is the only minority that operates a private security organization which works alongside the police—the Community Security Trust (CST). The CST also records incidents and operates as an information-gathering organization.[3]

The CST monitors and reports cases of verbal or physical assaults on Jews in Britain. According to CST publications and analysis, as shown in Figure 6.2, the trend of assaulting Jews increased after the outbreak of the second Intifada between the Palestinians and Israel; while only 350 cases were reported in 2002, this number increased to 1,652 in 2018. In 2018 most of these incidents were perpetrated by those who were described as "White-North-European" men.

The Case of the Jeremy Corbyn's Labour Party

The case of Jeremy Corbyn's Labour Party is one where a radical left which had existed in Britain for decades became mainstream when one of its members

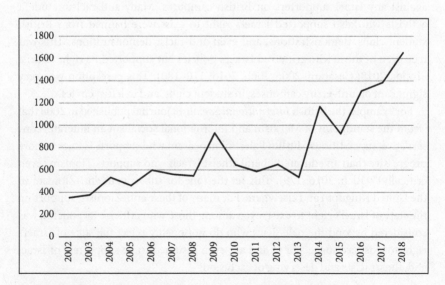

Figure 6.2 Anti-Semitic assaults in Britain (recorded by the CST).

became head of the Labour Party. On May 7, 2015, the United Kingdom held its general elections to elect 650 members to its House of Commons, a new government, leading party, and prime minister. The Labour Party was directed by Jewish member of Parliament and then leader of the opposition, Ed Miliband. However, Miliband's Labour Party had lost the elections to the Conservatives, led by David Cameron. Miliband decided to resign and quit his role as the leader of the Labour Party on May 8. Harriet Ruth Herman, MP, took his place as acting leader of the Labour Party, announcing that she would step down once a Labour leadership election would take place. The beaten Labour Party had no trust in its current leaders, after the loss in the general elections in May; Jeremy Corbyn, a backbencher and a controversial figure among many members, won the majority of votes on the first round (Wainwright, 2018).[4] On September 12, 2015, Jeremy Corbyn began his role as the leader of the Labour Party, the leader of the opposition. He remained leader of the party until he stepped down after the December 2019 elections in which the Labour Party was handed its worst defeat in a general election since 1935.

Interestingly, but maybe not surprisingly, some of Corbyn's supporters blamed Israel and the Jews for Labour's loss. Former MP Chris Williamson even blamed Israeli diplomats for intervening and preventing the creation of a Labour-led government. The French far-left politician Jean-Luc Melenchon also stated that "networks of influence from Likud" are responsible for Corbyn's defeat.[5]

Ideologically, Jeremy Corbyn is a socialist positioned on the left side of the central-left party. This ideology includes radical-left and post-colonial elements. For instance, he argues that both the United States and the state of Israel are colonial states to some extent[6] (Shindler, 2018). Corbyn is an excellent example of the complex phenomena where many on Britain's left are overtly and ideologically against racism of all kinds, yet due to their attitudes toward Israel have acquired a questionable record when it comes to Jews. On the one hand, Corbyn has publicly stated on multiple occasions that he is opposed to any kind of discrimination and racism, including against Jews. On the other hand, he promotes or, more often, turns a blind eye to speech and acts that many consider anti-Semitic and openly associates with those who both discriminate against Jews and those who act with anti-Semitism (Rich, 2016: 1–30; Topor, 2018).

During the period when he led the party, Jeremy Corbyn's views did not represent those of all members of the Labour Party. However, during his leadership tenure, his actions caused the Labour Party to be labeled as an anti-Semitic party. While these accusations were likely extreme, Corbyn's tendency to turn a blind eye to anti-Semitic speech and acts and to support controversial figures certainly gave those who want to accuse Corbyn and the Labour Party during his tenure a basis to do so.

For example, Johnson (2019: 14) argues that under Corbyn,

> the Labour Party has become host to three types of anti-Semitism. First, there
> is what has long been called "the socialism of fools," i.e. seeing capitalism or
> globalization or the banks as in some way "Jewish." When you hear talk of
> "Rothschild capitalism" you know you are listening to the socialism of fools.
> Second, there is "classic racial anti-Semitism," sometimes but not always in-
> formed these days by Islamist ideas about Jews. Third, there is anti-Semitism
> dressed up as "anti-Zionism."

He further argues that the Labour Party under Corbyn failed to recognize this
issue and to develop a process to deal with it.

This accusation has been largely corroborated. In October 2020, the United
Kingdom's Equality and Human Rights Commission, a governmental body
which investigated the anti-Semitism complaints against the Labour Party
during this era, found that incidents of harassment against Jews occurred and
the party did not deal with them adequately. Specifically, the report states, "our
investigation has identified serious failings in leadership and an inadequate process for handling antisemitism complaints across the Labour Party, and we have
identified multiple failures in the systems it uses to resolve them. We have concluded that there were unlawful acts of harassment and discrimination for which
the Labour Party is responsible."[7] The report found this behavior to be a breach
of the United Kingdom's 2010 Equality Act. The report also found that the leadership, including Corbyn, inappropriately denied complaints by trying to paint
them as "fake" or "smears" and inappropriately interfered in party investigations
into complaints about anti-Semitism within its ranks.[8] Ironically, Corbyn was
suspended by the new Labour Party leadership precisely for declaring that this
report was politically motivated and "dramatically overstated" the incidents in
question.[9]

Many argue that this failure to recognize or acknowledge anti-Semitism in the
left is a result of a blind spot in many brands of left-wing ideology. On the one
hand, since the ideology is explicitly anti-racist, those who believe in it, from
their perspective, cannot be racist and therefore cannot be anti-Semitic. On the
other hand, Israel is considered by many on the left, likely including Corbyn, to
be an illegitimate state. Setting aside the issue of whether this is in and of itself
anti-Semitic, while this does not necessarily lead to spillover against non-Israeli
Jews, it often does. Blaming all Jews for the behavior or existence of Israel is anti-
Semitic, according to the IHRA definition used in this study (Topor, 2018, 2019;
Geras, 2013; Rich, 2016: 1–30).

This occurs often. Many of those in the United Kingdom who argue against
Zionism clearly and overtly extend their criticism of Israel to British Jews as well.

This has occurred to the extent that British Jews are accused of being a "Zionist" fifth column in Britain, regardless of their actual beliefs on the state of Israel. This can also lead to "whitewashing," a process where other forms of anti-Semitism are legitimized and normalized under the umbrella of criticizing Israel[10] (Topor, 2018; Gerstenfeld, 2015: 50–52).

In the following we discuss some of the details of Corbyn's behavior surrounding the issues of Jews and Israel. We argue that this behavior is consistent with what Norman Geras calls the "alibi phenomenon" in which Israel provides an alibi for anti-Semitism. As discussed in more detail in Chapter 4, this involves blaming Israel for any anti-Semitic views held and expressed by those who oppose Israel and generally turning a blind eye to anti-Semitism expressed by them. Acts and speech that in any other context would be inexcusable are considered understandable because of their intense and justified hatred toward Israel.[11]

Association with Overt Anti-Semites

While a full history of Jeremy Corbyn's activities is beyond the scope of this chapter, some brief examples of his history regarding this intersection between Israel and Jews provide a good illustrative example. Like many of the New Left, Corbyn has repeatedly criticized Israel's policies, but has combined this with associating with and praising those who are more explicitly anti-Semitic. For instance, in 2009 Corbyn gave a speech at a Parliamentary event where he criticized Israeli policies toward the Palestinians, but also named the terror organizations Hamas and Hizballah as "friends," despite their being organizations whose leaders regularly engage in openly anti-Semitic speech and are declared terrorist groups by the European Union and the United States. He also invited representatives of these organizations to visit the British Parliament as his guests.[12]

In May 2012, Jeremy Corbyn gave a tour to a Palestine Solidarity Campaign (PSC) group inside the British Parliament. One of the group's members, Tapash Abu Shaim, enjoyed the tour and thanked Corbyn publicly. Abu Shaim shared articles on social media claiming that Israel is the entity truly behind most terror attacks. These includes articles claiming that Israel was behind the Charlie Hebdo killings and the ISIS terror group, as well as the 9/11 terror attacks.[13] Later that year, in November, Corbyn hosted a PSC member in the British Parliament with Mousa Abu Maria, an activist for the proscribed terrorist organization Palestinian Islamic Jihad (PIJ). Abu Maria spent several years in prison in Israel for his membership in the PIJ and for throwing Molotov cocktails.[14]

In that year, Corbyn, on video, called the Muslim hate preacher Sheikh Raad Salah an "honored citizen" and invited him for "tea on the terrace" at the House of Commons. Salah was unable to accept this invitation because he was excluded from Britain due to his "virulent anti-Semitism" and conspiracy theories blaming Israel for ISIS and the 9/11 terror attack.[15]

Between 2012 and 2013, Jeremy Corbyn, alongside his wife, Laura Alvarez, flew to the Gaza strip with the financial aid of Interpal, a declared terrorist organization sanctioned by the United States, and the Palestinian Return Centre. Corbyn met with several Hamas officials, such as Dr. Essam Mustapha, a close ally and advisor to the Hamas leader Ismail Haniyeh.[16]

In October 2014, Corbyn attended a memorial and wreath-laying ceremony for the terrorists who perpetrated the attack at the 1972 Munich Olympics. After he returned to the United Kingdom, he wrote a short article for the *Morning Star* newspaper in which he stated "wreaths were laid to mark the 1985 bombing of the PLO HQ and on the graves of others killed by Mossad agents in Paris in 1991."[17,18]

Support for Purveyors of Anti-Semitic Tropes

In 2011, Corbyn "wrote the foreword for a new edition of J. A. Hobson's *Imperialism: A Study*, in which the author argues European finance was controlled by 'men of a single and peculiar race.'" This book, while never using the word "Jew," expressed the conspiracy theories that Jews control finance and the policy of nations.[19] Corbyn's spokesman said that the foreword relates only to the theories on imperialism, which is of significant scholarly importance, and not minor issues such as Hobson's anti-Semitic remarks.[20] This particular incident is interesting in two respects. First, it directly demonstrates the phenomenon of excusing the anti-Semitism of an author whose other opinions fit with Corbyn's ideology. Second, as the book was written in 1902, it is difficult to argue that Hobson's views are in any way related to the state of Israel.

In 2012, in a Facebook post, Corbyn offered his support to the Los Angeles–based street artist Mear One, whose mural, featuring several known anti-Semitic tropes, was due to be removed after complaints. The mural, which was eventually scrubbed off, pictured several apparently Jewish bankers playing a game of Monopoly, while their tabletop rested on the bowed naked backs of several workers, with the all-seeing-eye behind them.[21]

In April 2013, Corbyn visited and donated in a Dier Yassin Remembered event led by the Holocaust denier Paul Eisen. While there is no indication that Corbyn himself is a Holocaust denier, it is unusual for Western politicians to openly associate with known Holocaust deniers.[22]

In March 2018, an investigative blogger named David Collier exposed that Jeremy Corbyn was a member of an anti-Semitic Facebook group named "Palestine Live" from 2013 until 2015, the year in which he became Labour leader. Many of the posts and debates in the group were explicitly anti-Semitic. These posts included Holocaust denial, accusation of Israel for supporting terror organizations and incidents such as the 9/11 attacks and the creation of ISIS, and comparisons of Israeli polices to Nazi policies, among others.[23]

The Labour Party under Corbyn repeatedly interfered in party investigations into anti-Semitism within its ranks. Many of these cases involved the use of anti-Semitic tropes. Such complaints about anti-Semitism are "the most common type of complaint received by the Party."[24]

Failure to Address Anti-Semitism in the Labour Party

In 2016, Corbyn assigned Baroness Shami Chakrabati to inquire into allegations of anti-Semitism in the Labour Party. The report was delivered on June 30, 2016. It concluded that there was no anti-Semitism in the party. "The Labour Party is not overrun by antisemitism, Islamophobia or other forms of racism" (Chakrabati, 2016: 1). Chakrabati concludes the report with 20 key recommendations, most of which focus on avoiding anti-Semitic language. For example, the first recommendation reads, "epithets such as 'Paki', 'Zio' and others should have no place in Labour Party discourse going forward" (Chakrabati, 2016: 27–28).

This report was widely criticized as a whitewash of anti-Semitism in the Labour Party. The report's failure to address the issue is threefold. First, it directly and explicitly denied that there is a problem. Second, its recommendations focus on how to change behavior but do not address the causes of the behavior. However, the core problem is acknowledged briefly in the body of the report. In the following brief passage, the report acknowledges a widespread problem of blaming Jews for actions taken by the state of Israel and the word "Zionist" being used as a synonym for Jew:

> I have heard testimony and heard for myself first-hand, the way in which the word "Zionist" has been used personally, abusively or as a euphemism for "Jew," even in relation to some people with no stated position or even a critical position on the historic formation or development of modern Israel. This has clearly happened so often over a number of years as to raise some alarm bells in Jewish communities, including amongst highly orthodox people who, whilst perhaps most "visibly Jewish" (e.g. in dress and or observance), would never see themselves as Zionists. (Chakrabati, 2016: 12).

Third, most of the recommendations carefully avoid addressing anti-Semitism directly and rather place it only in the context of racism in general. For example, Recommendation 2 reads, "critical and abusive reference to any particular person or group based on actual or perceived physical characteristics cannot be tolerated" (Chakrabati, 2016: 27).

The whitewashing criticism resurfaced when a few months after the report was released, Corbyn offered peerage to Shami Chakrabati. Marie van der Zyl, who served as the vice president of the board of deputies of British Jews, the leading group representing the Jewish community, commented on the report:

> It is beyond disappointing that Shami Chakrabarti has been offered, and ac-cepted, a peerage from Labour following her so-called "independent" in-quiry. . . . The report, which was weak in several areas, now seems to have been rewarded with an honour. This "whitewash for peerages" is a scandal that surely raises serious questions about the integrity of Ms Chakrabarti, her inquiry and the Labour leadership.[25]

This charge of whitewashing resurfaced again in 2019 in an hour-long report on the BBC that Jeremy Corbyn had repeatedly interfered in disciplinary cases in which Labour members were accused of anti-Semitism. The report included testimonies by eight former members of Labour's Disputes Committee, the com-mittee responsible for investigating violations of Labour Party rules by members of the Labour Party. They

> accused Labour senior officials of interfering with the party's anti-Semitism investigations and grossly misleading the public about their handling of mounting complaints. The former staffers gave harrowing accounts of an "insti-tutionally racist" party in which Jewish members were subjected to abuse. One interviewee said it was "self-destroying to be a member of the Labour Party and Jewish." They spoke of a complaints department team so undermined by party leader Jeremy Corbyn's aides that its members suffered mental breakdowns, with one contemplating suicide. . . . Meddling was intended to let anti-Semites off with the lightest possible punishment, often overriding complaint team's recommendations and dismissing their investigations.[26]

The former members of the committee, including two former heads of the com-mittee, accused Corbyn of normalizing anti-Semitism in the party and being more concerned "with public relations and damage control rather than investi-gating complaints and getting to the root of the growing problem."[27]

The report also included multiple testimonies by individual Jewish Labour Party members. The incidents reported mirror those briefly noted in the Chakrabati report quoted previously. They involve Jewish members being called "Zionists" in a manner reminiscent of "dirty Jew" in contexts completely unrelated to discussions of Israeli politics. They also involve Jewish members discussing how Labour Party meetings are becoming, from their perspective, an increasingly hostile environment.[28] These reports were later corroborated by a government investigation.[29]

The "British Irony" Incident

While there is clearly a trend that Jeremy Corbyn associates with and even endorses individuals who express ideas that are considered anti-Semitism based on the IHRA definition, overt anti-Semitic expressions by Corbyn himself are rare. What is perhaps the most well-known incident where Corbyn is accused of directly expressing anti-Semitic tropes occurred during a speech to a meeting convened by the Palestinian Return Centre in 2013. In that speech Corbyn spoke about the importance of history and the necessity for people to understand the origins of the Israeli-Palestinian conflict. During this speech Corbyn said,

> They [British Jews] clearly have two problems. One is that they don't want to study history, and secondly, having lived in this country for a very long time, probably all their lives, don't understand English irony either. Manuel [Hassassian] does understand English irony, and uses it very effectively. So I think they needed two lessons, which we can perhaps help them with.[30]

While the words themselves are vague, many took them to mean that Corbyn was accusing Jews of not being real Brits. For example, one such critic responded, "I am English. I have been part of English irony, humor, culture, for the last 50 years. It just seems to be that I am not part of Jeremy Corbyn's Britain."[31]

Corbyn's Labour Party and Defining Anti-Semitism

As noted in Chapter 1, this study uses the International Holocaust Remembrance Alliance (IHRA) definition of anti-Semitism. This definition has been widely adopted by Western governments and political entities including, eventually, the British Labour Party in 2018. However, before doing so, there was considerable resistance. The resistance surrounded one of the examples of anti-Semitism included in the definition regarding Israel: "denying the Jewish people their right to self-determination, e.g., by claiming that the existence of a State of Israel is a racist endeavor."

This resistance is well summarized by the following statement that Corbyn unsuccessfully attempted to include in the party's definition of anti-Semitism:

It cannot be considered racist to treat Israel like any other state or assess its conduct against the standards of international law. Nor should it be regarded as anti-Semitic to describe Israel, its policies or the circumstances around its foundation as racist because of their discriminatory impact, or to support another settlement of the Israel-Palestine conflict.[32]

Corbyn, Labour, Israel, and Discrimination against the Jews

It is not the purpose of this discussion to determine whether Jeremy Corbyn is himself anti-Semitic or behaves in a manner that could be considered anti-Semitic. Nor is it our purpose to determine the accuracy of accusations that the British Labour Party was institutionally anti-Semitic under Corbyn's tenure as leader (e.g., Johnson, 2019). However, we believe that the example of Jeremy Corbyn and the Labour Party under his leadership is an excellent example of the relationship between anti-Israel views and discrimination against Jews. More specifically, while the questions of whether anti-Zionism is always anti-Semitism and whether Corbyn's anti-Zionism is anti-Semitic are likely to be debated for some time, it is possible to focus on some objective facts.

First, Jeremy Corbyn holds anti-Israel views. He, on multiple occasions, has criticized the Israeli government, as well as expressing the view that Zionism is a racist endeavor; that is, he posits that the way in which Israel was founded is illegitimate and inherently racist. He has consistently and openly expressed these views. He also seems willing to overlook anti-Semitic views in those with whom he associates, especially if they are also active opponents of Israel. Essentially, the preponderance of evidence suggests that Corbyn allows others to use Israel as an alibi for anti-Semitism.

Second, under Corbyn's leadership, incidents of harassment of Jews increased significantly within the British Labour Party, as well as in Britain in general. There are numerous reports of harassment of Jewish members of the Labour Party from rank-and-file members to officials at the highest level, including elected members of Parliament. In February 2019, nine Labour members of Parliament quit the party over the issues of anti-Semitism and Brexit. One of them, Luciana Berger, who is Jewish, stated, "I cannot remain in a party that I have today come to the sickening conclusion is institutionally anti-Semitic . . . I am leaving behind a culture of bullying, bigotry and intimidation."[33] "When she described bullying and bigotry in her speech, Berger was speaking from her experience within the Labour Party, and the abuse she has received both on and offline."[34] Some of the documented comments sent to her on Twitter included common tropes related to anti-Zionism, including calling her a fifth columnist or an agent of a foreign power.[35] Others were more generally anti-Semitic or just threatening, such as "Jewish scum" and "Hitler was right."[36] Berger is not alone. Other Jewish Labour Party members and officials resigned from the party due to abuse. For example, "two Jewish Labour Councilors in Haringey resigned, saying it had become impossible to do their jobs due to overwhelming anti-Semitic abuse. Joe Goldberg and Natan Doron said that 'many members have repeated to me assertions about Jews having big noses, controlling the media and being wealthy'" (Johnson, 2019: 37).

As was the case for Luciana Berger, in many cases this harassment was directed at those who expressed views on Israel-related issues. Berger was among those in Labour who openly advocated for adoption the IHRA definition of anti-Semitism. In other cases, as noted in BBC's Panorama documentary and the Chakrabati report, both described in more detail earlier, it was due to assumptions that Jews are pro-Israel, blaming Jews for Israel, or simply Israel being used as a cover for other forms of Jew-hate. All of these types of harassment are actions that are considered societal discrimination by the empirical measures used in this study.

Johnson (2019: 32–50) also documents 70 examples (some of them including multiple incidents) of overt and public expressions of anti-Semitism by Labour Party members and officials. These include:

- Calling party officials who are not allied with Corbyn "Jewish" as a form of insult;
- Holocaust denial and blaming Jews for the Holocaust, usually through some conspiracy theory that the Jews originally supported Hitler;
- Comparisons between Jews or Israel and Nazis;
- References to Jewish control of finance with frequent mention of "the Rothschilds";
- Jewish control of the media, the UK and US governments, various UK political parties including the Labour Party, and world politics;
- Conspiracy theories regarding Jews or Israel controlling ISIS and being responsible for other terror attacks such as the 9/11 terror attacks;
- Jewish involvement in the slave trade;
- Jews as agents of exploitation;
- Memes depicting hook-nosed Jews engaging in various forms of malfeasance;
- Jews perverting democracy.

A government report similarly documented widespread comments on social media by Labour Party members that

- "diminished the scale or significance of the Holocaust,
- expressed support for Hitler or the Nazis,
- compared Israelis to Hitler or the Nazis,
- described a 'witch hunt' in the Labour Party, or said that complaints had been manufactured by the 'Israel lobby',
- referenced conspiracies about the Rothschilds and Jewish power and control over financial or other institutions,
- blamed Jewish people for the 'anti-Semitism crisis' in the Labour Party,
- blamed Jewish people generally for actions of the state of Israel,
- used 'Zio' as an anti-Semitic term, and
- accused British Jews of greater loyalty to Israel than Britain."[37]

There was also a wide range of use of general insults. For example, one Labour parish councilor posted on social media that "Jewish people 'drink blood and suck baby's dick,' that Jewish people are 'murdering bastards' who 'should be gassed,' and that 'Hitler would have a solution to the Israel problem'" (Johnson, 2019: 37).

Third, at the very least, there are serious questions as to whether the Labour Party under Corbyn made any serious efforts to reduce these incidents of harassment. As noted, the UK Government's Equality and Human Rights Commission determined that the Labour Party's efforts to deal with these incidents experienced "serious failings" during the Corbyn era.

In Chapter 4, we found a statistical relationship between anti-Israel views and government-based discrimination against Jews and a weak relationship between pro-Palestine views and societal discrimination against Jews. We also argued in Chapter 4 that much of the Israel-based discrimination against Jews outside of Israel is elite driven. As will be recalled, the empirical evidence in this study is only current though 2014. Most of the incidents of harassment of Jews began after Corbyn became leader of the Labour Party in 2015, so it does not coincide with our empirical study. In Chapter 5 we found that belief in conspiracy theories about Jews leads to both societal and government-based discrimination against Jews.

It is often ill advised to assume that correlation means causation. This is especially true when looking at a single case study. However, in this case there are two reasons to believe that anti-Israel sentiment is a cause of discrimination against Jews within the Labour Party. First, much of the harassment of Jews during this period involved language and behavior that is specifically anti-Israel. Furthermore, much of it took place in contexts where Israel was not being discussed and was often directed at Jews who did not openly support Israel.

Second, the Corbyn-era behavior that occurred in the context of Britain's Labour Party is consistent with the empirical results of this study. As the leadership of the party became more anti-Israel—which is what essentially occurred when Jeremy Corbyn became the party's leader—discrimination against Jews within the party became more common, more intense, and arguably was tolerated. Furthermore, we argue in this study that discrimination is often an elite-driven process where elites through speech acts and other signals can stigmatize a minority for discrimination. It is not difficult to argue that many took Corbyn's public acts and speech both before and after he became the party's leader as license to engage in overt harassment of Jews as long as it was expressed in the language of anti-Zionism or criticism of Israel.

It is impossible to know the true inner minds of the many perpetrators of this harassment. Nevertheless, given this evidence, the causes of this harassment are likely a combination of anti-Israel sentiment and deeper anti-Semitic motives which use Israel as an alibi. Both of these types of harassment were almost certainly facilitated by the speech acts and other enabling behavior of Jeremy Corbyn and the Labour leadership during his tenure as party leader.

What is most important for our purposes is that these observations remain true whether or not Corbyn himself is an anti-Semite or Britain's Labour Party under his tenure was institutionally anti-Semitic. Put differently, our argument is about the dynamics of discriminatory behavior toward Jews, rather than how the motives of this behavior or even the behavior itself is labeled. We argue that Corbyn's actions and his views on Israel certainly coincide with and are most likely among the causes of a highly increased level of harassment of Jews within the Labour Party. These actions are possibly also among the causes of the general rise in anti-Semitic incidents in the United Kingdom. This one narrow finding is consistent with the wider empirical results of this study.

Conclusions

The history of the Jews in Britain from 1070 until today provides a good case study. Anti-Semitism in Britain began with a combination of classic religious-based anti-Semitism with the general societal animus against Jews that grew out of this religious anti-Semitism, and then grew beyond it. Anti-Zionism had a steady presence in the country after the founding of the state of Israel in 1948, though it has likely reached its highest levels thus far during Jeremy Corbyn's term as the leader of the Labour Party. Corbyn's overt anti-Zionism and anti-Israel views are likely a cause, though certainly not the only one, for increasing discrimination and harassment of Jews in Britain, both within the Labour Party and in general, during that period.

7

Conclusions

The Passover Seder ends with the *Chad Gadya* song, in which a goat is eaten by a cat, which is bitten by a dog, who is beaten by a stick, which is burned by a fire, which is doused by water, which an ox drinks. The ox is then slaughtered by a butcher, who is himself killed by the angel of death, who, finally, is smitten by God. This song is relevant to this study in at least three ways. First, like the events in the song, the causes of discrimination against any minority are complex and crosscutting. As we demonstrate in this book, discrimination against Jews is no exception.

Second, no matter how powerful we are in one context, we are often vulnerable in another. Groups which are majorities in one country are often minorities in others. In the case of this study, the fact the Jews are a majority in Israel is related to levels of discrimination against Jews in the 76 countries where Jews are present as a significant minority. Third, Jews currently, despite experiencing significant levels of discrimination in many countries, are not goats led to the slaughter. However, the memory of when this was true remains strong among Jews, as does the fear that those times will return.

Given this, we posit that a study which uses an empirical comparative politics approach to examine the causes of discrimination against Jews is an important endeavor. The theories we examine are not new but, until it was generated by the Religion and State-Minorities round 3 data set (RASM3), the data necessary to thoroughly test these theories in a cross-country context were not available. Understanding the causes of discrimination against Jews is an important step in preventing similar discrimination in the future.

In this chapter we place these results in context. First, we summarize and discuss the findings themselves. Second, we ask what this study and the general literature on religious discrimination tell us about these causes of discrimination against Jews. Third, we ask what the findings of this study and the literature on anti-Semitism can tell us about discrimination in general, not just discrimination against Jews. These latter two questions are particularly important because, as we note throughout this book, the literatures on anti-Semitism and religious discrimination have many parallels, but often do not sufficiently relate to each other. We argue that a dialogue between these bodies of thought could benefit both.

Finally, we address what our findings tell us about anti-Semitism. As we discussed in detail in Chapter 1, this study focuses specifically on the causes of discrimination against Jews. However, we examine anti-Semitism as a potential cause of discrimination against Jews. The literature on anti-Semitism has multiple relevant theories on what might cause discrimination against Jews. Most of these theories posit that different manifestations of anti-Semitism are causes of discrimination against Jews. Thus, anti-Semitism is an essential component of the independent variables which relate to the causes of discrimination against Jews. Also, our findings have important implications for our understanding of the causes and nature of anti-Semitism.

What Did We Find?

This book has three goals. The first goal is to provide a thorough discussion of the levels of discrimination against Jews worldwide. In Chapter 2 we showed that patterns of discrimination against Jews, while related to those against other minorities in the 76 countries where Jewish minorities are present, are nevertheless unique and distinct. While levels of government-based religious discrimination (GRD) are not particularly high compared to other religious minorities, they are present. In contrast, societal religious discrimination (SRD) against Jews is relatively high compared to other religious minorities. In Muslim-majority countries, SRD is higher than against all religious minorities other than Christians; in Christian-majority countries, it is higher than against all other religious minorities. This pattern of high SRD combined with below average levels of GRD is unique to Jewish minorities.

The second goal is to analyze the causes of discrimination against Jews, focusing on three potential causes posited in the anti-Semitism and religious discrimination literatures. We do not claim that these are the only causes. Rather, these are the three causes on which we choose to focus our attention. We focus on these causes because we feel they are among the most important causes, or at least those which are most important to study given the current literatures on anti-Semitism and general discrimination. These are also the three causes for which cross-national data are available, which allows us to measure and test whether they actually cause discrimination against Jews. We also emphasize that these causes are not mutually exclusive. In fact, it is clear that they are interrelated and can act in concert to cause discrimination against Jews.

In Chapter 3 we examined the impact of religious ideologies and beliefs on discrimination against Jews. We find that, as expected, in states where the government is more closely associated with a religion, both SRD and GRD are higher. Thus there is considerable support for this aspect of the religious motive for discrimination against Jews.

Interestingly, SRD is lower in countries where the population is more religious. We argue that this is likely due to two dynamics. First, in the modern era where many religious people of all religions see modernity and secularism as a challenge to religion, those who so believe are more likely to be sympathetic to religious people from other religions or even to seek them out as allies in the struggle against secularism. Second, a less religious population means that there are more secular people in a country. This means the SRD may be inspired by anti-religious secular ideologies and attitudes. We discuss this issue in more detail later in this chapter.

In Chapter 4 we examined whether anti-Israel attitudes and behavior influence discrimination against Jews. We find that the presence of anti-Israel and pro-Palestine views in society are associated with higher levels of GRD. We also find that anti-Israel voting in the UN General Assembly is associated with higher levels of GRD, but only in Christian-majority countries. While in Chapter 4 we discussed anti-Zionism, these measures do not specifically measure anti-Zionism.

We argue that this in many ways simplifies the issue. This is because these relationships are present regardless of whether these anti-Israel attitudes and behavior are or are not anti-Zionist. That is, we can set the questions of what constitutes anti-Zionism and whether anti-Zionism is anti-Semitic aside and simply say that the anti-Israel factor is linked to discrimination against Jews. These other issues do not in any way influence this result.

However, this result does shed some light on these issues. The presence of this relationship between the anti-Israel factor and discrimination against Jews implies that at least some portion of those who hold anti-Israel sentiments and or engage in anti-Israel behavior associate Jews with their negative views of Israel and act on that association in the form of discrimination. Thus, this study provides evidence that Jews are being punished by governments in the form of discrimination because of anti-Israel sentiment. This is certainly consistent with the predictions in the literature on anti-Zionism. It also qualifies as anti-Semitism based on the International Holocaust Remembrance Alliance (IHRA) definition of anti-Semitism, which specifically considers it anti-Semitic when one holds "Jews collectively responsible for actions of the state of Israel."

However, we found insufficient evidence to support that the Israel factor causes more SRD. Thus, societal actions taken against Jews are likely driven primarily by other motivations.

In Chapter 5 we examined the influence of belief in conspiracies of Jewish power on discrimination against Jews. We find that tropes of Jewish power and control are strongly associated with both SRD and GRD. In fact, these are the most consistent results presented in this study. As we noted, it is likely that religious ideologies and anti-Zionism can contribute to belief in these conspiracy theories. Thus, these results demonstrate that when negative attitudes about Jews that are present in society reach the level at which they inspire widespread belief in this type of conspiracy theory, a critical threshold has been crossed. Once this threshold is crossed, discrimination becomes far more common and severe. As we discuss in the following sections, this has significant implications not just for Jews, but also for our understanding of the causes of discrimination in general.

The third goal is to examine the larger implications of our findings. The rest of this chapter focuses on this issue.

How Do Our Findings and the General Discrimination Literature Impact on the Anti-Semitism Literature?

As we note throughout the book, the literature on anti-Semitism and the general literature on the causes of discrimination, including the religious discrimination literature, are distinct. While the anti-Semitism literature does draw on many aspects of the general literatures, this occurs sporadically. That is, there has been no systematic effort to compare the insights contained in these two literatures, despite the obvious potential for these literatures to inform each other. This is likely at least in part because the anti-Semitism literature focuses on the causes and consequences of anti-Semitism, which is unique to Jews, and rarely frames its inquiries in a more general context that is comparable across cases, such as examining the causes of discrimination against religious minorities. It is also likely at least in part because the anti-Semitism literature is located largely in the humanities, and the general theories we highlight here come largely from the social sciences.

Accordingly, throughout this book we attempt to more systematically compare the anti-Semitism literature's insights on the causes of discrimination against Jews to the insights of the general literature on the causes of discrimination both in general and against religious minorities. In addition, we use empirical evidence, primarily from the RASM3 data set, World Values Survey (WVS), and the ADL Global 100 Survey, to test these propositions.

The implications of the empirical findings of the study for the anti-Semitism literature are straightforward. We find evidence to support all three theories of the causes of discrimination against Jews which are the focus of this book, all of which have deep roots in the anti-Semitism literature. However, in the case of two of them, the religious ideology and beliefs theory and the anti-Zionism theory, the results include some nuances and exceptions that have significant implications for our understanding of the causes of discrimination against Jews and, by implication, the causes of anti-Semitism. We also argue that while the results for conspiracy theories of Jewish power as a cause of discrimination are largely what one would expect, the strength and consistency of these findings have important implications for our understanding of the causes of anti-Semitism, including religious and anti-Zionist anti-Semitism. In addition, the general literature on conspiracy theories also adds depth to our understanding of how conspiracy theories about Jews influence discrimination against them.

Religious and Secular Causes of Discrimination

Both the anti-Semitism and religious discrimination literatures predict that religious belief and ideology are a potential cause of discrimination. This is perhaps among the least controversial arguments regarding the causes of discrimination against Jews, as well as against religious minorities in general. Yet we find that this assumption does not always hold, at least with regard to some aspects of discrimination against Jews between 1990 and 2014. Specifically, while governments which are more closely associated with a single religion behave as expected, in countries with more religious populations there is less, rather than more, SRD against Jews; that is, religious societies engage in less societal discrimination against Jews.

As both surveys of societal religiosity and detailed data on SRD against Jews are not available for past centuries, it is not possible to test to see if this was always the case. However, anecdotal evidence that in the past religion was a motivation for societal actions taken against Jews is abundant. Our discussion in Chapter 3 certainly implied such a correlation, and our discussion in Chapter 6 indicated that this was likely the case in England. This means that the relationship between religion and discrimination against Jews has changed in recent years. While this, in and of itself, is an important finding, it has larger implications.

This result shows that while religiously inspired discrimination against Jews and anti-Semitism have been constants historically, the dynamics which cause it and the motivations behind it can change. This is not a new insight. The anti-Semitism literature is quite clear that the ideologies which motivate anti-Semitism change and evolve over time.

However, the finding that a form of ideology that in the past caused *more* discrimination and more anti-Semitism against Jews is now responsible for *less* discrimination is a new finding. The anti-Semitism literature discusses how new ideologies can take the place old ones as a motivation for anti-Semitism. This means that as the influence of one ideology declines, another will take its place. However, it does not predict that ideologies which caused discrimination against Jews in the past can transform to factors that will lower the levels of discrimination. Consequently, this is an exceptional finding. It runs completely counter to a general consensus that was rarely, if ever, questioned within the anti-Semitism literature, or in the general literature on religion and discrimination for that matter.

There is a growing acknowledgment that the role of religion in society is changing in the modern era. One aspect of this change is that secularism has emerged as a coherent family of ideologies which challenge religion in society and politics (Taylor, 2007). Fox (2015, 2019) calls this the *secular-religious competition perspective*. In this perspective, religious and secular political actors compete to influence various aspects of politics and society, particularly government religion policy. In addition, the limitations paced on religion inspired by secular ideologies can often apply across religions. For example, restrictions on infant male circumcision and ritual slaughter of meat which are gaining popularity in Western democracies apply to both Muslims and Jews.

Given this, it is possible that religious members of a country's majority see in members of religious minorities potential allies in this secular-religious competition. When Jews are perceived as allies, there is less of a desire to discriminate against them. Also, Jewish religious acts may be seen in a new perspective, one in which religious Christians, for example, understand the importance of following the tenets of one's religion, even if some of the Jewish practices in question have no parallel in Christian religious practice.

In addition, to the extent that Jews are perceived as religious and engaging in practices counter to secular ideology, this could increase SRD in countries with fewer religious people and, by implication, a greater number of secular people. This is because secularism is more than just an absence of religion and religiosity. It is also an ideology with its own beliefs, many of which are either anti-religious in and of themselves or paint certain religious practices as immoral and unethical. Put simply, countries with a larger proportion of religious people will likely have fewer who follow secular ideologies. This can explain why in countries with a larger religious population there is less societal discrimination against Jews.

Given the results of this study, which show that this new dynamic is present in societal actions but not government actions, this is likely a new and emerging dynamic. Societal changes in patterns of behavior toward religious minorities can change more rapidly and often precede changes in government policy (Grim & Finke, 2011). This implies that inter-religious alliances between Jews and members of other religions who are themselves religious are a potential avenue to reduce discrimination against Jews and perhaps also reduce religion-based anti-Semitism. These alliances would be built on the common ground of the need to protect against limitations on the right to religious freedom that are motivated by secular ideologies. Put differently, this study suggests that religious people across religions are finding a common cause in fighting their common enemy of secularism and the anti-religious political agenda of secular political actors.

This can also be a reflection of the changing nature of secularism. Taylor (2007) argues that the rise of secularism as an ideology has changed the nature of religion. However, it is also arguable that it has changed the nature of those who are not religious; that is, those who are not religious now have an ideology known as secularism. In the past, those who were not religious were simply not religious. With the rise of secularism as an ideology of modern times, those who are not religious have available to them a family of ideologies that includes a family of belief systems. While, like religion, secularism is by no means a monolithic ideology, some versions of secularism are anti-religious in general. Others include beliefs that brand certain religious practices such as infant circumcision and kosher slaughter as immoral. This explains not only why secularism might be a common enemy to all religious people, but also why Jews, if they are perceived as religious or engaging in religious practices considered immoral by some secular ideologies, are targeted for more SRD.

Given this, with the exception of communism, which has received considerable attention, secular anti-religious ideologies deserve more consideration as a source of both anti-Semitism and discrimination against Jews. In addition, we need to take a more nuanced view of how religious ideologies and beliefs motivate discrimination against Jews which takes into account circumstances where religious Christians, for example, might find it in their interest to treat religious Jews as allies.

Anti-Zionism, Discrimination, and Securitization

This study, in its examination of the anti-Zionism theory, similarly finds that while anti-Israel attitudes and government behavior can predict levels of discrimination against Jews, this dynamic has nuances. Essentially, the link between anti-Israel sentiment and government behavior and GRD is as expected by the theory, but the results for SRD are not.

Let us start by discussing the influence of anti-Israel sentiment and a government's Israel policy on GRD. The larger the proportion of the population which express negative attitudes about Israel, as well as the larger the proportion of the population which express positive views of Palestine, the higher the levels of GRD against Jews. The results for UN General Assembly voting are present but more limited. Pro-Israel voting has no statistically significant influence on discrimination against Jews. Anti-Israel voting increases levels of discrimination, but only in Christian-majority countries. This is likely because

Muslim-majority countries nearly uniformly vote against Israel on all relevant UN General Assembly votes, so there is no variation across these countries.

Anti-Israel and pro-Palestine views have little influence on SRD, though there is a weakly significant increase in SRD in countries where a higher proportion of the population has a positive attitude toward Palestine. UN voting interestingly has the opposite predicted correlation. Countries which more often vote against Israel have lower levels of SRD. This may be because the most consistent pro-Israel voting countries in the United Nations are Australia, Canada, and the United States. In all of these countries, Jews experience relatively high levels of SRD. Be that as it may, this finding underlines the finding that the anti-Israel causes of discrimination against Jews are mostly limited to discrimination by governments and, at most, apply weakly to discrimination by society.

These results, when viewed from a broader perspective, have at least one interesting implication for the nature of anti-Zionism. We argue that these findings indicate that anti-Zionism, or at least its impact on discrimination, is an elite phenomenon. Anti-Israel societal attitudes and government behavior have influence, but this influence mostly manifests in the behavior of government elites in the form of GRD. Given this, when governments discriminate against Jews, it is reasonable to conclude that anti-Israel sentiments among government elites may be part of the reason.

There are two mechanisms by which societal attitudes against Israel may influence GRD. First, the attitudes of government elites likely reflect those of their constituents. Second, even if they do not, government elites often take the preferences of their constituents into account when making policy decisions.

However, there is insufficient empirical evidence to support the proposition that anti-Israel sentiment is an important motivation behind societal actions against Jews. Thus when synagogues are vandalized, Jews attacked, and anti-Jewish riots and protests occur, even if the participants use anti-Israel language, the evidence presented here suggests that this is not the true motivation, or at least not the most important motivation. Thus, at least with regard to societal actions, the evidence presented here supports the argument that Israel is used as an alibi to cover up other motives for discriminating against Jews.

The anti-Semitism and anti-Zionism literatures can also benefit from cross-fertilization with the general literature on the causes of discrimination. While we are able to identify no other case where an entire identity group has been consistently blamed across time in many locations for the behavior of a single country to the extent that Jews have been held responsible for Israel, there are some parallels. A comparison of similarities and differences between the Jew-Israel case and other cases can only increase our understanding.

In Chapter 4 we examined a number of these parallels. Perhaps the most prominent case currently is the blaming of all Muslims for the behavior of Muslim terrorists. This is different from the Jew-Israel case in at least two respects. First, it is a more recent phenomenon, as non-nationalist-inspired terror by Muslims is historically a more recent phenomenon (Rapoport, 2017). Second, this parallel is tied to the behaviors of non-state actors who are members of a particular religion rather than a particular state.

Yet an entire body of theory has developed around this case. Securitization theory has been developed to discuss how leaders use "speech acts" to "securitize" a group seen as a security risk and how this can help to justify actions against that group that would otherwise be considered outside of societal and political norms. While this body of theory was developed to explain behavior toward immigrant minorities in the West including Muslims, it can be used to understand the processes which cause discrimination against Jews.

While Jews outside of Israel are rarely presented as security threats, we argue that at least two securitization mechanisms might be occurring to Jews living outside of Israel. First, speech acts accusing Jews of dual loyalties can frame them as a danger in a manner analogous to the security threats and other threats posed by immigrants. In fact, an element of the perceived security threats posed by Muslims and other immigrants which can lead to their "securitization" is the question of their loyalty. Second, speech acts presenting Israel as a threat to world peace, combined with holding all Jews responsible for Israel's actions, can securitize Jews living outside of Israel. The conspiracy theory literature has it that these speech acts can be particularly potent because mere exposure to conspiracy theories, including conspiracy theories about Jews, makes people more likely to believe them (Lantian, 2013). Thus the use of conspiracy theories in speech acts used to securitize Jews, or any other minority, can be particularly potent.

Both of these mechanisms can also be accurately seen as simply the use of age-old tropes about Jews that are not particularly security-related. Given this, how does adding this extra layer of theory enhance our understanding? First, securitization theory describes a detailed process for how leaders mobilize sentiment against a minority to justify hostile actions taken against them. This can provide insight into how similar processes are applied to Jews. That is, it adds understanding to how leaders go about stigmatizing Jews. It likely can provide insight into the process by which Jews have been stigmatized historically as well as in modern times.

Second, it taps into a more general theory which allows a broader comparison of discrimination against Jews to discrimination against other minorities. In fact, we argue not only that the application of the insights of securitization theory is a useful theoretical framework to understand the causes of discrimination against Jews, but also that other theories can also serve this role. In Chapter 4 we discussed other bodies of theory, including how countries discriminate against groups perceived as threats to national culture, groups associated with foreign threats, and groups from other "civilizations," as well as other cases of states whose legitimacy are challenged. As we discussed more detail in Chapter 4, all of these cases and bodies of theory have the potential to add insight into the causes of discrimination against Jews in general and the dynamics of anti-Zionist-inspired discrimination in particular, through the methodology of comparison.

Third, on a normative level, securitization theory, as well as other more general theories, link discrimination against Jews to discrimination against other minorities. This can evoke sympathy among those who oppose discrimination against other securitized minorities and perhaps can be the basis for reducing anti-Semitism among those minorities, or even can serve as the basis for an alliance between Jews and other oppressed minorities. Fourth, as we discuss in more detail in Chapter 4 and the next section of this chapter, we argue that securitization theory can be broadened to understand how minorities are stigmatized, even when the basis for this stigmatization is not security related.

Conspiracy Theories

The finding in Chapter 5 that the proportion of a population which believes in conspiracy theories of Jewish power is a strong and consistent predictor of discrimination against Jews is not surprising. However, it does provide some important insights: that is, of the three theories tested in this study, the conspiracy theory factor is the most reliable predictor of discrimination against Jews. This is because in all tests without exception using these variables, they significantly predict both SRD and GRD. This cannot be said for any other set of variables in this study.[1]

This says much about the processes that lead to discrimination against Jews. For example, it suggests that discrimination against Jews is intrinsically linked to the popularity of certain types of anti-Semitic tropes. Also, of the three theories tested here, it is in particular the only one which consistently predicts higher SRD against Jews. As SRD against Jews is far higher than GRD, this makes it a particularly important indicator that requires further data collection and study.

The three theories we test here are not mutually exclusive. It is possible for all three to cause discrimination simultaneously. That being said, whatever the root causes of discrimination may be, it is clear that there is a line which, once crossed, leads to higher levels of discrimination against Jews. We are not able to determine from the available data whether belief in conspiracy theories against

Jews is in and of itself that line, or if it is a consequence of that line. Put differently, it may be the belief in conspiracy theories itself which is causing discrimination against Jews, or it may be that these beliefs and the discrimination are a consequence of some abstract level of prejudice and hatred toward Jews.

In either case, this finding, if nothing else, identifies an important, practical, and accurate method to forecast levels of discrimination against Jews. In theory, it also provides a potentially fruitful avenue for reducing this discrimination—countering these conspiracy theories. The general literature on conspiracy theories is pessimistic with regard to this avenue. This is because conspiracy theories are notoriously resistant to even empirical evidence which falsifies them, and countering them exposes more people to them, which can increase their popularity. In addition, as noted, the conspiracy theories may themselves be a symptom of underlying prejudices rather than a prime cause of discrimination. Despite this high bar for success, this finding does provide both evidence of the dynamics which cause discrimination against Jews and a path to mitigating it.

This is an important insight. There is much discussion in the anti-Semitism literature on how anti-Semitic tropes, including conspiracy theories, can travel from one ideology to the next, such as from religious-based anti-Semitism to anti-Zionist forms of anti-Semitism. However, this finding that belief in conspiracy theories of Jewish power transforms behavior toward Jews places this understanding in a new light. It demonstrates that when conspiracy theories of Jewish power become part of an anti-Semitic discourse, treatment of Jews is likely to worsen significantly.

As the general literature on conspiracy theories pays little attention to what happens to the objects of these conspiracy theories, the additional insights that can be transferred from this literature to the anti-Semitism literature are limited but still present. The study of what types of personalities are more likely to believe in conspiracy theories can help efforts to undermine the belief in conspiracy theories of Jewish power. Also, a close examination of those cases where the objects of conspiracy theories, other than Jews, have been subject to retaliation can shed light on how this process influences discrimination against Jews.

For example, in Chapter 5 we discussed how stereotypes of advantaged minorities in developing countries parallels stereotypes of Jews and can similarly lead to discrimination. We also discussed how the "white genocide" and "replacement" conspiracy theories have been applied by Western white supremacists to both Jews and Muslims. Jews are regarded as an entrenched powerful minority, as opposed to Muslims, who are portrayed as a foreign underclass seeking to dominate through demographic change. Thus, a detailed comparison of these two related cases would likely provide important insights.

Some Additional Empirical Insights

While the focus of this study has been these three theories of the causes of anti-Semitism as they apply to discrimination against Jews, this study has revealed some additional important findings. That is, we controlled for other factors in the multivariate analyses presented in Appendix A and found three additional interesting results.

First, SRD is more common in countries with larger Jewish populations—measured as the percent of the population which is Jewish. This is likely because SRD is often an act of opportunity. That is, societal actors who in the course of their day run across Jews or live in their vicinity are more likely to engage in acts like harassment, vandalism, and violence against them. Also, larger minorities tend to be more visible, which can attract SRD.

Second, while we would expect democracies to engage in less GRD against Jews, the results consistently show no support for this proposition. This is consistent with findings based on all 771 minorities in the RASM3 data set, where democracy is a poor predictor of GRD. In fact, Fox (2020) finds that Western democracies discriminate far more often than Christian-majority non-democracies in Asia, Africa, and Latin America.

Third, SRD is more common in more populous countries. Fox (2020: 255) argues that this phenomenon "may be because in smaller countries, people, especially group leaders, are more likely to know one another and have more contact across religious traditions. It is more difficult to discriminate against people one knows than a minority that one sees more in the abstract."

Some Broader Observations

If one looks more broadly at all three general literatures addressed here, as a whole they provide at least two additional and important insights that can inform the anti-Semitism literature. First, a common theme across literatures is that when a minority is seen as a threat, this can lead to discrimination. All three bodies of theory bring up the concept of threat, though the specific types of threat and how they are theorized differ across literatures. Second, while anti-Semitism and the causes of discrimination against Jews are likely unique, they are not so unique that there is an absence of parallels and basis for comparison. Jews are not alone in experiencing discrimination, and general theories on the causes of discrimination can be applied to deepen our understanding of why people and governments discriminate against Jews.

How Do Our Findings and the Anti-Semitism Literature Impact on the General Discrimination Literature?

Just as the literature on anti-Semitism has much to learn from the general literature on the causes of discrimination, so too the general literature can gain significant insights from both this study and the literature on anti-Semitism.

Religion, Secularism, and Discrimination

In some cases, the lessons are the same. For example, the changing nature of religion, secularism, and discrimination due to secular-religious competition is an important insight for theories of religion and discrimination. That, at least in some cases, increased religiosity, or perhaps decreased secularism, among a population leads to less discrimination against at least one religious minority is a significant finding. This is likely part of a larger trend. As noted in Chapter 3, other studies show that religious Europeans are more likely to be tolerant of Muslim religious practices such as women's head coverings than are secular Europeans (Helbling, 2014; Bohman & Hjerm, 2013).

However, this finding is limited in at least two interrelated respects. First, this study looks only at Jewish minorities. Second, most of the cases are in Christian-majority countries, and all of the rest, other than Singapore and Bosnia,[2] are Muslim-majority countries. Thus this increased tolerance at the societal level in recent years is specific to relations among Abrahamic religions. Hurd (2004a, 2004b) argues that even in secularized societies, shared religious values across the Abrahamic religions can be incorporated into the sociopolitical culture. This is especially true when the religions have shared origins, shared values, and a historical presence in a country. Judaism meets all three criteria for both Muslim-majority and Christian-majority countries. Given this, further study is necessary to determine to what extent this phenomenon is more widely applicable.

Conspiracy Theories as a Cause of Discrimination

Perhaps the most fruitful avenue for further research and discussion revealed by this study as well as the anti-Semitism literature is the potential role of conspiracy theories in causing discrimination. We are aware of no broad general discussion of this topic, much less cross-country empirical testing of this potential relationship, other than this study. This is likely because, other than the ADL Global 100 data set's data on conspiracy theories of Jewish power, we know of no cross-national survey measuring the presence of conspiracy theories about any religious minority or, for that matter, any type of group which might experience discrimination. In addition, the conspiracy theory literature rarely addresses this issue directly. In fact, as Sunstein and Vermeule (2009: 203) argue,

> most of the academic literature directly involving conspiracy theories falls into one of two classes: (1) work by analytic philosophers, especially in epistemology and the philosophy of science, that explores a range of issues but mainly asks what counts as a "conspiracy theory" and whether such theories are methodologically suspect; (2) a smattering of work in sociology and Freudian psychology on the causes of conspiracy theorizing.

Since Sunstein and Vermeule's (2009) article, the literature has advanced somewhat. It includes research on what type of person is more likely to believe in conspiracy theories and how conspiracy theories relate to each other in people's minds. However, we found little empirical study of the real-world consequences of conspiracy theories to the objects of those conspiracy theories.

In retrospect, the argument that the societal level of belief in conspiracy theories about a minority should be related to levels of discrimination against that minority has considerable face validity; that is, it seems like something that ought to be true. This can be due to a direct influence, or that the presence of a conspiracy theory is an indicator of high levels of prejudice and hatred toward a minority which are the base causes of discrimination. This study's findings of such a link with regard to Jews constitutes an excellent test case which delivers a proof of concept. This suggests that there is a possibility this link is also present for other minorities and other categories of people who are objects of conspiracy theories, though at this time no cross-country data exist to test that possibility.

Conspiracy Theories and the "Canary in the Coal Mine"

The anti-Semitism literature contains another relevant proposition: that the presence of anti-Semitism is an indicator that there is a generally high level of intolerance in a society. More specifically,

> Jew-hatred—in the present as well as the past—reveals something fundamentally wrong with its host society. In this sense, anti-Semitism . . . stem[s] from broader social, political, economic, and ideological failures. . . . Anti-Semitism is the "*canary in the coal mine*," the harbinger of a more general danger. (Kressel, 2007: 201)

Previous studies provide some evidence for this contention. For example, Zick, Küpper, and Hövermann (2011) found in a survey-based study in eight European countries that anti-Semitism is strongly correlated with homophobia, anti-immigrant attitudes, racism, anti-Muslim attitudes, and sexism. They also found that all of these attitudes became more common as respondents placed themselves father toward the right end of the political spectrum. However, their study focuses on attitudes, not actions such as discrimination.

Based on this, one would expect that the presence of conspiracy theories about Jewish power would also be correlated with discrimination against religious minorities other than Jews. This is a testable proposition. As discussed in Chapter 2, all of the 76 countries with Jewish minorities also have other religious minorities. Accordingly, Table 7.1 examines the influence of conspiracy theories of Jewish power on discrimination against religious minorities other than Jews in the countries included in this study. It also compares these results to the results from Chapter 5 on whether belief in these conspiracy variables influences discrimination against Jews.[3]

Table 7.1 demonstrates that the "canary in the coal mine" argument is accurate in this respect. The percentage of a country's population which believes in conspiracy theories about Jews also predicts levels of discrimination not only against Jews, but also against non-Jewish religious minorities. That prejudice against one minority makes more likely prejudice against other minorities is, as noted, not a new finding. But that prejudices against Jews, including several which are not conspiracy theory–type prejudices, are predictors of real-world discrimination against other religious minorities is to our knowledge an unprecedented finding. Most past studies are based on surveys which map prejudice and discriminatory attitudes among individuals. This study takes this finding a step further by demonstrating that prejudices against one minority have significant real-world consequences, including discrimination, against other minorities who are not the object of these prejudices.

In order to further test the "canary in the coal mine" argument, also in Table 7.1, we examine the impact of SRD and GRD against Jews on SRD and GRD against other religious minorities. If the argument is correct, we would expect discrimination against Jews to predict discrimination against non-Jewish religious minorities. Interestingly, both SRD and GRD against Jews predict GRD against non-Jewish religious minorities but not SRD against them. Thus, belief in conspiracy theories about Jews are actually better predictors of SRD against non-Jewish religious minorities than actual levels of SRD against Jews. This makes societal attitudes toward Jews a more accurate "canary in the coal mine" than are societal actions taken against Jews.

All of this has broad implications for the general literature on the causes of discrimination against religious minorities and perhaps discrimination in general.

Table 7.1 Summary of Views on ADL 100 Significantly Correlated with Discrimination

ADL Survey Question	Jews		All Other Minorities	
	Societal Discrimination	Government-Based Discrimination	Societal Discrimination	Government-Based Discrimination
Global ADL Score	✓	✓	✓	✓
Jews are more loyal to Israel than to this country.	✓	✓	✓	✓
Jews have too much power in the business world.	✓	✓	✓	✓
Jews have too much power in international finance markets.	✓	✓		✓
Jews still talk too much about what happened to them in the Holocaust.	✓			✓
Jews don't care about what happens to anyone but their own kind.	✓	✓	✓	✓
Jews have too much control over global affairs.	✓	✓		✓
Jews have too much control over the United States government.	✓	✓		✓
Jews think they are better than other people.	✓	✓	✓	✓
Jews have too much control over the global media.	✓	✓	✓	✓
Jews are responsible for most of the world's wars.	✓	✓	✓	✓
People hate Jews because of the way they behave.		✓	✓	✓
Israel unfavorable	✓	✓	✓	✓
Palestine favorable				✓
Societal discrimination against Jews	na	na	✓	✓
Government-based discrimination against Jews	na	na		✓

The full multivariate analyses represented in this table are presented in Appendix A.

This study shows that some types of prejudice are more likely to influence discrimination than others and that these prejudices can have an impact on groups other than the object of these prejudices. However, all of this is tested only in a specific set of cases. This finding begs a broader empirical review of this phenomenon. Such a review would require a broader data collection than is currently available.

In addition, this study bolsters the argument in the anti-Semitism literature that Jews are, in fact, the "canary in the coal mine." This suggests two research agendas. The first is a broader review of the impact of prejudice and discrimination against Jews on other important social and political factors. This study focuses on discrimination against religious minorities. Does this canary predict other forms of abuses, such as discrimination and violence against other groups, such as ethnic minorities, the LGBTQ community, or women? Does it predict general levels of repression, restrictions on freedom, or human rights violations?

Previous studies show that prejudices against Jews are related to homophobia, anti-immigrant attitudes, racism, anti-Muslim attitudes, and sexism. However, it is important to study whether these prejudices lead to action in the real-world against these groups. As this study shows that anti-Jewish prejudices lead to discrimination against Muslims, for example, examining whether it also influences levels of discrimination against other groups should be an important research agenda.

The second agenda is even broader. This study begs the question of whether Jews are uniquely a "canary in the coal mine." It is also possible that this is a specific example of a broader phenomenon where all forms of prejudice, discrimination, repression, human rights violations, and restrictions on freedoms are interconnected. If so, to what extent, and what are the paths of these interconnections? It is worth noting that this argument is consistent with the basic premise of the intersectionalism literature discussed in Chapter 4. Also, the findings in Chapter 2 show that a good portion of GRD against Jews takes place in the context of GRD against multiple minorities in the same country.

As shown in Table 7.2, it is possible to begin to answer these questions using the data from this study. SRD and GRD against Christians predicts GRD against all non-Christian religious minorities. Similarly, GRD against Muslims predicts both SRD and GRD against all non-Muslim religious minorities, and SRD against Muslims predicts SRD (but not GRD) against all non-Muslim religious minorities.[4]

This indicates that while the "canary in the coal mine" theory is correct, it is not unique to Jews. Discrimination against any religious minority is likely to predict discrimination against other religious minorities in a country. Thus, it can be said that all religious minorities are canaries in coal mines. To be clear, this does not in any way take away from the finding that discrimination against Jews

Table 7.2 Summary of Discrimination against Muslim and Christian Minorities as Causes of Discrimination against Other Minorities

	SRD	GRD
Societal discrimination against Christians		✔
Government-based discrimination against Christians		✔
Societal discrimination against Muslims	✔	
Government-based discrimination against Muslims	✔	✔

The full multivariate analyses represented in this table are presented in Appendix A.

is likely a sign of a malaise in society and politics which can affect other groups. It just means that this insight is part of a larger phenomenon where this is true of discrimination against any religious minority.

That being said, this study confirms the findings of previous studies (Fox, 2016, 2020) that most countries discriminate unequally. That is, in most countries which discriminate, some minorities are subject to more discrimination than others. Thus, while there is an interconnectedness between discrimination against different religious minorities in the same country, patterns of discrimination usually vary from minority to minority. Thus, there is much we do not know about the extent, limitations, and dynamics of this "canary in the coal mine" phenomenon.

Anti-Israel Attitudes and a Broader "Stigmatization Theory"

The final set of findings in this book are from Chapter 4 and examine the impact of anti-Israel attitudes and anti-Israel voting in the UN General Assembly on discrimination against Jews. This study finds a link between these factors and GRD against Jews. Despite the discussion in Chapter 4 which outlines parallel situations, the general literature on the causes of discrimination has little focused discussion of how the actions of a country whose majority religion is a minority religion in other countries might influence discrimination against members of that religion where they constitute a minority. If one looks, it is possible to find relevant material in the general literature. However, few if any of these discussions focus on this issue.

Given this, the case of Jews being blamed and punished for the perceived behavior of Israel can provide the seed to grow a new avenue of study. As we discussed in Chapter 4, this pattern of blaming and engaging in collective punishment against an entire group for the real or perceived behavior of some members of that group is present with other minorities, particularly Muslims and other immigrant minorities in the West. While theories like securitization theory discuss the mechanism of how leaders engage in this blaming process, there is limited systematic discussion of when such a process might be invoked. That is, securitization theory focuses far more on how leaders create this perception and use it to justify discrimination than on why a minority is targeted for this process. Both securitization theory and the results presented here indicate that this is likely an elite-driven process, but securitization theory focuses on the narrow example of when a minority becomes associated with being a security risk.

While in Chapter 4 we argued that applying the dual loyalty trope to Jews or associating Jews with Israel's perceived threat to world security and peace might create an analogous process, it is difficult to argue that Jews in the West constitute a security risk. However, the dual loyalties trope, as applied to Jews, associates Jews living outside of Israel with Israel and its policies, and presenting Muslims and other immigrant minorities as a security threat are arguably examples of a larger phenomenon where leaders choose to target and perhaps scapegoat minorities. The anti-Semitism literature addresses the scapegoating issue, but focuses more on for what Jews are blamed than why or how the scapegoating occurs.

It is also possible to divest of the security analogies altogether. Specifically, the combination of the securitization literature with the Jewish case suggests that the securitization literature needs to be broadened beyond security issues. It needs to see security issues as one of multiple types of issues or motivations where elites may invoke a process using speech acts to stigmatize a minority and justify discrimination. The process described in the securitization literature can be applied to other motivations for stigmatizing a minority and is, therefore, a subset of a larger phenomenon. Using this framework, the insights of the securitization literature can be used to apply the use of any type of trope, prejudice, conspiracy theory, or other mode of speech act to stigmatize a minority and thereby bring it out of the realm of normal politics and justify acts against this minority that would otherwise be beyond the pale.

This would result in a "stigmatization" theory that allows for a broader array of reasons or excuses for stigmatizing a minority. Securitization theory focuses less on why elites "securitize" a minority than on the process by which they accomplish this task. This new stigmatization theory would argue that this same process of stigmatization could be used for a broader array of reasons and motivations.

This would explicitly include religious and ideological motivations, among many others. That is, a religion or an ideology, such as anti-Zionism, can paint a minority as somehow deserving of this stigmatization, and this initiates the speech act process which accomplishes this task. In addition, the finding in Chapter 5 that conspiracy theories are strong causes of discrimination against

Jews suggests that the use of conspiracy theories is likely among the most potent type of speech act that can be used in this securitization/stigmatization process.

The literature on genocide provides a useful list of other circumstances under which minorities might be similarly targeted, including when societies are divided, when governments are seeking to expand their control of society, when governments are implementing a belief or ideology, retribution for perceived past acts, and during or just after times of war or political upheaval (Fein, 1990). Yet even this list does not determine why particular groups might be targeted as opposed to others. Given this, the likely unique case of Jews can potentially be part of the foundation of a new more general "stigmatization" theory of the process by which minorities are targeted by leaders.

Given all of this, the findings of this study, which are mostly specific to Jewish minorities and the anti-Semitism literature, potentially have much to contribute to our understanding of the causes of discrimination in general.

What Does This Study Have to Say about Anti-Semitism?

While the purpose of this study is to determine the causes of discrimination against Jews, it also inevitably addresses the causes and nature of anti-Semitism. One example of this interconnected distinction is that we draw from the anti-Semitism literature as part of this study's theoretical foundation, but the empirical portion of the study and the questions we ask focus specifically on the causes of discrimination against Jews. This discrimination is present, as are the potential causes we identify in this study regardless of whether the discrimination itself or any of the causes involve or are labeled as anti-Semitism. This is one of the major advantages of this study. It can examine relationships while avoiding messy debates over the normative and sometimes factual issues surrounding anti-Semitism. Nevertheless, anti-Semitism is an integral element of this study.

We do not believe this study provides any definitive answers to the questions of what anti-Semitism is, what types of actions are anti-Semitic, and who is an anti-Semite. Such an outcome is inevitably improbable for three reasons. The first is the contested nature of the term, which is wrapped up in a complex web of history and politics. The second is that this study is neither designed nor intended to answer these types of questions. Third, in the end, the question of what is anti-Semitism is more of a normative question, and less an empirical one. That being said, we posit that the results from this study can contribute to this already lively debate.

One major point of contention is whether anti-Israel views or anti-Zionism constitute anti-Semitism. If Jews living outside of Israel are, in fact, held responsible for Israel's behavior, whether that behavior is perceived or real, and punished for this behavior in the form of discrimination, that would be anti-Semitic as defined by the IHRA definition used in this study. In fact, we argue that when Jews living outside of Israel are punished for the behavior of Israel, by any reasonable definition of the term, this is anti-Semitic. However, it is certainly possible to criticize and oppose Israel's policies and not be anti-Semitic. Otherwise Israel's political opposition would all be anti-Semites and this is clearly not the case. But this is a well-worn argument, and we prefer to stick to the empirical evidence and its implications.

This study empirically links anti-Israel views in society and anti-Israel government policies to discrimination by governments against Jews. While this unavoidably has implications for our understanding of what constitutes anti-Semitism, to place this in its proper context, it is important to unpack what this means. The social science methods used in this study are based on probability, not determinism. This means that, for example, a government which votes more often than average against Israel in the UN General Assembly is more likely to engage in higher levels of GRD against Jews. This does not mean that all governments with anti-Israel policies do so. It is similarly more probable that the governments of states in which a high proportion of the population views Israel unfavorably will engage in higher levels of GRD than states where the population has a more favorable attitude toward Israel.

However, again, this relationship is not a math formula, where a country's treatment of its Jewish minority is determined solely and exactly by its Israel policy and the views of its population. For example, in 2014, Andorra, Barbados, Singapore, and Suriname all voted against Israel in the UN General Assembly 100% of the time, but engaged in no GRD against their Jewish minorities. Similarly, Macedonia and Paraguay never once voted against Israel in the UN General Assembly in 2014 but do engage in some GRD against their Jewish minorities, though mostly in the context of policies that discriminate against multiple religious minorities. Canada, the United States, Egypt, and Iran were more typical. In 2014, Canada and the United States never voted against Israel and engaged in no GRD against Jews, while Egypt and Iran voted against Israel in all of the votes and engaged in high levels of GRD against Jews. Thus, enough states follow this pattern for there to be a statistically significant relationship, but there are exceptions.

Similarly, in the country of Georgia, only 9% of respondents had an unfavorable view of Israel, but it engaged in high levels of GRD against Jews (a score of 14). In contrast, in Morocco, 80% of respondents had an unfavorable view of Israel, but GRD against Jews was far lower (a score of 3). Again, the United States (13% Israel unfavorable), Canada (15%), Egypt (81%), and Iran (80%) were more typical.

In this context, anti-Israel attitudes and activities have a high likelihood to lead to GRD against Jews, but do not necessarily do so, and GRD is possible in their absence. This implies that anti-Israel attitudes and activities are often linked to anti-Semitism, at least among government elites, but this is certainly not always the case. This means that the combination of anti-Israel activities and attitudes, combined with overt discrimination against Jewish minorities, is certainly sufficient to, at the very least, raise suspicion of anti-Semitism. However, in and of itself, it is-not sufficient to categorically determine that such anti-Semitism is present.

That being said, there is an additional piece of evidence that anti-Israel sentiment may be anti-Semitic in some cases. As discussed earlier, the evidence shows that levels of anti-Israel sentiment in society are not significantly correlated with societal actions taken against Jews, such as vandalism of religious property and attacks on Jews. Yet, often the perpetrators of these actions claim to do so based on anti-Israel sentiment. This suggests that when this occurs, there is a strong likelihood that Israel is being used as a cover for other motivations. We posit that if the true motivations for this behavior were socially and politically acceptable, there would be no need to use criticism of Israel as an alibi. The most likely motivation, which is not politically and socially acceptable, is old-fashioned anti-Semitism.

To further complicate matters, it is clear from this study, as well as others which look at the causes of religious discrimination more broadly, that there are many interrelated causes of discrimination against religious minorities (Grim & Finke, 2011; Fox, 2016, 2020). In addition, most countries which discriminate against Jews also discriminate against other religious minorities, and often the motivations to discriminate are not specific to Jews but apply to multiple religious minorities. This discrimination and the motivations behind it are by no means commendable, but as they are not specific to Jews it is difficult to paint them as anti-Semitic.

Another important finding of this study is that some aspects of anti-Semitism are more likely to have consequences if it is present among elites than when present in society. The findings for the link between anti-Israel attitudes and politics, on one hand, and discrimination, on the other, apply nearly exclusively to discrimination by governments (GRD) rather than discrimination in society (SRD). Similarly, a government's connection with religion leads to more discrimination against Jews, but societies which are more religious engage in less discrimination against Jews. All of this indicates that anti-Semitism has substantial elite-driven elements. This also fits well with our argument that elite speech acts which stigmatize Jews are a significant cause of discrimination against Jews.

Finally, this study's examination of the ADL Global 100's 11 measures for anti-Semitism sheds some light on what types of anti-Semitism are more dangerous.

These 11 measures look at various classic anti-Semitic tropes. This study found that while all but one of them lead to at least some form of discrimination, only seven are linked to both GRD and SRD. These seven include all six tropes which focus on conspiracy theories of Jewish power. The final one is blaming the victim, or more specifically, "people hate Jews because of the way Jews behave." This shows that while most anti-Semitic tropes have real-world consequences, tropes of Jewish power and control and tropes which blame the victim are particularly dangerous. It also shows that some forms of anti-Semitism present in society do influence societal and government behavior.

Thus, not only are the dynamics which cause discrimination against Jews complex, these dynamics differ for SRD and GRD.

Some Final Thoughts

As we have argued at several points in this book, the Passover Seder provides a number of good analogies for the findings from this study. On a more general level, the Seder has a set text and ceremonies, yet it also is designed to inspire a broader discussion of a wide range of issues. Like the Seder, the basic findings of this study are important, but the discussion surrounding them and the discussion and research agendas this study will, we hope, inspire are an integral part of this study's larger context.

While religious discrimination is likely more straightforward to define, measure, and address than anti-Semitism, it is still a complex phenomenon with even more complex causes. This book is not intended to be a thorough examination of the causes of religious discrimination in general, though it certainly addresses that issue. Rather, we seek to examine the patterns and causes of discrimination against one particular group, Jews. There is a well-developed literature on anti-Semitism that discusses these causes, but this study adds two elements that we argue have been missing from that literature or are at least in need of further development and integration into it. First, we include a thorough cross-national analysis of three core theories of the causes of discrimination against Jews found in the anti-Semitism literature. Second, we increase the cross-fertilization between the anti-Semitism literature and the general literature on the causes of discrimination and religious discrimination.

We also view this book as being about more than just discrimination against Jews. While our focus is on discrimination against Jews, in the process of this study we uncover information relevant to the causes of discrimination in general. As we have discussed throughout this book, while all religious minorities, including Jews, are unique, discrimination is common against religious minorities. These causes of discrimination are similar across religious minorities and, therefore, comparable. Thus, without in any way denying that the Jewish experience has been historically unique and should be treated as such, we posit that much can be learned about the general causes of religious discrimination from the more specific case of discrimination against Jews. The other side of that coin is that the insights gained from general studies of the causes of discrimination against other religious minorities, as well as other types of minorities, can help us better understand the causes of discrimination against Jews. We believe that this study's empirical tests, combined with the theoretical discussion which informed these tests, as well as our discussion of the implications of our findings, demonstrate this principle.

Put differently, this book has been written in the tradition of comparative politics. An essential foundational principle of the field of comparative politics is that we can gain insight and understanding through comparing different cases. Each case is unique, but it is this very uniqueness which allows us to compare and contrast what is similar and what is different across cases and gain understanding. Discrimination against Jews has likely existed as long as Jews have lived in countries other than their own. While the specifics have evolved over time, this central element has remained true. However, this can be said of most religious groups who live in lands where they are not the majority.

Finally, according to the Haggadah, once, around two millennia ago in the town of Benei Brak, the Passover discussion at a Seder was attended by some of the day's most important and influential rabbis, Rabbi Joshua, Rabbi Elazar ben Azaryah, Rabbi Akiva, and Rabbi Tarphon. The discussion lasted all night and ended only when their students came to tell them the sun had risen, and it was time for morning prayers. Yet the conversation did not end. It simply paused because there is always another Passover Seder the following year, when the conversation will continue. Similarly, we do not consider this book to be the final word in the discussion of what causes discrimination against Jews and what this says about discrimination in general. However, we fully expect it to contribute to the conversation and anticipate that the conversation will continue.[5]

Multivariate Analyses and Technical Details

This appendix includes the technical details of the multivariate analyses in the body of the book. It is divided by chapter. The tables are labeled with the letter A, followed by the number of the chapter in which the discussion appears, followed by the table number. For example, the first table for Chapter 3 would be Table A3.1.

Chapter 3

The World Values Study (WVS) includes 87 countries, though no wave of the survey contains all 87 countries. To date, seven waves of data are publicly available, collected from 1981–1984, 1990–1994, 1995–1998, 1999–2004, 2005–2009, 2010–2014, and 2017–2019. As the Religion and State-Minorities round 3 (RASM3) data used in this study range from 1990 to 2014, we use WVS data from waves two through six. We include each country in which the RASM3 data set includes a Jewish minority and is included in the WVS. Each country is included separately for each wave of the WVS in which there are data and is matched with the relevant RAS3 and RASM3 variables for that year. These cases are listed in Table A3.1. A total of 56 countries are included between one and five times for a total of 142 cases. These case are analyzed together because there are too few cases in any one wave to analyze separately.

We also use the following control variables based largely on those factors found in Fox (2015, 2016, 2020) to be important predictors of GRD and SRD:

- The majority religion in the country: we control specifically for whether the majority is Orthodox Christian or Muslim. Each of these variables is coded as 1 if the country has a majority of the specified religion and otherwise as 0. This is because Muslim-majority and Orthodox-majority countries have a distinct patterns of GRD and SRD.
- We use the log of per capita GDP to measure economic development.[1] Past studies have shown that more developed countries engage in higher levels of GRD, perhaps because they have more resources to do so (Fox, 2015, 2016, 2020).
- We control for the country's population using the log of the population[2] because past studies have shown that GRD is higher in more populous countries (Fox, 2015, 2016, 2020).
- We control for the size of the Jewish minority. While most past studies show no correlation between the minority size and GRD and SRD (Fox, 2016; 2020), it is important to test this also for Jewish minorities specifically. This is especially true of SRD since with smaller populations there would be less opportunity to engage in many of the categories of SRD unless one is seeking out Jews to harass.
- Democratic regimes are generally argued to be more tolerant of religious minorities. However, previous studies of GRD and SRD in general show this relationship can be more complex (Fox, 2020). We use the Polity score to measure democracy.[3]

Table A3.1 WVS Cases Included in the Study

Country	Two	Three	Four	Five	Six	Times Included
Algeria			X		X	2
Andorra				X		1
Argentina	X	X	X	X	X	5
Armenia				X	X	2
Australia		X		X	X	3
Azerbaijan		X			X	2
Belarus	X	X			X	3
Bosnia		X	X			2
Brazil	X	X		X	X	4
Bulgaria		X		X		2
Canada			X	X		2
Chile	X	X	X	X	X	5
Colombia		X			X	2
Croatia		X				1
Cyprus, Greek				X	X	2
Czech Republic	X	X				2
Egypt	X			X	X	3
Estonia	X				X	2
Mexico	X	X	X	X	X	5
Moldova		X	X	X		3
Montenegro		X	X		X	2
Morocco			X	X	X	3
Netherlands					X	1
New Zealand		X		X	X	2
Norway		X	X		X	2
Peru		X	X	X	X	4
Poland		X	X	X	X	4
Romania		X		X	X	3
Russia	X	X		X	X	3
Serbia (Yugoslavia)	X	X	X	X	X	3
Singapore			X		X	2
Slovak Rep.		X	X		X	2
Slovenia		X	X	X	X	3
South Africa	X	X	X	X	X	5
Spain	X	X	X	X	X	5

						Total
Finland	X		X	X	X	2
Georgia	X	X	X	X	X	3
Germany	X	X	X		X	3
Hungary	X		X	X	X	1
Iran			X			1
Italy	X		X	X	X	1
Kazakhstan				X	X	1
Kyrgyzstan		X		X		2
Latvia	X		X		X	1
Lithuania	X			X		1
Macedonia	X		X	X	X	2
Sweden		X	X	X	X	4
Switzerland	X	X		X	X	3
Tunisia					X	1
Turkey	X	X	X	X	X	5
Ukraine		X	X	X	X	3
Uruguay		X	X	X	X	3
United States		X	X	X	X	4
Uzbekistan			X		X	1
Venezuela		X		X	X	2
Yemen					X	1
Total	13	41	22	30	36	142

Table A3.2 Multivariate Analysis of Causes of GRD and SRD focusing on Government Support for Religion in 2014

	SRD		GRD	
	Beta	Sig	Beta	Sig
Government support	0.212	.056	0.361	.001
Majority Orthodox	0.222	.055	0.330	.003
Majority Muslim	0.168	.293	0.096	.523
Per capita GDP-log	0.280	.033	−0.077	.529
Population of country-log	0.360	.001	−0.046	.627
Jews percent of population	0.263	.012	−0.113	.241
Polity	0.211	.105	−0.176	.150
df		75		75
r-squared		.298		.377

While this is a smaller number of controls than is often used in this type of study, given the relatively low number of cases, using more would undermine the reliability of the study.

The first set of tests do not include the WVS data in order to test whether government support for religion influences GRD and SRD for all Jewish minorities and are presented in Table A3.2. This analysis looks at all 76 cases in 2014, the most recent year available. The results show that government support for religion increases levels of GRD with high statistical significance. It is also positively correlated with SRD but the level of significance is 0.56, which is just over the generally accepted cutoff of .05. Thus this relationship can be considered of borderline significance. The only other variable which significantly predicts GRD is whether the state has an Orthodox majority. This is consistent with previous studies (Fox, 2020). Like support for religion, Orthodox majorities increase levels of SRD but with borderline significance. However, SRD is more common against Jews in wealthier and more populous countries. It is also more common against larger Jewish minorities.

Table A3.3 presents the results including the measures for religiosity from the WVS data set predicting SRD. There are three models for each set of tests. The first uses both WVS variables. Models 2 and 3 test whether the results when using the attendance and importance variables individually (that is, each model includes only one of these variables) in order to make sure the results are not influenced by an interaction between the two variables. Finally, all three models are repeated looking only at Christian-majority countries in order to assess whether the results are driven by Muslim-majority countries.

Both the attendance and importance variables are strongly but negatively significant in all six tests. This means that in countries where the population is more religious, there is less SRD. This is the opposite of what the theories based on both anti-Semitism and the general literature predict. This result is robust. In addition to the tests presented in Table A3.3, this result holds up when controlling for the year of the sample and when removing government support for religion form the test (on the grounds there may be an interaction between government support for religion and religiosity). Finally, when controlling

Table A3.3 The Influence of Religiosity on SRD

	Model 1		Model 2		Model 3	
	Beta	Sig	Beta	Sig	Beta	Sig
All Cases						
Government Support	0.216	.003	0.214	.004	0.216	.004
WVS: Attend at least once a month	−0.094	.578	−0.418	.000		
WVS: Religion important	−0.365	.032			−0.437	.000
Majority Orthodox	0.274	.009	0.136	.102	0.301	.000
Majority Muslim	0.152	.224	−0.034	.714	0.187	.053
Per capita GDP-log	0.070	.433	0.070	.442	0.061	.485
Population of country-log	0.582	.000	0.613	.000	0.557	.000
Jews percent of population	0.267	.000	0.240	.001	0.276	.000
Polity	0.218	.007	0.230	.005	0.223	.007
df	131		131		136	
r-squared	.525		.511		.508	
Christian-Majority Countries Only						
Government support	0.251	.001	0.246	.002	0.255	.001
WVS: Attend at least once a month	−0.101	.598	−0.448	.000		
WVS: Religion important	−0.342	.046			−0.404	.000
Majority Orthodox	0.217	.068	0.063	.492	0.244	.004
Per capita GDP-log	0.049	.609	0.053	.590	0.040	.676
Population of country-log	0.588	.000	0.623	.000	0.559	.000
Jews percent of population	0.342	.000	0.311	.000	0.356	.000
Polity	−0.026	.740	−0.033	.673	−0.030	.698
df	109		109		112	
r-squared	.554		.540		.531	

for the influence of religiosity, the religious support variable becomes an important predictor of SRD.

The results for the non-WVS variables are similar to those in Table 3.2 (Chapter 3), with the exceptions that government support for religion is fully significant in all six tests and Orthodox-majority fully significant in three of them. In addition, the polity variable is not significant in the regressions only for Christian-majority countries, but this is likely due to the fact that most of these countries are democratic so there is little variation. The most striking difference is that per capita GDP is not significant in any of these tests.

Table A3.4 presents the results predicting GRD using the same models as for SRD, except it adds SRD as a control variable for GRD because Grim and Finke (2011) predict that SRD is a cause of GRD. In contrast, Fox (2020) finds that this relationship exists only

Table A3.4 The Influence of Religiosity on GRD

	Model 1		Model 2		Model 3	
	Beta	Sig	Beta	Sig	Beta	Sig
Government support	0.362	.000	0.365	.000	0.344	.000
WVS: Attend at least once a month	−0.006	.976	0.090	.375		
WVS: Religion important	0.113	.577			0.082	.425
Majority Orthodox	0.250	.049	0.294	.003	0.265	.006
Majority Muslim	0.127	.394	0.184	.087	0.129	.263
Per capita GDP-log	−0.071	.499	−0.070	.503	−0.079	.448
Population of country-log	−0.187	.092	−0.190	.086	−0.179	.083
Jews percent of population	0.016	.856	0.027	.755	0.010	.910
Polity	−0.146	.136	−0.147	.133	−0.109	.274
Societal Discrimination	0.096	.371	0.084	.421	0.096	.361
df	131		131		136	
r-squared	0.34		0.343		0.311	

for some religious minorities. The tests here show that like Fox (2020), this study finds no SRD-GRD link for Jewish minorities.

The results show that neither religiosity variable has a significant influence on GRD in any of the models. This result is robust in that it remains the same in tests (not presented here) looking at Christian-majority countries only and including the year as a control. However, government support for religion does have a significant influence in all three models. The results for the other variables in these tests are similar to those in Table 3.2.

Chapter 4

This study uses two types of measures of anti-Zionism. The first uses UN General Assembly votes on Israel. For each year between 1990 and 2014, each state is assigned two scores based on its voting record on votes pertaining to Israel. The first is the percentage of votes which are pro-Israel. The second is votes which are anti-Israel. As many states abstain on these votes or miss votes, the two measures, while similar, are not reciprocal. These tests combine all years into a single test and include a variable measuring the year to control for change over time. All other controls are the same as those included in Chapter 3.

The second set of measures are taken from a survey on anti-Semitism. The Anti-Defamation League performed a survey in over 100 countries which seeks to measure anti-Semitism called the ADL Global 100.[4] While the survey had two waves, we use the first wave from 2014, so it is in the same time frame as our dependent variables. These data include a full survey for each country included; 63 of these 100 countries overlap with the 76 countries with Jewish minorities included in the RASM3 data set, but not all variables

Table A4.1 UN Voting and Societal Discrimination against Jews, 1990–2014

	Model 1		Model 2		Model 3	
	Beta	Sig	Beta	Sig	Beta	Sig
All Cases						
Government support	0.093	.000	0.099	.000	0.095	.000
Majority Orthodox	0.223	.000	0.218	.000	0.222	.000
Majority Muslim	−0.026	.404	−0.028	.354	−0.027	.383
Per capita GDP-log	0.299	.000	0.290	.000	0.296	.000
Population of country-log	0.572	.000	0.566	.000	0.568	.000
Jews percent of population	0.229	.000	0.221	.000	0.226	.000
Polity	0.034	.209	0.025	.351	0.034	.212
Year	−0.015	.432	−0.003	.877	−0.014	.465
Anti-Israel			−0.052	.005		
Pro-Israel					0.013	.503
df	1,759		1,759		1,759	
Adjusted r-squared	0.490		0.490		0.488	
Christian-Majority Countries Only						
Government support	0.096	.000	0.099	.000	0.099	.000
Majority Orthodox	0.211	.000	0.198	.000	0.210	.000
Per capita GDP-log	0.350	.000	0.330	.000	0.347	.000
Population of country-log	0.584	.000	0.573	.000	0.581	.000
Jews percent of population	0.242	.000	0.232	.000	0.240	.000
Polity	−0.136	.000	−0.147	.000	−0.137	.000
Year	−0.025	.202	−0.007	.727	−0.024	.221
Anti-Israel			−0.067	.001		
Pro-Israel					0.012	.552
df	1,459		1,459		1,459	
Adjusted r-squared	.519		.522		.519	

are available for all countries. We use two variables from the ADL Global 100 to measure levels of anti-Zionism in a country. The first measures the percent of respondents in a country who express an unfavorable opinion of Israel. The second measures the percent of respondents in a country who express a favorable opinion of Palestine. While the two are correlated (.686 significance <.001), they are not identical, so it is worthwhile examining both. The controls are the same as those used in Chapter 3.

The tests based on UN voting are presented in Tables A4.1 and A4.2 and provide mixed support for the anti-Zionism explanation for discrimination against Jews. As shown in Table A4.1, anti-Israel UN voting by a state is associated with lower levels of societal

Table A4.2 UN Voting and Government-Based Discrimination against Jews, 1990–2014

	Model 1		Model 2		Model 3	
	Beta	Sig	Beta	Sig	Beta	Sig
All Cases						
Government support	0.378	.000	0.376	.000	0.377	.000
Majority Orthodox	0.344	.000	0.346	.000	0.344	.000
Majority Muslim	0.039	.218	0.040	.207	0.040	.209
Per capita GDP-log	−0.108	.000	−0.105	.000	−0.106	.000
Population of country-log	−0.026	.275	−0.025	.295	−0.023	.331
Jews percent of population	−0.039	.047	−0.037	.062	−0.037	.065
Polity	−0.243	.000	−0.241	.000	−0.243	.000
Year	0.049	.011	0.045	.023	0.048	.013
Societal discrimination	0.071	.004	0.073	.003	0.071	.004
Anti-Israel			0.018	.348		
Pro-Israel					−0.008	.670
df	1,759		1,759		1,759	
Adjusted r-squared	.463		.462		.462	
Christian-Majority Countries Only						
Government support	0.323	.000	0.319	.000	0.325	.000
Majority Orthodox	0.378	.000	0.389	.000	0.378	.000
Per capita GDP-log	0.020	.456	0.038	.173	0.018	.520
Population of country-log	−0.013	.611	−0.006	.802	−0.016	.549
Jews percent of population	0.001	.955	0.010	.660	0.000	.983
Polity	−0.449	.000	−0.438	.000	−0.450	.000
Year	0.014	.496	−0.004	.849	0.015	.475
Societal discrimination	0.001	.978	0.009	.755	0.001	.984
Anti-Israel			0.068	.001		
Pro-Israel					0.010	.658
df	1,459		1,459		1,459	
Adjusted r-squared	.476		.479		.476	

religious discrimination (SRD) both when looking at all states and when looking only at Christian-majority states. However, pro-Palestine voting has no correlation with SRD. In contrast, anti-Israel voting by a state is associated with higher levels of GRD, but only in tests that are limited to Christian-majority countries.

As the UN voting measure focuses on one form of government behavior, it is logical that it would be more likely to be associated with GRD, which is another form of government behavior. However, that higher levels of anti-Israel voting by a government are statistically associated with lower levels of SRD requires some explanation. The pattern is largely explained by the behavior of Western governments. Western democracies voted against Israel an average of just under 70% of the time between 1990 and 2014, which is the least anti-Israel voting record by world region. They also have the highest mean-level of SRD over time at a score of 6.75.

Thus, if we assume anti-Zionism is a motivation for SRD, there is a disconnect between leadership and society in the West, at least for the 1990–2014 period. While there is a significant correlation between societal unfavorable attitudes toward Israel and anti-Israel UN voting (.333, significance = .009 for all states), this is driven largely by Muslim-majority countries, which almost universally vote against Israel in the United Nations and have levels of societal anti-Israel attitudes (from the ADL Global 100 data) more than double those of most-anti-Israel societies among Christian-majority countries. When looking at Christian-majority countries only, there is no significant correlation between anti-Israel UN voting and anti-Israel societal attitudes (correlation of .121, significance = .408). However, we have no explanation for why anti-Israel UN voting would cause or be associated with lower levels of SRD.

The finding that among Christian-majority states, anti-Israel UN voting predicts GRD shows that these two forms of government policy are connected. The likely reason the correlation becomes insignificant when including Muslim-majority states is because those states consistently vote against Israel in the United Nations, so there is no variation.

The tests using the ADL Global 100 data are presented in Tables A4.3 and A4.4. In each of these tests we use two models. The first uses all control variables. The second removes the control variables that prove not to be significant in model 1. This is because with the low number of cases, too many variables can camouflage the significance of other variables.

The results show at most a weak connection between anti-Israel and pro-Palestine views in society and SRD. The pro-Palestine variable does predict SRD against Jews, but its significance of 0.54 in model two is past the generally accepted 0.50 cutoff for statistical significance. However both anti-Israel and pro-Palestine views are associated with higher levels of GRD.

Chapter 5

The ADL 100 creates a measure of "anti-Semitism" by reading the following 11 statements to respondents and asking them whether they agree or disagree:

1. Jews are more loyal to Israel than to this country.
2. Jews have too much power in the business world.
3. Jews have too much power in international finance markets.
4. Jews still talk too much about what happened to them in the Holocaust.
5. Jews don't care about what happens to anyone but their own kind.
6. Jews have too much control over global affairs.
7. Jews have too much control over the United States government.
8. Jews think they are better than other people.
9. Jews have too much control over the global media.
10. Jews are responsible for most of the world's wars.
11. People hate Jews because of the way they behave.

Table A4.3 The Influence of Anti-Israel and Pro-Palestinian Attitudes on SRD

	Model 1		Model 2	
Government support	0.095	.465		
Majority Orthodox	0.233	.040	0.193	.126
Majority Muslim	0.069	.763		
Per capita GDP-log	0.313	.010	0.277	.039
Population of country-log	0.576	.000	0.296	.010
Jews percent of population	0.344	.001		
Polity	0.215	.133	0.368	.002
Israel unfavorable	0.033	.862	0.190	.124
df	62		62	
Adjusted r-squared	.452		.287	
Government support	0.059	.630		
Majority Orthodox	0.218	.053	0.178	.138
Majority Muslim	−0.012	.949		
Per capita GDP-log	0.292	.015	0.264	.037
Population of country-log	0.559	.000	0.260	.023
Jews percent of population	0.333	.002	0.362	.002
Polity	0.201	.138		
Palestine favorable	0.157	.292	0.224	.054
df	62		62	
Adjusted r-squared	.463		.304	

According to the ADL 100's global score, a respondent is considered anti-Semitic if they answer "true" or "probably true" to a majority of these statements. This study looks at both the percentage of people in a country considered anti-Semitic based on these criteria, as well as, for each score individually, the percentage of respondents in a country who answered "true" or "probably true." This study examines the impact of the percentage of a country's population which agrees with each of these statements on discrimination.

Tables A5.1 and A5.2 present the results predicting government-based religious discrimination (GRD) and societal religious discrimination (SRD), respectively, using the same controls as in previous chapters. However, we removed nonsignificant variables due to the low number of cases. We discuss the results and their implications in more detail in Chapter 5.

Table A4.4 The Influence of Anti-Israel and Pro-Palestinian Attitudes on GRD

	Model 1		Model 2	
Government support	0.229	.097	0.272	.045
Majority Orthodox	0.340	.005	0.420	.000
Majority Muslim	−0.275	.260		
Per capita GDP-log	−0.045	.718		
Population of country-log	−0.005	.968		
Jews percent of population	−0.122	.257		
Polity	−0.273	.073		
Israel unfavorable	0.441	.034	0.336	.015
df	62		62	
Adjusted r-squared	.387		.369	
Government support	0.276	.042	0.331	.011
Majority Orthodox	0.335	.007	0.398	.000
Majority Muslim	−0.089	.662		
Per capita GDP-log	−0.044	.728		
Population of country-log	−0.054	.639		
Jews percent of population	−0.137	.212		
Polity	−0.205	.163		
Palestine favorable	0.278	.087	0.268	.038
df	62		62	
Adjusted r-squared	.384		.367	

Chapter 7

The tables measuring the impact of conspiracy theories about Jews (Tables A7.1 and A7.2), anti-Israel views, pro-Palestine views, and discrimination against Jews on discrimination against non-Jewish religious minorities (Tables A7.3 and A7.4) in the 76 countries included in this study are presented in the following. This includes the 194 minorities in the 62 countries where both Jewish minorities are included in the RASM data set and ADL Global 100 data are available for the conspiracy theory and anti-Israel variables. For SRD and GRD against Jews as causes of discrimination, the tests use all 274 minorities in all 76 countries included in this study. These tests use the same control variables as those used in Chapter 6.

Table A5.1 ADL Global 100 and SRD in 2014, Significant Variables

	Beta	Sig	Beta	Sig	Beta	Sig	Beta	Sig	Beta	Sig	Beta	Sig	Beta	Sig
Majority Orthodox	0.214	.044	0.254	.012	0.231	.030	0.207	.043	0.217	.034	0.200	.061	0.264	.015
Per capita GDP-log	0.335	.003	0.577	.000	0.429	.001	0.553	.000	0.543	.000	0.340	.003	0.515	.001
Population of country-log	0.537	.000	0.537	.000	0.552	.000	0.556	.000	0.557	.000	0.545	.000	0.534	.000
Jews percent of population	0.325	.001	0.353	.000	0.350	.001	0.325	.001	0.339	.001	0.330	.001	0.346	.001
Global ADL Score	0.355	.004	0.354	.004										
Jews loyal to Israel					0.161	.169								
Too much power in business							0.297	.030						
Too much power in finance									0.294	.026				
Talk about Holocaust too much											0.091	.344		
Care only about own kind													0.239	.081
df	62		62		62		62		62		62		62	
Adjusted r-squared	.524		.526		.467		.493		.496		.458		.478	

	Beta	Sig	Beta	Sig	Beta	Sig	Beta	Sig	Beta	Sig	Beta	Sig
Majority Orthodox	0.227	.023	0.251	.013	0.230	.028	0.236	.015	0.291	.008	0.278	.010
Per capita GDP-log	0.569	.000	0.474	.000	0.509	.001	0.557	.000	0.535	.000	0.506	.000
Population of country-log	0.534	.000	0.529	.000	0.540	.000	0.501	.000	0.515	.000	0.521	.000
Jews percent of population	0.354	.000	0.365	.000	0.336	.001	0.354	.000	0.353	.000	0.348	.001
Too much global power	0.355	.004										
Too much power in US			0.303	.003								
Think they are better than us					0.237	.078						
Too much power in the media							0.386	.001				
Cause wars									0.280	.033		
Anti-Semitism due to their behavior											0.267	.026
df	62		62		62		62		62		62	
Adjusted r-squared	.524		.526		.479		.553		.492		.495	

Table A5.2 ADL Global 100 and GRD in 2014, Significant Variables

	Beta	Sig	Beta	Sig	Beta	Sig	Beta	Sig	Beta	Sig	Beta	Sig	Beta	Sig
Government support	0.489	.000	0.339	.004	0.381	.001	0.432	.000	0.410	.000	0.502	.000	0.395	.000
Majority Orthodox	0.378	.001	0.319	.003	0.336	.002	0.302	.007	0.307	.006	0.370	.001	0.346	.001
Global ADL Score			0.308	.009										
Jews loyal to Israel					0.250	.030								
Too much power in business							0.230	.041						
Too much power in finance									0.241	.035				
Talk about Holocaust too much											0.049	.660		
Care only about own kind													0.298	.006
df	62		62		62		62		62		62		62	
Adjusted r-squared	.352		.393		.402		.366		.369		.321		.402	

	Beta	Sig	Beta	Sig	Beta	Sig	Beta	Sig	Beta	Sig	Beta	Sig
Government support	0.379	.001	0.264	.039	0.383	.001	0.335	.007	0.293	.014	0.322	.005
Majority Orthodox	0.314	.004	0.340	.001	0.310	.004	0.321	.003	0.365	.000	0.364	.000
Too much global power	0.252	.033										
Too much power in US			0.363	.005								
Think they are better than us					0.278	.015						
Too much power in the media							0.283	.023				
Cause wars									0.362	.003		
Anti-Semitism due to their behavior											0.352	.002
df	62		62		62		62		62		62	
Adjusted r-squared	.370		.404		.384		.406		.416		.420	

Table A7.1 ADL Global 100 and SRD in 2014 for Non-Jewish Religious Minorities, Significant Variables

	Beta	Sig	Beta	Sig	Beta	Sig	Beta	Sig	Beta	Sig	Beta	Sig	Beta	Sig
Majority Orthodox	0.152	.016	0.158	.012	0.156	.013	0.144	.023	0.145	.022	0.161	.011	0.156	.015
Per capita GDP-log	-0.070	.263	0.030	.692	0.006	.933	-0.012	.886	0.009	.908	-0.084	.188	-0.048	.556
Population of country-log	0.159	.007	0.162	.006	0.178	.003	0.165	.005	0.169	.004	0.150	.011	0.159	.007
Minority percent of population	0.137	.021	0.140	.018	0.141	.017	0.144	.016	0.147	.014	0.126	.036	0.138	.020
Global ADL Score			0.164	.024										
Jews loyal to Israel					0.147	.032								
Too much power in business							0.091	.250						
Too much power in finance									0.126	.101				
Talk about Holocaust too much											-0.079	.195		
Care only about own kind													0.033	.670
df	194		194		194		194		194		194		194	
Adjusted r-squared	.070		.084		.083		.088		.076		.072		.067	

	Beta	Sig	Beta	Sig	Beta	Sig	Beta	Sig	Beta	Sig	Beta	Sig
Majority Orthodox	0.148	.018	0.167	.007	0.147	.020	0.148	.018	0.184	.004	0.170	.008
Per capita GDP-log	0.008	.911	0.032	.626	-0.001	.991	0.026	.717	0.032	.680	-0.003	.966
Population of country-log	0.160	.006	0.165	.004	0.159	.007	0.145	.013	0.146	.013	0.153	.009
Minority percent of population	0.141	.018	0.128	.027	0.140	.019	0.134	.023	0.134	.024	0.135	.023
Too much global power	0.132	.072										
Too much power in US			0.259	.000								
Think they are better than us					0.110	.153						
Too much power in the media							0.190	.005				
Cause wars									0.159	.031		
Anti-Semitism due to their behavior											0.120	.081
Israel unfavorable												
df	194		194		194		194		194		194	
Adjusted r-squared	.078		.125		.074		.093		.083		.077	

Table A7.2 ADL Global 100 and GRD in 2014 for Non-Jewish Religious Minorities, Significant Variables

	Beta	Sig	Beta	Sig	Beta	Sig	Beta	Sig	Beta	Sig	Beta	Sig	Beta	Sig
Government support	0.484	.000	0.395	.000	0.424	.000	0.456	.000	0.439	.000	0.482	.000	0.440	.000
Majority Orthodox	0.358	.000	0.315	.000	0.329	.000	0.299	.000	0.303	.000	0.360	.000	0.334	.000
Global ADL Score			0.236	.000										
Jews loyal to Israel					0.185	.000								
Too much power in business							0.193	.000						
Too much power in finance									0.203	.000				
Talk about Holocaust too much											-0.009	.854		
Care only about own kind													0.212	.000
df	194		194		194		194		194		194		194	
Adjusted r-squared	.354		.398		.381		.385		.388		.351		.394	

	Beta	Sig	Beta	Sig	Beta	Sig	Beta	Sig	Beta	Sig	Beta	Sig
Government support	0.418	.000	0.337	.000	0.405	.000	0.366	.000	0.360	.000	0.387	.000
Majority Orthodox	0.310	.000	0.332	.000	0.281	.000	0.303	.000	0.350	.000	0.344	.000
Too much global power			0.204	.000								
Think they are better than us					0.286	.000						
Too much power in the media							0.266	.000				
Cause wars									0.284	.000		
Anti-Semitism due to their behavior											0.275	.000
df	194		194		194		194		194		194	
Adjusted r-squared	.386		.408		.422		.406		.417		.418	

Table A7.3 Anti-Israel Sentiments and Discrimination against Jews as Causes of SRD in 2014 against Non-Jewish Religious Minorities, Significant Variables

	Beta	Sig	Beta	Sig	Beta	Sig	Beta	Sig
Majority Orthodox	0.221	.001	0.182	.004	0.124	.056	0.086	.169
Per capita GDP-log	0.008	.904	−0.046	.459	−0.129	.072	0.008	.901
Population of country-log	0.157	.006	0.129	.028	0.068	.389	0.133	.020
Minority percent of population	0.120	.039	0.120	.041	0.134	.024	0.120	.039
Israel unfavorable	0.238	.000						
Palestine favorable			0.187	.002				
SRD against Jews					0.143	.093		
GRD against Jews							.273	.000
df		194		194		273		273
Adjusted r-squared		.117		.110		.076		.127

Table A7.4 Anti-Israel Sentiments and Discrimination against Jews as Causes of Discrimination in 2014 against All Other Religious Minorities, Significant variables

	Beta	Sig	Beta	Sig	Beta	Sig	Beta	Sig
Government support	0.346	.000	0.366	.000	.492	.000	.236	.000
Majority Orthodox	0.396	.000	0.381	.000	.361	.000	.166	.000
Israel unfavorable	0.237	.000						
Palestine favorable			0.228	.000				
SRD against Jews					−.054	.273		
GRD against Jews							.544	.000
df		194		194		273		273
Adjusted r-squared		.387		.389		.354		.552

Tables A7.5 and A7.6 measure whether SRD and GRD against Muslims and Christians predict SRD and GRD against all other minorities. These tests include all religious minorities on the 76 countries in these studies, other than the ones measured in the independent SRD or GRD variable. They also exclude all cases where no independent variable is coded because the relevant minority is not present on the country. We discuss the results in more detail in Chapter 7.

Table A7.5 Discrimination against Christians and Muslims as Causes of SRD in 2014 against Non-Jewish Religious Minorities, Significant Variables

	Beta	Sig	Beta	Sig	Beta	Sig	Beta	Sig
Majority Orthodox	0.104	.153	0.092	.239	0.212	.001	.131	.053
Per capita GDP-log	0.233	.001	0.244	.001	−0.117	.101	.067	.307
Population of country-log	0.292	.000	0.286	.000	0.136	.030	.167	.005
Minority percent of population	0.163	.014	0.163	,014	−0.040	.497	−0.037	.521
SRD against Christians	0.062	.405						
GRD against Christians			0.076	.381				
SRD against Muslims					.249	.000		
GRD against Muslims							.333	.000
df		204		204		253		253
Adjusted r-squared		.134		.134		.137		.173

Table A7.6 Discrimination against Christians and Muslims as Causes of GRD in 2014 against Non-Jewish Religious Minorities, Significant Variables

	Beta	Sig	Beta	Sig	Beta	Sig	Beta	Sig
Government support	0.485	.000	0.280	.000	0.415	.000	0.230	.000
Majority Orthodox	0.217	.000	−0.034	.556	0.431	.000	0.291	.000
SRD against Christians	0.174	.006						
GRD against Christians			0.602	.000				
SRD against Muslims					−0.032	.531		
GRD against Muslims							0.460	.000
df	204		204		253		253	
Adjusted r-squared	.380		.556		.350		.510	

Notes

Chapter 1

1. "Anti-Semitic Incidents Remained at Near-Historic Levels in 2018: Assaults against Jews More than Doubled," https://www.adl.org/news/press-releases/anti-semitic-incidents-remained-at-near-historic-levels-in-2018-assaults; "Antisemitism Rising Sharply across Europe, Latest Figures Show," *The Guardian*, February 15, 2019.
2. Translation by the authors.
3. It is our contention that one can find an academic to dispute nearly anything.
4. https://www.holocaustremembrance.com/node/196.
5. https://www.holocaustremembrance.com/node/196.
6. For a review of these studies, see Tausch (2018).
7. See AMHCA's reports on anti-Semitic activities on campus. There are multiple reports each year. https://amchainitiative.org/reports.
8. For a discussion of this theory and tis critics, see Fox (2004).

Chapter 2

1. While Muslims in Bosnia are a plurality, they do not constitute a majority. In fact, the country has three major religious groupings: Bosnians, who are Muslim; Croats, who are Catholic; and Serbs, who are Orthodox Christian. The country has a complicated governing arrangement where Bosnians control the government for some areas of the country, while Serbs and Croats jointly control other areas. We posit that this is better described as a state with a mixed majority rather than a single majority.
2. "Government Minister's Slurs Anger South African Jews," *Jewish Standard*, http://jewishstandard.timesofisrael.com/government-ministers-slurs-anger-south-african-jews/.
3. Anastasia Sampson, "Hunting in Sweden," https://www.sweden.org.za/hunting-in-sweden.html.
4. "Law Forcing Jews to Obtain Permits for Kosher Meat Proposed by Austrian Politician," *The Independent*, July 18, 2018, https://www.independent.co.uk/news/world/europe/kosher-meat-ban-permits-register-jews-lower-austria-freedom-party-gottfried-waldhausl-a8453011.html.
5. Milan Schreuer, "Belgium Bans Ritual Slaughter," *New York Times*, January 6, 2019. https://www.nytimes.com/2019/01/05/world/europe/belgium-ban-jewish-muslim-animal-slaughter.html.

6. "Sweden Restricts Circumcision," *BBC News*, October 1, 2001; "Ritual Circumcision Ban Recommended in Sweden and Denmark by Medical Associations," *Huffington Post*, January 27, 2014, https://www.huffpost.com/entry/circumcision-ban-sweden-denmark_n_4674547; J. Deisher, "Sweden Children's Rights Official Calls for Ban on Infant Male Circumcision," *Jurist: University of Pittsburgh's School of Law*, September 29, 2013, http://jurist.org/paperchase/2013/09/sweden-childrens-rights-official-calls-for-ban-on-infant-male-circumcision.php.

7. "Norway Passes Act Regulating Circumcision," *Times of Israel*, June 28, 2014, https://www.timesofisrael.com/norway-passes-act-regulating-circumcision/

8. https://www.retsinformation.dk/Forms/R0710.aspx?id=162591; https://stps.dk/da/nyheder/2013/omskaering-af-drengeboern/~/media/92A1A9B3C9E34F22A855659470CD81FE.ashx.

9. Nicholas Kulush, "German Ruling against Circumcising Boys Draws Criticism," *New York Times*, June 26, 2012, https://www.nytimes.com/2012/06/27/world/europe/german-court-rules-against-circumcising-boys.html; Judy Dempsey, "Germany, Jews and Muslims, and Circumcision," *New York Times*, September 17, 2012, https://www.nytimes.com/2012/09/18/world/europe/18iht-letter18.html; Melissa Eddy, "Germany Clarifies Its Stance on Circumcision," *International Herald Tribune*, December 13, 2012.

10. "Denmark Refuses to Ban the Ritual Circumcision on Boys," *CPH Post Online*, September 11, 2020. http://cphpost.dk/?p=118305.

11. "Norway Passes Act Regulating Circumcision," *Times of Israel*, June 28, 2014. https://www.timesofisrael.com/norway-passes-act-regulating-circumcision/

12. *Changed Relations between the State and the Church of Sweden*, Ministry of Culture, Sweden, https://www.legislationline.org/download/id/5811/file/Factsheetaboutstate-churchrelations_2000_en.pdf.

13. M. Bayram, "Kyrgyzstan: Complaining to Local Authorities about Burial Violations Is "Useless," *Forum 18 News Service*, June 6, 2014. https://www.refworld.org/docid/5391b0d64.html

14. Zagreb, *International Jewish Cemetery Project*, 2014, http://www.iajgsjewishcemeteryproject.org/croatia/zagreb.html; US Department of State, *Religious Freedom Report Croatia 2010*. www.state.gov

15. S. Isaacson, *A Practical Comparison of the Laws of Religion of Colombia and Chile*, International Center for Not-for-Profit Law, September 2003, https://www.icnl.org/resources/research/ijnl/a-practical-comparison-of-the-laws-of-religion-of-colombia-and-chile.

16. US Department of State, *Religious Freedom Report, Azerbaijan 2010, 2011, 2012, 2013*; W. Fautré et al., *Annual Report: In Prison for Their Religion or Beliefs*, Human Rights without Frontiers, 2015. https://hrwf.eu/

17. Louis Fishman, "Turkey's Symbolic Measures Toward Jews Neglect to Address Real Anti-Semitism," *HaAretz*, April 15, 2015, http://www.haaretz.com/opinion/.premium-1.651649; Ceylan Yeginsumay, "Sephardic Jews Feel Bigotry's Sting in Turkey and a Pull Back to Spain," *New York Times*, May 26, 2015, http://www.nytimes.com/2015/05/27/world/europe/sephardic-jews-feel-bigotrys-sting-in-turkey-and-a-pull-back-to-spain.

html; Yair Rosenberg, "Will Obama Condemn the Mainstreaming of Anti-Semitism by Turkey's Ruling Party?," *Tablet*, March 20, 2015; http://www.tabletmag.com/scroll/189783/will-obama-condemn-the-mainstreaming-of-anti-semitism-by-turkeys-ruling-party.

18. Sam Sokol, "Venezuelan Government Accused of Doing Little to Curb Anti-Semitism," *Jerusalem Post*, January 5, 2015; http://www.jpost.com/Diaspora/Venezuelan-government-accused-of-doing-little-to-curb-anti-Semitism-386731.

19. European Commission against Racism and Intolerance, *Report on Greece*, 2009, http://www.coe.int/t/dghl/monitoring/ecri/Country-by-country/Greece/GRC-CbC-IV-2009-031-ENG.pdf.

20. Ari Soffer, "British MP George Galloway Declares His City 'Israeli-Free,'" *Arutz Sheva*, August 7, 2014, http://www.israelnationalnews.com/News/News.aspx/183832#.VJga_sAKA

21. Judy Maltz, "Iceland Jews Are Left Out in the Cold," *HaAretz*, December 23, 2011, http://www.haaretz.com/weekend/week-s-end/iceland-jews-are-left-out-in-the-cold-1.403142; "Anti-Semitic Incident in Iceland," *Artuz Sheva*, February 1, 2009, http://www.israelnationalnews.com/News/Flash.aspx/160118#.VJ_NxsAKA.

22. K. Clarke & G. Hamilton, "Jews Pull the Strings: Québec Media Personality; Anti-Semitic Rant," *National Post*, August 14, 2014, https://nationalpost.com/news/canada/quebec-jewish-community-disturbed-by-lack-of-outrage-over-columnists-anti-semitic-radio-rant.

23. 1996 US State Department Human Rights Report, https://1997-2001.state.gov/global/human_rights/1996_hrp_report/czechrep.html.

24. *25 Months of Anti-Semitic Invective in Greece*: A report compiled in cooperation with the Greek Helsinki Monitor, presented at the OSCE Conference on Antisemitism in Berlin, April 28–29, 2004, by Dr. Shimon Samuels, director for International Liaison of the Simon Wiesenthal Centre, Paris, http://www.wiesenthal.com/atf/cf/%7BDFD2AAC1-2ADE-428A-9263-35234229D8D8%7D/25Months.pdf.

25. Jonathan Pearlman, "Australia's Most Senior-Ranked Catholic Says Jews 'Intellectually and Morally Inferior,'" *The Telegraph*, April 12, 2012, https://www.telegraph.co.uk/news/religion/9199453/Australias-most-senior-ranked-Catholic-says-Jews-intellectually-and-morally-inferior.html.

26. Rajeev Syal, "Priest Known for Extreme Views Invited to European Parliament by MEPs," *The Guardian*, June 21, 2011, https://www.theguardian.com/world/2011/jun/21/priest-european-paliament-extremist-polish; "Poland Complains to Vatican over Priest's Anti-Semitic Remarks," *Haaretz*, June 27, 2011, https://www.haaretz.com/jewish/1.5023945.

27. M. Goldfarb, "Rise of Hungary's Right-Wing Jobbik Party Bodes Poorly for Jews and Roma," *GlobalPost*, May 22, 2014, https://www.pri.org/stories/2014-05-22/rise-hungarys-right-wing-jobbik-party-bodes-poorly-jews-and-roma.

28. "Bulgarian 'Ataka' Party Follows Neo-Nazi Trends," *Artutz Sheva*, May 16, 2013, https://www.israelnationalnews.com/News/News.aspx/168042.

29. Anti-Defamation League, "ADL Welcomes Russian Government Response to Accusations Against Jews," January 26, 2005, http://www.adl.org/PresRele/ASInt_13/4631_13.htm.

30. "Finland Has Its Own Anti-Semitism," *Arutz Sheva*, July 3, 2013.

31. For a detailed listing of similar incidents in the United States, see the Anti-Defamation League's listing of Anti-Semitic Incidents in 2017 at https://www.adl.org/media/10943/download.

32. Statistics Canada, *Police-Reported Hate Crime in Canada 2012*, http://www.statcan.gc.ca/pub/85-002-x/2014001/article/14028-eng.pdf; Statistics Canada, *Police-Reported Hate Crime in Canada 2011*, http://www.statcan.gc.ca/pub/85-002-x/2013001/article/11822-eng.pdf.

33. For a detailed listing of similar incidents in the United States, see the Anti-Defamation League's listing of Anti-Semitic Incidents in 2017 at https://www.adl.org/media/10943/download.

34. Dan Goldberg, "Rising Anti-Semitism in Australia Leaves Jews Feeling Vulnerable," *Haaretz*, August 28, 2014, http://www.haaretz.com/jewish-world/jewish-world-news/.premium-1.612430.

35. Mansfred Gerstenfeld, "The Broad Array of Belgian Anti-Semitism," *Besa Perspectives*, February 10, 2019, https://besacenter.org/perspectives-papers/belgium-antisemitism/.

36. Shaul Walker, "Jews in Germany Warned of Risks of Wearing Kippah Cap in Public," *The Guardian*, May 26, 2019, https://www.theguardian.com/world/2019/may/26/jews-in-germany-warned-of-risks-of-wearing-kippah-cap-in-public.

37. European Union Agency for Fundamental Rights, *Discrimination and Hate Crime against Jews in EU Member States: Experiences and Perceptions of anti-Semitism*, 2013, http://fra.europa.eu/sites/default/files/fra-2013-discrimination-hate-crime-against-jews-eu-member-states-0_en.pdf; J. Yardley, "Europe's Anti-Semitism Comes out of the Shadows," *New York Times*, September 24, 2014, A.1, https://www.nytimes.com/2014/09/24/world/europe/europes-anti-semitism-comes-out-of-shadows.html; "Gaza conflict: France Jails Pro-Palestinian Rioters," *BBC News*, July 23, 2014, https://www.bbc.com/news/world-europe-28439988; Jocelyn Gecker, "French Political and Religious Leaders Join in Prayer for Stabbed Paris Rabbi," *Associated Press International*, January 8, 2003; Cox News Service, "With Rising Muslim Population, A Rise in Anti-Jewish Sentiment," April 26, 2006.

38. K. Willsher, "Armed Man Kills 4 at French Jewish school; One of the Guns Matches a Weapon Used in the Slayings of Three Soldiers Last Week in the Same Area," *Los Angeles Times*, March 20, 2012, A.3; S. Sayar & S. Erlanger, "Killer Sought in 3rd Attack in France; 4 Die at School: 3 Victims Are Children; Killings Follow Similar Attacks on Soldiers," *International Herald Tribune*, March 20, 2012, 4.

39. "Obituary: Toulouse Gunman Mohammed Merah," *BBC News*, March 22, 2012.

40. Society for the Protection of Jewry in France, *Report on Anti-Semitism in France 2012*, http://antisemitisme.org/dl/SPCJ-2012-EN.pdf.

41. C. Daley, "Anti-Semitism Reported in Rape in Paris Suburb," *International New York Times*, December 4, 2014, 4.

42. European Union Agency for Fundamental Rights, *Discrimination and Hate Crime against Jews in EU Member States: Experiences and Perceptions of Anti-Semitism*, 2013.

43. L. Hoare, "Brazen Anti-Semitism Sends French Jews Racing to Leave in Record Numbers: Aliyah Figures Soar above Total for Americans," *The Forward*, July 16, 2014, http://forward.com/articles/202126/brazen-anti-semitism-sends-french-jews-racing-to-l/#ixzz3MEWCch5S; "Anti-Semitic Attacks on Rise in France, Says Minister," *Reuters*, December 7, 2014.

Chapter 3

1. This means that the legal/social status of Jews was not defined. They had no regulations, so people could treat Jews as they wished, for better or for worse.

2. *Greek Reporter*, http://greece.greekreporter.com/2013/11/11/religious-icons-in-courtrooms-case-rejected-by-judges/.

3. Greek Helsinki Monitor (January 29, 2010), "Greece: Conviction of 'Apollonio Fos' Publisher for Anti-Semitic Pamphlets in Plevris Trial; European Network of Legal Experts in the Non-Discrimination Field," *Court Conviction of Editor of Neo-Nazi Magazine for Distribution of Anti-Semitic Pamphlets*, http://www.non-discrimination. net/content/media/EL-15-EL_Apollonio%20Fos.pdf; M. Shamee, "Greek Neo-Nazi Plevris Acquitted of Incitement against: Jews," *Jerusalem Post*, March 29, 2009.

4. N. Stamouli & A. Granitsas, "Greece's Parliament Approves Hate-Crime Law; Law Stiffens Penalties for Racially Motivated Crime and Genocide and War-Crime Denial," *Wall Street Journal*, September 9, 2014.

5. European Commission against Racism and Intolerance (2009), *Report on Greece*, http://www.coe.int/t/dghl/monitoring/ecri/Country-by-country/Greece/GRC-CbC-IV-2009-031-ENG.pdf.

6. Amnesty International (2014), *A Law Unto Themselves: A Culture of Abuse and Impunity in the Greek Police*, http://www.amnesty.org/en/library/asset/EUR25/005/2014/en/47005cd7-f536-4c21-851f-e595076dcaef/eur250052014en.pdf.

7. European Commission against Racism and Intolerance (2009), *Report on Greece*, http://www.coe.int/t/dghl/monitoring/ecri/Country-by-country/Greece/GRC-CbC-IV-2009-031-ENG.pdf; Human Rights Watch (2013), *Unwelcome Guests: Greek Police Abuses of Migrants in Athens*, http://www.refworld.org/docid/51bae3274. html; Amnesty International (2014), *A Law Unto Themselves: A Culture of Abuse and Impunity in the Greek Police*, http://www.amnesty.org/en/library/asset/EUR25/005/2014/en/47005cd7-f536-4c21-851f-e595076dcaef/eur250052014en.pdf; Hellenic League for Human Rights (2010) *Racist and Related Hate Crimes in EU Country Report Greece 2010*, http://www.academia.edu/6336019/Racist_and_related_hate_crimes_in_Greece

8. United Nations Human Rights Commission (2014), *Neo-Nazis Are Raising Their Heads in Greece*, http://www.unhcr.gr/1againstracism/en/neo-nazis-are-raising-their-heads-in-greece/; European Commission against Racism and Intolerance (2009), *Report on Greece*, http://www.coe.int/t/dghl/monitoring/ecri/Country-by-country/Greece/GRC-CbC-IV-2009-031-ENG.pd.

9. A. Faiola, "Golden Dawn Rises in Greece: Critics Fear Anti-Immigrant Party's Gains in Struggling Nation," *Chicago Tribune*, October 24, 2012, 16.
10. Religion and State codebook. Available at www.religionandstate.org. Each of these components is coded as 1 if it is present in a country and 0 otherwise. The resulting scale ranges from 0 to 52. For a more thorough discussion of this variable including a distribution for each component, see Fox (2015, 2019) and http://www.thearda.com/Archive/Files/Codebooks/RAS3COMP_CB.asp.
11. http://www.worldvaluessurvey.org/wvs.jsp.
12. The variable represents the percentage of respondents in a country that said religion was either "very important" or "rather important."
13. The relationship between government support for religion and SRD becomes statistically significant at the .05 level only when controlling for the religiosity variables. In these tests, as measured by Beta values, the religiosity variables have a substantially larger impact on the results than does government support for religion. For more details, see Appendix A.
14. The religious support variable is significant in predicting GRD in both tests, including the religiosity variables and those not including them. In these tests, as measured by Beta values, the religious support variable is the strongest significant influence on GRD. For more details, see Appendix A.

Chapter 4

1. Daniel Staetsky, "Anti-Zionism and Anti-Semitism: Are They Related?" *Times of Israel*, March 6, 2019, https://blogs.timesofisrael.com/anti-zionism-and-anti-semitism-are-they-related/.
2. A video of this episode is available at https://www.youtube.com/watch?v=KHqXt_JNSt8.
3. United Nations General Assembly Resolution 3379. The full Resolution of the United Nations General Assembly can be found at https://www.un.org/documents/ga/res/30/ares30.htm.
4. Office of the Historian, "The Madrid Conference," 1991, https://history.state.gov/milestones/1989-1992/madrid-conference.
5. United Nations General Assembly Resolution 46/86. The full Resolution of the United Nations General Assembly can be found at https://www.un.org/documents/ga/res/46/a46r086.htm.
6. UNSCR 242; a resolution adopted by the UN Security Council after the Six Day War in 1967 for an Israeli withdrawal from occupied territories with a Palestinian recognition of Israel.
7. UNSCR 338; a resolution adopted by the UN Security Council after the Yom Kippur War in 1973 calling for a ceasefire from all sides as well as the implementation of UNSCR 242.

8. Rachel L. Swarns, "The Racism Walkout: The Overview; U.S. and Israelis Quit Racism Talks over Denunciation," *New York Times*, September 4, 2001, https://www.nytimes.com/2001/09/04/world/racism-walkout-overview-us-israelis-quit-racism-talks-over-denunciation.html.

9. Eugene Kontorovich, "Guest Post: Iran's Relief Ship and the Blockade of Yemen," *Opinion Juris*, May 11, 2015, http://opiniojuris.org/2015/05/11/guest-post-irans-relief-ship-and-the-blockade-of-yemen/.

10. Norman Geras, "Alibi Antisemitism," *Fathom*, 2013, http://fathomjournal.org/alibi-antisemitism/.

11. Geras, "Alibi Antisemitism."

12. For a discussion of the history of Zionism among Jewish feminists and lesbians, see Lober (2018).

13. "After Banning Jewish Flags Last Year, Chicago Dyke March Displays Palestinian Flags," *Haaretz*, June 26, 2018, https://www.haaretz.com/us-news/chicago-dyke-march-flies-palestinian-flags-after-banning-jewish-ones-1.6216718.

14. Trudy Ring, "D.C. Dyke March Band Rainbow Star of David Flag," *The Advocate*, June 6, 2019, https://www.advocate.com/news/2019/6/06/dc-dyke-march-bans-rainbow-star-david-flag.

15. Erin Calabrese and Bob Fredericks, "Pro-Palestinian Activists Leave 'Eviction' Notices for Jewish NYU Students," *New York Post*, April 24, 2014, https://nypost.com/2014/04/24/jewish-nyu-students-targeted-by-pro-palestine-activists-report/.

16. Jeremy Sharon, "Pro-Palestinian Activists Post Evictions Notices on Jewish Students' Doors," *The Jerusalem Post*, April 4, 2019, https://www.jpost.com/diaspora/pro-palestinian-activists-post-eviction-notices-on-jewish-students-doors-585761.

17. Adam Nagourney, "In U.C.L.A. Debate over Jewish Student, Echoes on Campus of Old Biases," *New York Times*, March 5, 2015, https://www.nytimes.com/2015/03/06/us/debate-on-a-jewish-student-at-ucla.html.

18. Amrita Bhattacharyya, "Jewish Students File Complaint against UI, Allege Anti-Semitic Environment," *The Daily Illini*, November 5, 2020. https://dailyillini.com/news/2020/11/05/jewish-students-file-complaint-against-ui-allege-anti-semitic-environment/.

19. Nagourney "In U.C.L.A. Debate over Jewish Student."

20. See AMHCA's reports on anti-Semitic activities on campus. There are multiple reports each year. https://amchainitiative.org/reports.

21. Non-anti-Semitic theories do exist, but they are mostly argued by ultra-religious Jews who oppose a Jewish state because of religious beliefs (e.g., establishing a Jewish state can be done only after the arrival of the Messiah), or by secular Jews who argue for assimilation, such as the Jewish Bund movement (The General Jewish Labour Bund in Lithuania, Poland, and Russia). For more information, see Bernard McGinn et al., eds., *The Continuum History of Apocalypticism* (A&C Black, 2003); Jack Jacobs, *Jewish Politics in Eastern Europe: The Bund at 100* (Springer, 2001).

22. Michael Koziol & Leila Abdallah, "We Are the Ones Being Terrorized, Muslims Say," *The Sydney Morning Herald*, September 21, 2014, https://www.smh.com.au/politics/federal/we-are-the-ones-being-terrorised-muslims-say-20140920-10jdkw.html; "Rise in Attacks against Aussie Muslims," September 24, 2014, http://www.watoday.com.au/wa-news/rise-in-attacks-against-aussie-muslims-20140924-10lhl9.html; Neil Doorley, "Logan Mosque Bombarded with Anti-Islamic Leaflets in Latest Hate Attack," *The Courier Mail*, September 15, 2014, https://www.couriermail.com.au/news/queensland/logan-mosque-bombarded-with-antiislamic-leaflets-in-latest-hate-attack/news-story/505cc360194b9d2d2cb6a84e7954ce7c.

23. See, for example, the 2017–2018 Arab Opinion Index, https://www.theguardian.com/world/2003/nov/03/eu.israel, and "EU Poll Sees Israel as Peace Threat," *The Guardian*, November 3, 2003, https://www.couriermail.com.au/news/queensland/logan-mosque-bombarded-with-antiislamic-leaflets-in-latest-hate-attack/news-story/505cc360194b9d2d2cb6a84e7954ce7c.

24. "'I Felt the Hatred' Says Philosopher Attacked by Gilets Jaunes," *The Guardian*, February 24, 2019, https://www.theguardian.com/world/2019/feb/24/alain-finkielkraut-winds-of-antisemitism-in-europe-gilets-jaune; "French Jewish Intellectual Attacked by Anti-Semites during Yellow Vest Protest," *The Times of Israel*, March 3, 2019, https://www.timesofisrael.com/french-jewish-intellectual-attacked-by-anti-semites-during-yellow-vest-protest/.

25. For example, Huntington's (1996: 252–254) discussion of the characteristics of fault line wars refers repeatedly to conflicts within states.

26. For a more detailed discussion of the theory and its critics, see Fox (2004).

27. These data were collected by Tanya Haykin and Ron Tubman.

28. In these tests, as measured by beta values, the UN voting variable, while significant, has a lower impact on the results than do other significant influences, such as government support for religion. For more details, see Appendix A.

29. In these tests, as measured by beta values, the UN voting variable, while significant, has a lower impact on the results than do other significant influences, such as government support for religion, the country's economic performance, and the size of the country's Jewish minority. For more details, see Appendix A.

30. In these tests, as measured by beta values, pro-Israel variable has a greater impact on the results than do some other significant influences, such as government support for religion, but a lower impact than a measure for whether the country has a Christian Orthodox majority. For more details, see Appendix A.

31. In these tests, as measured by beta values, the pro-Palestine variable, while significant, has a lower impact on the results than do other significant influences, such as government support for religion. For more details, see Appendix A.

32. This result has a statistical significance of .054, which is slightly higher than the conventional .05 cutoff for statistical significance. Therefore we inter-operate this as a weak result. As measured by beta values, this result has a lower impact on the results as compared to other significant influences, including the size of the Jewish minority and democracy.

Chapter 5

1. Lev Topor, "COVID-19: Blaming the Jews for the Plague, Again," *Fathom*, March 2020, https://fathomjournal.org/covid-19-blaming-the-jews-for-the-plague-again/.
2. This list is largely taken form the Wikipedia page, "Anti-Semitic Canards," https://en.wikipedia.org/wiki/Antisemitic_canard. While this list looks at various forms of anti-Semitic accusations, not all of them can be classified as conspiracy theories. We use the Sunstein and Vermule (2009: 205) definition of conspiracy theory discussed at the outset of this chapter to distill this list into conspiracy theories regarding Jews.
3. Topor, "COVID-19: Blaming the Jews for the Plague, Again.".
4. Dirk Johnson, "Black-Jewish Hostility Rouses Leaders in Chicago to Action," *New York Times*, July 29, 1988, https://www.nytimes.com/1988/07/29/us/black-jewish-hostility-rouses-leaders-in-chicago-to-action.html.
5. For further read into Islamic Anti-Semitism, see Bostom (2008).
6. "Contemporary imprints of *The Protocols of the Elders of Zion*," https://en.wikipedia.org/wiki/Contemporary_imprints_of_The_Protocols_of_the_Elders_of_Zion.
7. https://dailystormer.name/donald-trump-should-be-forced-to-register-as-an-agent-of-a-foreign-government/.
8. Bari Weiss, "Ihlan Omar and the Myth of Jewish Hypnosis: A Conspiracy Theory with Ancient Roots and a Bloody History," *New York Times*, January 21, 2019.
9. Mark Landler, "Trump, No Stranger to Jewish Stereotypes, Rejects Ilhan Omar's Apology," *New York Times*, February 12, 2019, https://www.nytimes.com/2019/02/12/us/politics/trump-omar-anti-semitism.html.
10. Michael S. Rosenwald, "The Rothschilds, a Pamphlet by 'Satan' and Anti-Semitic Conspiracy Theories Tied to a Battle 200 Years Ago," *Washington Post*, April 20, 2018 https://www.washingtonpost.com/news/retropolis/wp/2018/03/19/the-rothschilds-a-pamphlet-by-satan-and-conspiracy-theories-tied-to-a-battle-200-years-ago/.
11. Andreas Gergley, "Orban Accuses Soros of Stoking Refugee Wake to Weaken Europe," *Bloomberg*, October 30, 2015 https://www.bloomberg.com/news/articles/2015-10-30/orban-accuses-soros-of-stoking-refugee-wave-to-weaken-europe.
12. Marton Dunai, "Hungary Approves 'STOP Soros' Law, Defying EU, Rights Groups," *Reuters*, June 20, 2018 https://www.reuters.com/article/us-hungary-soros-idUSKBN1JG1VN.
13. Shaun Walker, "'Dark Day for Freedom': Soros-Affiliated University Quits Hungary," *The Guardian*, December 3, 2018 https://www.theguardian.com/world/2018/dec/03/dark-day-freedom-george-soros-affiliated-central-european-university-quits-hungary.
14. Kenneth P. Vogel, Schott Shane, & Patrick Kingsley, "How Vilification of George Soros Moved from the Fringes to the Mainstream," *New York Times*, October 31, 2018.
15. Ben Sales, "Top GOP Pols Accused of Encouraging Anti-Semitism," *Haaretz*, October 25, 2020. https://thehill.com/homenews/administration/414171-trump-i-wouldnt-be-surprised-if-soros-were-paying-for-migrant-caravan
16. For example, in October 2018 both President Trump and *Fox News* hosts Laura Ingraham, Maria Bartiromo, and Lou Dobbs raised the idea that George Soros

was funding migrant caravans headed to the United States. Brett Samules, "Trump: 'I Wouldn't Be Surprised if Soros Was Paying for Migrant Caravans,'" *The Hill*, October 31, 2018, https://thehill.com/homenews/administration/ 414171-trump-i-wouldnt-be-surprised-if-soros-were-paying-for-migrant-caravan.

17. Ben Zimmer, "The Origins of the 'Globalist' Slur," *The Atlantic*, March 14, 2018, https://www.theatlantic.com/politics/archive/2018/03/the-origins-of-the-globalist- slur/555479/.

18. Zimmer, "The Origins of the 'Globalist' Slur."

19. Zimmer, "The Origins of the 'Globalist' Slur"; Sergei Klebnikov, "Right-Wing Conspiracists Pull from Old Playbook Blame George Soros for Riots," *Forbes*, May 30, 2020, https://www.forbes.com/sites/sergeiklebnikov/2020/05/30/right- wing-conspiracists-pull-from-old-playbook-blame-george-soros-for-riots/ ?sh=3aa0c6b74100; Vogel, Shane, & Kingsley, "How Vilification of George Soros Moved from the Fringes to the Mainstream." *New York Times*, October 31, 2018, https://www.nytimes.com/2018/10/31/us/politics/george-soros-bombs-trump.html

20. Davey Alba, "Misinformation about George Floyd Protests Surges on Social Media" *New York Times*, June 1, 2020, https://www.nytimes.com/2020/06/01/technology/ george-floyd-misinformation-online.html.

21. Eric Cortellessa, "Rising Conspiracy Theory Claims George Soros Behind US Unrest ADL Says," *Times of Israel*, June 2, 2020, https://www.timesofisrael.com/rising- conspiracy-theory-claims-george-soros-behind-us-unrest-adl-says/.

22. Joe Croncha, "Fox News Anchor Addresses Cutting of Gingrich Linking Soros to Violent Protests," *The Hill*, September 17, 2020, https://thehill.com/homenews/media/ 516961-fox-news-anchor-addresses-cutting-off-gingrich-linking-soros-to-violent.

23. Amir Tibon, "Newt Gingrich Shares Conspiracy Theory with Anti-Semitic Roots, Draws Warning from ADL," *Haaretz*, November 11, 2020, https://www.haaretz.com/ jewish/.premium-newt-gingrich-shares-conspiracy-theory-with-antisemitic-roots- draws-warning-by-adl-1.9301257.

24. John Bingham, "Vicar Investigated over '9/11 Israel Did It' Posting," *The Telegraph*, January 29, 2015, https://www.telegraph.co.uk/news/religion/11378475/Vicar- investigated-over-911-Israel-did-it-posting.html.

25. Jessica Chasmar, "Louis Farrakhan: 'Israelis and Zionist Jews' Played Key Roles in 9/ 11 Attacks," *The Washington Times*, March 5, 2015, https://www.washingtontimes. com/news/2015/mar/5/louis-farrakhan-israelis-and-zionist-jews-played-k/.

26. Hagay Hacohen, "Mossad Blamed by Muslim Leader in New Zealand for Mass Killing," *The Jerusalem Post*, March 28, 2019, https://www.jpost.com/Israel-News/ Mossad-blamed-by-Muslim-leader-in-New-Zealand-for-mass-killing-584965.

27. Mathilde Frot, "NUS Candidate Disqualified over 'ISIS Leader Trained by Israel' Post," *Jewish News*, April 10, 2019, https://jewishnews.timesofisrael.com/nus- student-disqualified-from-running-over-isis-leader-trained-by-israel-post/.

28. Sophie Rosenbaum, "Professor Says Jews Are Behind 9/11 Attacks and She's Keeping Her Job," *New York Post*, March 12, 2016 https://nypost.com/2016/03/02/oberlin- college-president-stands-by-anti-semitic-professor/; David Gerstman, "Oberlin Professor Claims Israel Was Behind 9/11 ISIS, Charlie Hebdo Attack," *The Tower*,

February 25, 2016, http://www.thetower.org/3012-oberlin-professor-claims-israel-was-behind-911-isis-charlie-hebdo-attack/.

29. Benjamin Weinthal, "Finnish MP under Fire for Comparing Israel to ISIS," *Jerusalem Post*, May 2, 2019 https://www.jpost.com/diaspora/antisemitism/finnish-mp-under-fire-for-comparing-israel-to-isis-588084.

30. Lee Harpin, "Jeremy Corbyn Suggested British Support for Israel Was 'Major Factor' in 7/7/ Bombers' Motives," *The Jewish Chronicle*, April 24, 2019 https://www.thejc.com/news/uk/jeremy-corbyn-suggested-british-support-for-israel-was-major-factor-in-7-7-bombers-motives-1.483368.

31. "With Whom Are Many U.S. Police Departments Training? With a Chronic Human Rights Violator—Israel," August 25, 2016, *Amnesty International*, https://www.amnestyusa.org/with-whom-are-many-u-s-police-departments-training-with-a-chronic-human-rights-violator-israel/.

32. Dominic Green, "Does Israel Train America's Police Forces?" *The Spectator*, June 25, 2020, https://www.spectator.co.uk/article/does-israel-train-america-s-police-forces-

33. Green, "Does Israel Train America's Police Forces?" The Spectator.

34. This claim is empirically dubious for at least four reasons. First, most Israeli training of US police, to the extent that it exists, focuses on anti-terror tactics, not how to restrain suspects. Second, there is no evidence that this tactic is included in any Israeli instruction or information sharing with US police. Third, the knee on the neck tactic has been present in US law enforcement since well before the establishment of the state of Israel and may date back to the "slave patrol" vigilante groups from as early as the 1700s. Fourth, many US police departments officially allow the tactic as a last resort or when an officer's life is threatened (Hadden, 2001); "Spokane Policy to Only Use Knee on Neck Tactic as a Last Resort," *KXLY News*, June 5, 2020, https://www.kxly.com/spokane-police-to-only-use-knee-to-neck-technique-as-a-last-resort/.

35. Benjamin Muller, "Labour's New Leader Fires Official over Chares of Anti-Semitism," *New York Times*, June 25, 2020; "Spokane Policy to Only Use Knee on Neck Tactic as a Last Resort."

36. "Syrian-Produced Hizbullah TV Ramadan Series' VideoClip of a 'Blood Libel,'" The Middle East Media Research Institute, December 8, 2003, https://www.memri.org/reports/syrian-produced-hizbullah-tv-ramadan-series-video-clip-blood-libel.

37. See, for example, "Egyptian Professor of Hebrew Dr. Fouad Abdelwahed: Jews Eats Matzos Prepared with Human Blood (Donated by Jews) on Passover," *Middle East Research Institute TV Monitor Project*, June 3, 2019 https://www.memri.org/reports/egyptian-professor-hebrew-dr-fouad-abdelwahed-jews-eat-matzos-prepared-human-blood-donated; "Blood Libel by Kuwaiti Researcher Muhanna Hamad Al-Muhanna: The Jews Use Blood of Christian Children for Holiday Pastries," *Middle East Research Institute TV Monitor Project*, February 6, 2019, https://www.youtube.com/watch?v=kAESCb-GdIs; "Jordanian Cleric Abu Qatada Al-Filistini Discusses The Protocols of the Elders of Zion, States: Jews Use Blood for Passover Matzos," *Middle East Research Institute TV Monitor Project*, January 8, 2016, https://www.memri.org/tv/jordanian-cleric-abu-qatada-al-filistini-discusses-protocols-elders-zion-states-jews-use-blood; "Blood Libel on Hamas TV—President of the American

Center for Islamic Research Dr. Sallah Sultan: Jews Murder non-Jews and Use Their Blood to Knead Passover Matzos," *Middle East Research Institute TV Monitor Project*, March 20, 2010, https://www.memri.org/tv/blood-libel-hamas-tv-president-american-center-islamic-research-dr-sallah-sultan-jews-murder-non.

38. "Baroness Tonge Fired over Outburst against Israeli Soldiers in Haiti," *The Telegraph*, February 13, 2010, https://www.telegraph.co.uk/news/politics/liberaldemocrats/7225643/Baroness-Tonge-fired-over-outburst-against-Israeli-soldiers-in-Haiti.html.

39. "Iranian Ayatollah Ahmad Khatami: US Occupied Haiti; Reports That Israeli Relief Delegation Is Stealing Organs," *Middle East Media Research Institute*, January 22, 2010, https://www.memri.org/tv/iranian-ayatollah-ahmad-khatami-us-occupied-haiti-reports-israeli-relief-delegation-stealing

40. Donna R. Edmunds, "Coronavirus Is a Zionist Plot Say Turkish Politicians, Media, Public," *The Jerusalem Post*, March 18, 2020, https://www.jpost.com/diaspora/antisemitism/coronavirus-is-a-zionist-plot-say-turkish-politicians-media-public-621393.

41. "Coronavirus Crisis Elevates Anti-Semitic, Racist, Tropes," *ADL*, March 17, 2020, https://www.adl.org/blog/coronavirus-crisis-elevates-antisemitic-racist-tropes.

42. Anti-Semitic conspiracy theories often include triple-brackets around texts such as names of people or institutions. These are known as "echoes," a far-right invention. These "echoes" begun as an attempt to identify and mark Jewish Twitter users, so that other anti-Semites could then harass them online.

    Topor "COVID-19: Blaming the Jews for the Plague, Again."

43. This description also relies upon Minorities at Risk project reports on the Chinese in Indonesia, Thailand, and Vietnam by Deepa Khosla. This project was the basis for Gurr (1993, 2000).

44. "What Aren't They Telling Us? Chapman University Survey of American Fears," October 11, 2016, https://blogs.chapman.edu/wilkinson/2016/10/11/what-arent-they-telling-us/.

45. "Revealed: Populists Far More Likely to Believe in Conspiracy Theories," *The Guardian*, https://www.theguardian.com/world/2019/may/01/revealed-populists-more-likely-believe-conspiracy-theories-vaccines.

46. "Marjorie Taylor Greene Shared Antisemitic and Islamophobic Video" *The Jerusalem Post*, August 27, 2020, https://www.jpost.com/diaspora/antisemitism/marjorie-taylor-greene-shared-antisemitic-and-islamophobic-video-640093.

47. This is similar to other lists intended to measure anti-Jewish sentiments. For example, Swami (2012) uses a measure where respondents are asked to agree or disagree with 12 statements: (1) Jews have too much power and influence in the world; (2) world banking is dominated by Jewish families; (3) Jews use their positions in the world news media to foster a pro-Jewish agenda; (4) Jews have caused an economic crisis in this country for their own ends; (5) Jews are to blame for the detrimental effects of globalization in this country; (6) Jews are attempting to establish a secret world government; (7) Jews are secretly running the US government in collaboration with Israel; (8) Jews are manipulating capitalism to their own ends; (9) the Holocaust is a myth fabricated to serve Jewish interests; (10) Jews are responsible for the social and moral ills of this country; (11) Jews are using political groups and organizations

to destabilize this country; (12) organizations such as the Freemasons are a means for Jews to establish a secret world government. This measure is derived from taking questions from earlier similar measures.

48. In these tests, as measured by beta values, the ADL variables which are statistically significant have a lower impact on the results than do other significant influences such as the size of the Jewish minority. For more details, see Appendix A.

49. In these tests, as measured by beta values, the ADL variables which are statistically significant have a lower impact on the results than do other significant influences such as government support for religion. For more details, see Appendix A.

50. While government support for religion significantly predicts SRD in some models used on this study, in others it does not. Thus its ability to predict SRD is inconsistent. Also, the other religion-related factor, societal religiosity, predicts less SRD.

Chapter 6

1. Paul Vallely, "Dickens' Greatest Villain: The Faces of Fagin," *The Independent*, February 7, 2005.

2. Henry Bodkin, "Labour 'Too Tolerant' for Anti-Semitism—New Poll," *The Telegraph*, August 20, 2017.

3. For more about the CST, see https://cst.org.uk.

4. Ben Riley-Smith, "Jeremy Corbyn: Claims I Am Racist and Anti-Semite Are 'Deeply Offensive,'" *The Telegraph*, August 19, 2015.

5. Cnaan Lipshiz, "Anti-Israel Stalwarts Blame Zionists and Jews for Corbyn's Defeat," *Jerusalem Post*, December 18, 2019.

6. Brian Wheeler, "The Jeremy Corbyn Story: Profile of Labour Leader," *BBC*, September 24, 2016.

7. "Investigation into Antisemitism in the Labour Party," Equality and Human Rights Commission, October 2020, https://www.equalityhumanrights.com/sites/default/files/investigation-into-antisemitism-in-the-labour-party.pdf.

8. "Investigation into Antisemitism in the Labour Party."

9. "Labour Suspends Jeremy Cobyn over Reaction to Anti-Semitism Report," *BBC News*, October 29, 2020, https://www.bbc.com/news/uk-politics-54730425.

10. Norman Geras, "Alibi Antisemitism," *Fathom*, 2013, http://fathomjournal.org/alibi-antisemitism/.

11. Geras "Alibi Antisemitism."

12. "Jeremy Corbyn Regrets Referring to Hamas and Hizbollah as 'Friends,'" *Haaretz*, July 5, 2016.

13. Daniel Sugarman, "Why Was This Alleged Spreader of Anti-Semitic Conspiracy Theories Allowed at Labour Conference?" *The Jewish Chronicle*, October 8, 2017.

14. Samuel Westrop, "Providing a Platform for Terror," *Gatestone Institute*, November 29, 2012, https://www.gatestoneinstitute.org/3467/jeremy-corbyn-mousa-abu-maria

15. Jake Wallis, "Jeremy Corbyn Caught on Video Calling Muslim Hate Preacher 'Honoured Citizen' and Inviting Him to 'Tea on the Terrace' at the House of Commons," *Daily Mail*, August 15, 2015.

16. Andrew Giligan, "Jeremy Corbyn, Friend to Hamas, Iran and Extremists," *The Telegraph*, July 18, 2015.

17. Dan Sabbagh, "Labour Hits out at 'False' Claims over Corbyn Cemetery Visit," *The Guardian*, August 15, 2018.

18. Jeremy Corbyn made a mistake about the dates because the only person killed in Paris was Atef Bseiso, the PLO's head of intelligence, in 1992.

19. Lizzy Buchan, "Corbyn in Fresh Anti-Semitism Row over Endorsement of Book Suggesting Banks Controlled by Jews," *The Independent*, May 1, 2019.

20. Heather Stewart & Sarah Marsh, "Jewish Leaders Demand Explanation over Corbyn Book Foreword," *The Guardian*, May 1, 2019.

21. Heather Stewart, "Corbyn in Anti-Semitism Row after Backing Artist Behind 'Offensive' Mural," *The Guardian*, March 23, 2018.

22. Robert Mendick, "Jeremy Corbyn's 10-Year Association with Group Which Denies the Holocaust," *The Telegraph*, May 20, 2017.

23. David. Collier, "Anti-Semitism Inside Palestine Live (a Facebook Group)," March 6, 2018, http://david-collier.com/reports/

24. "Investigation into Antisemitism in the Labour Party."

25. Rowena Mason, "Corbyn's offer of Peerage to Shami Chakrabarti Causes Labour Tensions," *The Guardian*, August 4, 2016.

26. Hannah Gal, "BBC's Panorama—Is Labour Anti-Semitic: Analysis," *Jerusalem Post*, July 14, 2019.

27. Gal, "BBC's Panorama—Is Labour Anti-Semitic: Analysis."

28. "Is Labour Anti-Semitic," Panorama, July 10, 2019, https://www.conservativehome.com/video/2019/07/watch-is-labour-anti-semitic-yesterdays-panorama-in-full.html.

29. "Investigation into Antisemitism in the Labour Party."

30. Heather Stewart & Andrew Sparrow, "Jeremy Corbyn: I Used the Term 'Zionist' in Accurate Political Sense," *The Guardian*. August 24, 2018.

31. Heather Stewart & Andrew Sparrow, "Jeremy Corbyn: I Used the Term 'Zionist' in Accurate Political Sense," *The Guardian*, August 24, 2018.

32. Dan Sabbagh, "Labour Adopts IHRA Anti-Semitism Definition in Full" *The Guardian*, September 4, 2018.

33. Abnabelle Dickson & James Randerson, "7 UK Labour MPs Leave Party to Form Breakaway Group," *Politico*, February 18, 2019.

34. Karl Pike, "Independent Group: Why Seven Labour MPS Have Left the Party," *The Conversation*, February 19, 2019.

35. Jeremy Sharon, "Luciana Berger: 'Shocking' Anti-Semitism in my Party" *The Jerusalem Post*, February 22, 2019.

36. Owen Jones, "Whatever Luciana Berger's Politics, Labour Members Must Stand with Her against Anti-Semitism," *The Guardian*, February 8, 2019.

37. "Investigation into Antisemitism in the Labour Party."

Chapter 7

1. While government support for religion significantly predicts SRD in some models used in this study, including the primary analyses in Chapter 3, in others it does not. It is used as a control variable in both Chapters 4 and 5, and in some of those cases loses its significance when controlling for other variables. Thus its ability to predict SRD is inconsistent. Also, the other religion-related factor, societal religiosity, predicts less SRD. See Appendix A for more details.
2. While Muslims in Bosnia are a plurality, they do not constitute a majority. In fact, the country has three major religious groupings: Bosnians, who are Muslim; Croats, who are Catholic; and Serbs, who are Orthodox Christian. The country has a complicated governing arrangement where Bosnians control the government for some areas of the country, while Serbs and Croats jointly control other areas. We posit that this is better described as a state with a mixed majority rather than a single majority.
3. For a full discussion of this analysis, including the strength of these relationships, see Appendix A.
4. For a full discussion of this analysis, including the strength of these relationships, see Appendix A.
5. This book has been completed fully, correctly, and in accord with all the rules and procedures of empirical research.

Appendix A

1. These are taken from the World Bank at https://data.worldbank.org/.
2. These are taken from the World Bank at https://data.worldbank.org/.
3. See Jaggers & Gurr (1995).
4. http://global100.adl.org/. For an analysis of the ADL data, see Tausch (2014).

Bibliography

Abalakina-Paap, Marian, Walter G. Stephan, Traci Craig, & W. Larry Gredory. "Beliefs in Conspiracies." *Political Psychology*, 20 (3), 2002, 637–647.

Akbaba, Yasemin, & Zeynep Tydas. "Does Religious Discrimination Promote Dissent? A Quantitative Analysis." *Ethnopolitics*, 10 (3), 2011, 271–295.

Albertson, Daniel, & Indra de Soysa. "Oil, Islam and the Middle East: An Empirical Analysis of the Repression of Religion, 1980–2013." *Politics & Religion*, 11 (2), 2017, 249–280, doi:10.1017.

Alexander, Kathryn J. "Religiosity and Bellicosity: The Impact of Religious Commitment on Patterns of Interstate Conflict." *Journal of Global Security Studies*, 2 (4), 2017, 271–287.

Alexseev, Mikhail A., & Sufian N. Zhemukhov. "From Mecca with Tolerance: Religion, Social Recatagorization, and Social Capital." *Religion, State and Society*, 43 (4), 2016, 379–391. http://dx.doi.org/10.1080/09637494.2015.1127672.

Appleby, R. Scott. *The Ambivalence of the Sacred: Religion, Violence, and Reconciliation.* New York: Rowman and Littlefield, 2000.

Barak, Oren. "The Failure of the Israeli–Palestinian Peace Process, 1993–2000." *Journal of Peace Research*, 42 (6), 2005, 719–736.

Barro, Robert J., & Rachel M. McCleary. "Which Countries Have State Religions." *Quarterly Journal of Economics*, 120 (4), 2005, 1331–1370.

Bartov, Omer. "The New Anti-Semitism: Genealogy and Implications." In David I. Kertzer, ed., *Old Demons: New Debates: Anti-Semitism and the West.* Teaneck, NJ: Holmes & Meier, 2005, 9–26.

Basedau, Matthias, Birte Pfeiffer, & Johannes Vullers. "Bad Religion? Religion, Collective Action, and the Onset of Armed Conflict in Developing Countries." *Journal of Conflict Resolution*, July 23, 2014, 1–30, doi: 10.1177/0022002714541853.

Basedau, Matthias, & Johanna Schaefer-Kehnert. "Religious Discrimination and Religious Armed Conflict in Sub-Saharan Africa: An Obvious Relationship?" *Religion, State & Society*, 47 (1), 30–47, 2019. doi: 10.1080/09637494.2018.1531617.

Basedau, Matthias, Georg Strüver, Johannes Vüllers, & Tim Wegenast. "Do Religious Factors Impact Armed Conflict? Empirical Evidence from Sub-Saharan Africa." *Terrorism and Political Violence*, 23 (5), 2011, 752–779.

Bayefsky, Anne. "The UN World Conference against Racism: A Racist Anti-Racism Conference." In *Proceedings of the ASIL Annual Meeting*, vol. 96. Cambridge: Cambridge University Press, 2002, pp. 65–74.

Beit-Hallahmi, Benjamin. "The Return of Martyrdom: Honour, Death, and Immortality." *Totalitarian Movements and Political Religions*, 4 (3), 2003, 11–34.

Ben-Nun Bloom, Pazit. "State-Level Restriction of Religious Freedom and Women's Rights: A Global Analysis." *Political Studies*, 64 (4), 2015, 1–22, doi: 10.1111/1467-9248.12212.

Bergmann, Werner. "Antisemitism in Europe Today: The Phenomena, the Conflicts." *Conference paper från konferensen Antisemitism in Europe Today: The Phenomena, the Conflicts*, 2013.

Bilewicz, Michal, & Ireneusz Krzeminski. "Anti-Semitism in Poland and Ukraine: The Belief in Jewish Control as a Mechanism of Scapegoating." *International Journal of Conflict and Violence (IJCV)*, 4 (2), 2010, 234–243.

Bilewicz, Michal, Mikolaj Winiewski, Miroslaw Kofta, & Adrian Wojcik. "Harmful Ideas, the Structure and Consequences of Anti-Semitic Beliefs in Poland." *Political Psychology*, 34 (6), 2013, 821–839.

Blanchard, William H. "Karl Marx and the Jewish Question." *Political Psychology*, 5 (3) 1984, 365–374.

Bodansky, Yossef. *Islamic Anti-Semitism as a Political Instrument*. Houston, TX: Freeman Center for Strategic Studies, 1999.

Bohman, Andrea, & Mikhaek Hjerm. "How the Religious Context Affects the Relationship between Religiosity and Attitudes Toward Immigration." *Ethnic and Racial Studies*, 2013, 1–22, doi: 10.1080/01419870.2012.748210.

Boomgaarden, Hajo G., & Andreas M. Woost. "Religion and Party Positions towards Turkish EU Accession." *Comparative European Politics*, 10 (2), 2012, 180–197.

Bostom, Andrew G. *The Legacy of Islamic Antisemitism: From Sacred Texts to Solemn History*. Amherst, New York: Prometheus Books, 2008.

Boyer, John W. "Karl Lueger and the Viennese Jews." *The Leo Baeck Institute Yearbook*, 26 (1), 1981, 125–141.

Brahm, Gabriel N. "Intersectionality." *Israel Affairs*, 24 (2), 2019, 157–170.

Brand, Paul. "Jews and the Law in England, 1275–90." *The English Historical Review*, 115 (464), 2000, 1138–1158.

Brandenberger, David. "Stalin's Last Crime? Recent Scholarship on Postwar Soviet Antisemitism and the Doctor's Plot." *Kritika: Explorations in Russian and Eurasian History*, 6 (1), 2005, 187–204.

Brathwaite, Robert, & Andrew Bramsen. "Reconceptualizing Church and State: A Theoretical and Empirical Analysis of the Separation of Religion and State on Democracy." *Politics & Religion*, 4 (2), 2011, 229–263.

Breakwell, Glynis. *Coping with Threatened Identities*. London: Methuen, 1986.

Brotherton, Robert, Christpher C. French, & Allen D. Pickering. "Measuring Belief in Conspiracy Theories: The Generic Conspiracist Beliefs Scale." *Frontiers in Psychology*, 4, 2013, 279, https://doi.org/10.3389/fpsyg.2013.00279.

Brown, Davis. "The Permissive Nature of the Islamic War Ethic." *Journal of Religion and Violence*, 2 (3), 2015, 460–483.

Brown, Davis. "Religion and State Entanglement and Interstate Armed Conflict Initiation, 1990–2010." *Religion, State & Society*, 47 (1), 2019, 48–66, doi: 10.1080/09637494.2018.1528786.

Buzan, Berry, Ole Waever, & Jaap de Wilde. *Security: A New Framework for Analysis*. Boulder, CO; London: Lynne Rienner, 1998.

Canetti, Daphna, Stevan E. Hobfoll, Ami Pedahzur, & Eran Zaidise "Much Ado about Religion: Religiosity, Resource Loss, and Support for Political Violence." *Journal of Peace Research*, 47 (5), 2010, 1–13.

Carlo-Gonzalez, Celin, Christopher McKallagat, & Jenifer Whitten-Woodring. "The Rainbow Effect: Media Freedom, Internet Access, and Gay Rights." *Social Science Quarterly*, 98 (3), 2017, 1061–1077.

Casanova, Jose. "The Secular and Secularisms." *Social Research*, 76 (4), 2009, 1049–1066.

Cesarani, David. "Anti-Zionism in Britain, 1922–2002: Continuities and Discontinuities." *The Journal of Israeli History*, 25 (1), 2006, 131–160.

Cesari, Jocelyne. *Why the West Fears Islam: An Exploration of Islam in Liberal Democracies*. New York: Palgrave Macmillan, 2013.

Cesari, Jocelyne, & Jonathan Fox. "Institutional Relations Rather than Clashes of Civilizations: When and How Is Religion Compatible with Democracy?" *International Political Sociology*, 10 (3), 2016, doi: 10.1093/ips/olw011.

Chakrabati, Shami. "The Shami Chakrabati Inquiry." *The Labour Party*, 2016, https://labour.org.uk/wp-content/uploads/2017/10/Chakrabarti-Inquiry-Report-30June16.pdf.

Chebel d'Appollonia, Ariane. *Migrant Mobilization and Securitization in the US and Europe: How Does It Feel to Be a Threat?* New York: Palgrave-Macmillan, 2015.

Chesler, Phyllis. *The New Anti-Semitism*. Jerusalem: Gefen, 2014.

Cingranelli, David L., and David L. Richards. "The Cingranelli-Richards (CIRI) Human Rights Data Project." *Human Rights Quarterly*, 32 (2), 2010, 401–424.

Cohen-Zada, Danny, Yotam Margalit, & Oren Rigbi. "Does Religiosity Affect Support for Political Compromise?" *International Economic Review*, 57 (93), 2016, 1085–1106.

Cohen-Sherbok, Dan. *Anti-Semitism: A History*. Thrupp, Stroud, Gloucestershire: Sutton, 2002.

Cunningham, Philip, A. "Jews and Christians from the Time of Christ to Constantine's Reign." In Albert S. Lindemann & Richard S. Levy, eds., *Antisemitism: A History*. New York: Oxford University Press, 2010, 47–62.

Cunradi, Carol B., Raul Caetano, & John Schafer. "Religious Affiliation, Denominational Homogamy, and Intimate Partner Violence among US Couples." *Journal for the Scientific Study of Religion*, 41 (1), 2002, 139–151.

Davis, Frederick Bryant. *The Jew and Deicide: The Origin of an Archetype*. Lanham, MD: University Press of America, 2003.

De Juan, Alexander, & Andreas Hasenclever. "Framing Political Violence: Success and Failure of Religious Mobilization in the Philippines." *Civil Wars*, 17 (2), 2015, 201–221.

de Zavala, Agnieszka G., & Aleksandra Cichocka. "Collective Narcissism and Anti-Semitism in Poland." *Group Pressures and Intergroup Relations*, 15 (2), 2012, 213–229.

Djupe, Paul A., & Brian R. Calfino. "Religious Value Priming, Threat, and Political Tolerance." *Political Research Quarterly*, 66 (4), 2012, 768–780.

Donnelly, Jack. *International Human Rights*. Boulder, CO: Westview Press, 2007.

Douglas, Karen M., Joseph E. Uscinski, Robbie M. Sutton, Aleksandra Cichocka, Turkay Nefes, Chee Siang Ang, & Farzin Deravi. "Understanding Conspiracy Theories." *Advances in Political Psychology*, 40 (1), 2019, 3–35.

Douglas, Karen M., & Robbie M. Sutton. "Why Conspiracy Theories Matter: A Social Psychological Analysis." *European Review of Social Psychology*, 29 (1), 2018, 256–298.

Dyrendal, Asbjorn, David G. Robertson, & Egil Asprem, eds. *Handbook of Conspiracy Theory and Contemporary Religion*. Boston, MA: Brill, 2018.

Eisenstein, Marie A. "Rethinking the Relationship between Religion and Political Tolerance in the US." *Political Behavior*, 28, 2006a, 327–348.

Eisenstein, Marie A. "Religious Motivation vs. Traditional Religiousness: Bridging the Gap between Religion and Politics and the Psychology of Religion." *Interdisciplinary Journal of Research on Religion*, 2 (2), 2006b, 1–30.

Eisenstein, Marie A. *Religion and the Politics of Tolerance: How Christianity Builds Democracy.* Waco, TX: Baylor University Press, 2008.

Ellison, Christopher G., & Kristin L. Anderson. "Religious Involvement and Domestic Violence among US Couples." *Journal for the Scientific Study of Religion*, 40 (2), 2001, 269–286.

Elman, Miriam F., & Asaf Romirowski. "Postscript: BDS." *Israel Affairs*, 24 (2), 2019, 228–235.

Facchini, Francois. "Religion, Law and Development: Islam and Christianity: Why Is It in Occident and Not in the Orient That Man Invented the Institutions of Religious Freedom?" *European Journal of Law and Economy*, 29 (1), 2010, 103–129.

Fein, Helen. "Dimensions of Antisemitism: Attitudes, Collective Accusations, and Actions." In Helen Fein, ed., *The Persisting Question: Sociological Perspectives and Social Contexts of Modern Antisemitism.* Berlin; New York, 1987, 67.

Fein, Helen. "Genocide: A Sociological Perspective." *Current Sociology*, 38 (1), Spring 1990, 1–126.

Feinberg, Ayal K. "Explaining Ethnoreligious Minority Targeting: Variation in U.S. Anti-Semitic Incidents." *Perspectives on Politics*, 18 (3), 2020, 770–787, doi: 10.1017/S153759271900447X.

Feinberg, Ayal K. "Homeland Violence and Diaspora Insecurity: An Analysis of Israel and America Jewry." *Politics & Religion*, 13 (1), 2020a, 1–27.

Filote, Andra, Niklas Potrafke, & Heinrich Ursprung. "Suicide Attacks and Religious Cleavages." *Public Choice*, 166 (1), 2016, 3–28.

Fine, Robert, & Philip Spencer. *Antisemitism and the Left: On the Return of the Jewish Question.* Manchester University Press, 2018.

Finke, Roger, & Robert R. Martin. "Ensuring Liberties: Understanding State Restrictions on Religious Freedoms." *Journal for the Scientific Study of Religion*, 53 (4), 2014, 687–705.

Fisch, M. Steven, Francesca R. Jensenius, & Katherine E. Michel. "Islam and Large-Scale Political Violence: Is There a Connection?" *Comparative Political Studies*, 43 (11), 2010, 1327–1362.

Fox, Adam, & Tuang Thomas. "Impact of Religious Affiliation and Religiosity on Forgiveness." *Australian Psychologist*, 43 (3), 2008, 175–185.

Fox, Jonathan. *Religion, Civilization and Civil War: 1945 through the New Millennium.* Lanham, MD: Lexington Books, 2004.

Fox, Jonathan. *A World Survey of Religion and the State.* New York: Cambridge University Press, 2008.

Fox, Jonathan. *Political Secularism, Religion, and the State: A Time Series Analysis of Worldwide Data.* New York: Cambridge University Press, 2015.

Fox, Jonathan. *The Unfree Exercise of Religion: A World Survey of Religious Discrimination against Religious Minorities.* New York: Cambridge University Press, 2016.

Fox, Jonathan. *The Correlates of Religion and State.* London: Routledge, 2019.

Fox, Jonathan. *Thou Shalt Have No Other Gods Before Me: Why Governments Discriminate against Religious Minorities.* New York: Cambridge University Press, 2020.

Fox, Jonathan, & Yasemin Akbaba. "Securitization of Islam and Religious Discrimination: Religious Minorities in Western Democracies, 1990 to 2008." *Comparative European Politics*, 13 (2), 2015, 175–197.

Fox, Jonathan, Chris Bader, & Jennifer McClure. "Don't Get Mad: The Disconnect between Religious Discrimination and Individual Perceptions of Government." *Conflict Management & Peace Science*, 36 (5), 2017, 495–516, doi: 10.1177/0738894217723160.

Frieland, Roger. "Religious Nationalism and the Problem of Collective Representation." *Annual Review of Sociology*, 27, 2001, 125–152.

Frindte, Wolfgang, Susan Wettig, & Dorit Wammetsberger. "Old and New Anti-Semitic Attitudes in the Context of Authoritarianism and Social Dominance Orientation: Two Studies in Germany." *Peace and Conflict: Journal of Peace Psychology*, 11 (3), 2005, 239–266.

Froese, Paul. "After Atheism: An Analysis of Religious Monopolies in the Post-Communist World." *Sociology of Religion*, 65 (1), 2004, 57–75.

Gearty, Connor. "Terrorism and Human Rights." *Government and Opposition*, 42 (3), 2007, 340–362.

Geehr, S. Richard. *"I decide who is a Jew!": The Papers of Dr. Karl Lueger*. Washington, DC: University Press of America, 1982.

Gerstenfeld, Manfred. *The War of a Million Cuts: The Struggle against the Delegitimization of Israel and the Jews, and the Growth of Antisemitism*. New York: Rvp Press, 2015.

Gill, Anthony. "The Political Origins of Religious Liberty: A Theoretical Outline." *Interdisciplinary Journal of Research on Religion*, 1 (1), 2005, 1–35.

Gill, Anthony. *The Political Origins of Religious Liberty*. New York: Cambridge University Press, 2008.

Glassman, Bernard. *Anti-Semitic Stereotypes without Jews: Images of the Jews in England 1290–1700*. Detroit: Wayne State University Press, 2017.

Gleditsch, Nils P., & Ida Rudolfsen. "Are Muslim Countries More Prone to Violence." *Research and Politics*, 3 (2), 2016, 1–9, doi: 10.1177/2053168016646392.

Goertzel, Ted. "Belief in Conspiracy Theories." *Political Psychology*, 15 (4), 1994, 731–742.

Goodwin, Matthew J. *New British Fascism: Rise of the British National Party*. London: Routledge, 2011.

Gopin, Marc. *Between Eden and Armageddon: The Future of World Religions, Violence, and Peacemaking*. Oxford: Oxford University Press, 2000.

Gopin, Marc. *Holy War, Holy Peace: How Religion Can Bring Peace to the Middle East*. New York: Oxford University Press, 2002.

Green, David M. "The End of Identity? The Implications of Postmodernity for Political Identification." *Nationalism and Ethnic Politics*, 6 (3), 2000, 68–90.

Grim, Brian J., & Roger Finke. "International Religion Indexes: Government Regulation, Government Favoritism, and Social Regulation of Religion." *Interdisciplinary Journal of Research on Religion*, 2 (1), 2006, 1–40.

Grim, Brian J., & Roger Finke. "Religious Persecution on Cross-National Context: Clashing Civilizations or Regulating Religious Economies." *American Sociological Review*, 72 (4), 2007, 633–658.

Grim, Brian J., & Roger Finke. *The Price of Freedom Denied*. New York: Cambridge University Press, 2011.

Gurr, Ted R. "War Revolution, and the Growth of the Coercive State." *Comparative Political Studies*, 21 (1), April 1988, 45–65.

Gurr, Ted R. *Minorities at Risk*. Washington, DC: United States Institute of Peace, 1993.

Gurr, Ted R. *Peoples versus States: Minorities at Risk in the New Century*. Washington, DC: United States Institute of Peace, 2000.

Gurses, Mehmet. "Islamists and Women's Rights: Lessons from Turkey." *Journal of the Middle East and Africa*, 6 (1), 2015, 33–44.

Guth, James L. "Religion and American Public Attitudes on War and Peace." *Asian Journal of Peacebuilding*, 1 (2), 2013, 227–252.

Hadden, Sally E. Slave *Patrols: Law and Violence in Virginia and the Carolinas*. Cambridge, MA: Harvard University Press, 2001.

Harrison, Bernard. *The Resurgence of Anti-Semitism: Jews, Israel, and Liberal Opinion*. Lanham, MD: Rowman & Littlefield, 2006.

Hay, Malcolm Vivian. *The Roots of Christian Anti-Semitism*. New York: Freedom Library Press, 1981.

Haynes, Jeffrey. From *Huntington to Trump: Thirty Years of the Clash of Civilizations*. Lanham, MD: Lexington University Press, 2019.

Hazan, Baruch A. *Soviet Propaganda: A Case of the Middle East Conflict*. London: Routledge, 2017.

Helbling, Marc. "Opposing Muslims and the Muslim Headscarf in Western Europe." *European Sociological Review*, 30 (2), 2014, 242–257, doi: 10.1093/esr/jct038.

Helbling, Marc, & Richard Traunmuller "How State Support for Religion Shapes Attitudes toward Muslim Immigrants: New Evidence from a Sub-National Comparison." *Comparative Political Studies*, 49 (3), 2015, 391–424, doi: 10.1177/0010414015612388.

Heni, Clemens. *Antisemitism, a Specific Phenomenon: Holocaust Trivialization, Islamism, Post-colonial and Cosmopolitan Anti-Zionism*. Berlin: Edition Critic, 2013.

Henne, Peter S. "The Two Swords: Religion-State Connections and Interstate Disputes." *Journal of Peace Research*, 49 (6), 2012, 753–768.

Henne, Peter S. "Does the UN Human Rights Council Help or Hurt Religious Repression?" *Journal of Church and State*, 2018, 1–20, doi: 10.1093/jcs/csy005.

Henne, Peter S. "Government Interference in Religious Institutions and Terrorism." *Religion, State & Society*, 47 (1), 2019, 67–86, doi: 10.1080/09637494.2018.1533691.

Henne, Peter S., & Jason Klocek. "Taming the Gods: How Religious Conflict Shapes State Repression." *Journal of Conflict Resolution*, 63 (1), 2017, 112–138, doi: 10.1177/0022002717728104.

Hermann, Tamar, & David Newman. "A Path Strewn with Thorns: Along the Difficult Road of Israeli-Palestinian Peacemaking." In John Darby & Roger MacGinty, eds., *The Management of Peace Processes*. London: Palgrave Macmillan, 2000, pp. 107–153.

Hilberg, Raul. *The Destruction of the European Jews*. Vol. 3. New York: Holmes & Meier, 1985.

Hill, Kim Q., & Tetsuya Matsubayashi. "Church Engagement, Religious Values, and Mass-Elite Policy Agenda Agreement in Local Communities." *American Journal of Political Science*, 52 (3), 2008, 570–584.

Horowitz, Donald L. *Ethnic Groups in Conflict*. Berkeley: University of California Press, 1985.

Htun, Mala, & A. Laurel Weldon. "Religious Power, the State, Women's Rights, and Family Law." *Politics & Gender*, 11 (3), 2015, 451–477.

Huntington, Samuel P. "The Clash of Civilizations?" *Foreign Affairs*, 72 (3), 1993, 22–49.

Huntington, Samuel P. *The Clash of Civilizations and the Remaking of the World Order*. New York: Simon and Schuster, 1996.

Huntington, Samuel P. "Try Again: A Reply to Russett, Oneal, and Cox." *Journal of Peace Research*, 37 (5), 2000, 609–610.

Hurd, Elizabeth S. "The Political Authority of Secularism in International Relations." *European Journal of International Relations*, 10 (2), 2004a, 235–262.

Hurd, Elizabeth S. "The International Politics of Secularism: US Foreign Policy and the Islamic Republic of Iran." *Alternatives*, 29 (2), 2004b, 115–138.

Isaacs, Matthew. "Sacred Violence or Strategic Faith? Disentangling the Relationship Between Religion and Violence in Armed Conflict." *Journal of Peace Research*, 53 (2), 2016, 211–225.

Isani, Mujtaba, & Daniel Silverman. "Foreign Policy Attitudes towards Islamic Actors: An Experimental Approach." *Political Research Quarterly*, 69 (3) 2016, 571–582.

Jacobs, Dirk, Yoann Veny, Louise Caller, Barbara Herman, & Aurelie Descamps. "The Impact of the Conflict in Gaza on Antisemitism in Belgium." *Patterns of Prejudice*, 45 (4), 2011, 341–360.

Jacobs, Jack. *Jewish Politics in Eastern Europe: The Bund at 100*. New York: Palgrave Macmillan, 2001.

Jacobs, Steven L., & Mark Weitzman. *Dismantling the Big Lie: The Protocols of the Elders of Zion*. Jersey City, NJ: KTAV, 2003.

Jaggers, Keith, & Ted R. Gurr. "Tracking Democracy's Third Wave with the Polity III Data." *Journal of Peace Research*, 32, (4), 1995, 469–482.

Jelen, Ted G., & Clyde Wilcox. "Denominational Preference and the Dimensions of Political Tolerance". *Sociological Analysis*, 51 (1), 1990, 69–81.

Jikely, Gunther. "Is Religion Coming Back as a Source for Antisemitic Views." *Religions*, 2020, 11, 255, 1–8, doi:10.3390/rel11050255.

Johnson, Alan. "Antisemitic Anti-Zionism: The Root of Labour's Crisis." *bicom*, 2016, http://www.bicom.org.uk/wp-content/uploads/2016/06/Prof-Alan-Johnson-Chakrabarti-Inquiry-submission-June-2016.pdf.

Johnson, Alan. "Contemporary Left Antisemitism and the Crisis of the British Labour Party." *Fathom*, 2019, https://fathomjournal.org/fathom-report-institutionally-antisemitic-contemporary-left-antisemitism-and-the-crisis-in-the-british-labour-party/.

Johnstone, Naomi, & Isak Svenssom. "Belligerants and Believers: Exploring Faith-Based Mediation in Internal Armed Conflicts." *Politics, Religion, & Ideology*, 14 (4), 2013, 557–579.

Jolley, Danies, Rose Meleady, & Karen M. Douglas. "Exposure to Intergroup Conspiracy Theories Promotes Prejudice Which Spreads across Groups." *British Journal of Psychology*, 111 (1), 2019, 17–35, doi.org/10.1111/bjop.12385.

Juergensmeyer, Mark. *The New Cold War?* Berkeley: University of California, 1993.

Julius, Anthony. "Anti-Semitism and the English Intelligensia." In David I. Kertzer, ed., *Old Demons, New Debates: Anti-Semitism in the West*. Teaneck, NJ: Holmes & Meier, 2005, pp. 53–58.

Julius, Anthony. *Trails of the Diaspora: A History of Anti-Semitism in England*. Oxford: Oxford University Press, 2010.

Kalmar, Ivan. "Islamophobia and Anti-Antisemitism: The Case of Hungary and the 'Soros plot.'" *Patterns of Prejudice*, 54 (1–2), 2020, 182–198.

Kaplan, Edward H., & Charles A. Small. "Anti-Israel Sentiment Predicts Anti-Semitism in Europe." *Journal of Conflict Resolution*, 50 (4), 2006, 548–561.

Karagiannis, Evangelos. "Secularism in Context: The Relation between the Greek State and the Church of Greece in Crisis." *European Journal of Sociology*, 50 (1), 2009, 122–167.

Karakaya, Suveyda. "Religion and Conflict: Explaining the Puzzling Case of 'Islamic Violence.'" *International Interactions*, 41 (3), 2015, 509–538.

Karakaya, Suvedya. "Ethno-Political Organization in the Middle East: When Do They Opt for Violence?" *Politics & Religion*, 9 (2), 2016, 332–363.

Keen, Ralph. "Antisemitism in the Late Medieval and Early Modern Periods." In Albert S. Lindemann & Richard S. Levy, eds., *Antisemitism: A History*. New York: Oxford University Press, 2010, pp. 79–93.

Kim, Dongsuk, & Hyun Jin Choi. "Autocracy, Religious Restriction, and Religious Civil War." *Politics and Religion*, 10 (2), 29176, 311–388.

Klein, Ralph W. "Anti-Semitism as Christian Legacy: The Origin and Nature of our Estrangement from the Jews." *Currents in Theology and Mission*, 11 (5), 285–301, 1984.

Klier, John D. *State Policies and the Conversion of Jews in Imperial Russia*. 2001. In Robert P. Geraci & Michael Khodarkovsky, eds., *Of Religion and Empire: Missions, Conversion, and Tolerance in Tsarist Russia*. Ithaca, NY: Cornell University Press pp. 92–112.

Koesel, Karrie J. *Region and Authoritarianism: Cooperation, Conflict, and the Consequences*. New York: Cambridge University Press, 2014.

Kostyrchenko, Gennadiï. *Out of the Red Shadows: Anti-Semitism in Stalin's Russia*. Amherst, NY: Prometheus Books, 1995.

Kotek, Joël. *Major Anti-Semitic Motifs in Arab Cartoons*. Jerusalem: Jerusalem Center for Public Affairs, 2004.

Kressel, Neil J. "Mass Hatred in the Muslim and Arab World: The Neglected Problem of Anti-Semitism." *International Journal of Applied Psychoanalytic Studies*, 4 (3), 2007, 197–215.

Kunovich, Robert M. "An Exploration of the Salience of Christianity for National Identity in Europe." *Sociological Perspectives*, 49 (4), 2006, 435–460.

Lantain, Anthony. "A Review of Different Approaches to Study Belief in Conspiracy Theories." *Psypag*, 88, 2013, 19–21.

Laqueur, Walter. *The Changing Face of Anti-Semitism: From Ancient Times to the Present Day*. Oxford: Oxford University Press, 2006.

Laustsen, Carsten B., & Ole Waever. "In Defense of Religion: Sacred Referent Objects for Securitization." *Millennium*, 29 (3), 2000, 705–739.

Laythe, Brian, Deborah Finkel, & Lee A. Kirkpatrick. "Predicting Prejudice from Religious Fundamentalism and Right Wing Authoritarianism: A Multiple Regression Approach." *Journal for the Scientific Study of Religion*, 40 (1), 2002a, 1–10.

Laythe, Brian, Deborah G. Finkel, Robert G. Bringle, & Lee A. Kirkpatrick. "Religious Fundamentalism as a Predictor of Prejudice: A Two Component Model." *Journal for the Scientific Study of Religion*, 41 (4), 2002b, 623–635.

Lebzelter, Gisela. *Political Anti-Semitism in England 1918-1939*. New York, NY: Plagrave-Macmillan, 1978.

Linder, Amnon. "The Legal Status of Jews in the Roman Empire." In Steven T. Katz, ed., *Judaism*, Vol. 4. Cambridge, UK: Cambridge University Press, 2008, pp. 128–174.

Little, David. "Belief, Ethnicity, and Nationalism." *Nationalism and Ethnic Politics*, 1 (2), 1995, 284–301.

Litvak, Meir, & Esther Webman. "Israel and Antisemitism." In Albert S. Lindemann & Richard S. Levy, eds., *Antisemitism: A History*. New York: Oxford University Press, 2010, pp. 237–249.

Lober, Brooke. "Narrow Bridges: Jewish Lesbian Feminism, Identity, Politics, and the 'Hard Ground' of Alliance." *Journal of Lesbian Studies*, 23 (1), 2018, 83–101.

Lucas, Phillip. "The Future of New and Minority Religions in the Twenty-first Century: Religious Freedom under Global Siege." In Tom Robbins & Phillip Lucas, eds., *New Religious Movements in the 21st Century*. New York: Routledge, 2004, pp. 341–358.

Mabee, Bryan. "Re-imagining the Borders of US Security after 9/11: Securitization, Risk, and the Creation of the Department of Homeland Security." *Globalizations*, 4 (3), 2007, 385–397.

Marcus, Kenneth L. "Anti-Zionism as Racism: Campus Anti-Semitism and the Civil Rights Act of 1964." *William & Mary Bill of Rights Journal*, 15 (2), 2006, 837–891.

Marcus, Kenneth L. "The Definition of Antisemitism" In Asher Charles Small, ed., *Global Antisemitism: A Crisis of Modernity*. Leiden: Brill Nijhoff, 2013, pp. 97–109.

Marx, Karl. *On the Jewish Question (1844)*. Aristeus Books, 2012.

Mataic, Dane R., & Roger Finke. "Compliance Gaps and the Failed Promises of Religious Freedoms." *Religion, State & Society*, 47 (1), 2019, 124–150. doi: 10.1080/ 09637494.2018.1528788.

Mavrogordatos, George. "Orthodoxy and Nationalism in the Greek Case." *West European Politics*, 26 (1), 2003, 117–136.

McGinn, Bernard, et al., eds. *The Continuum History of Apocalypticism*. New York: Continuum, 2003.

Milligan, Scott, Robert Anderson, & Robert Brym. "Assessing Variation in Tolerance in 23 Muslim-Majority and Western Countries." *Canadian Review of Sociology*, 51 (3), 2014, 241–261.

Najeebabadi, Akbar Shah. *The History of Islam*, Vol. 1. Darusallam, 2000.

Nattrass, Nicoli. "Understanding the Origins and Prevalence of AIDS Conspiracy Beliefs in the United States and South Africa." *Sociology of Health & Illness*, 35 (1), 2012, 113–129.

Neuberg, Stephen L., Carolyn M. Warner, Stephen A. Mistler, Anna Berlin, Eric D. Hill, Jordan D. Johnson, Gabrielle Filip-Crawford, Roger E. Millsap, George Thomas, Michael Winkelman, Benjamin J. Broome, Thomas J. Taylor, & Juliane Schober. "Religion and Intergroup Conflict: Findings from the Global Relations Project." *Psychological Science*, November 21, 2013, doi: 10.1177/0956797613504303.

Nicholls, William. *Christian Antisemitism: A History of Hate*. Lanham, MD: Rowman & Littlefield, 1995.

Norris, Pippa, & Ronald Inglehart. *Sacred and Secular: Religion and Politics Worldwide*. New York: Cambridge University Press, 2004.

Nyhan, Brendan, & Thomas Zeitzoff. "Conspiracy and Misperception Belief in the Middle East and North Africa." *Journal of Politics*, 80 (4), 2018, 1400–1404.

O'Flaherty, Michael. "Young Jewish Europeans: Perceptions and Experiences of Anti-Semitism." *European Union Agency for Fundamental Rights*, 2019.

Parkes, James W. *The Conflict of the Church and Synagogue*. New York: Macmillan, 1969.

Pearce, Susanna. "Religious Rage: A Quantitative Analysis of the Intensity of Religious Conflicts." *Terrorism and Political Violence*, 17 (3), 2005, 333–352.

Pease, Joshua. "How You've been Conditioned to Love Conspiracy Theories." *Popular Mechanics*, December 17, 2019, https://www.popularmechanics.com/science/ a30119985/why-people-believe-conspiracy-theories/.

Perry, Marvin, & Frederick M. Schweitzer. *Antisemitic Myths: A Historical and Contemporary Anthology*. Bloomington: Indiana University Press, 2008.

Powell, Emilia J. *Islamic Law and International Law: Peaceful Resolution of Disputes.* New York: Oxford University Press, 2020.

Pulzer, Peter G. J., & Peter Pulzer. *The Rise of Political Anti-Semitism in Germany and Austria.* Cambridge, MA: Harvard University Press, 1988.

Rapoport, David C. "Terrorism as a Global Wave Phenomenon: Overview." In William R. Thompson, ed., *Oxford Research Encyclopedia of Politics*, New York, Oxford University Press, 2017, doi: 10.1093/acrefore/9780190228637.013.299.

Razack, Sherene H. *Casting Out: The Eviction of Muslims from Western Law and Politics.* Toronto: University of Toronto Press, 2008.

Rafferty, Yvonne. "International Dimensions of Discrimination and Violence against Girls: A Human Rights Perspective." *Journal of International Women's Studies*, 14 (1), 2013, 1–23.

Rebe, Ryan J. "Re-examining the Wall of Separation: A Cross-National Study of Religious Pluralism in Democracy." *Politics & Religion*, 5 (3), 2012, 655–670.

Reid, Anthony. "Jewish-Conspiracy Theories in Southeast Asia: Are Chinese the Target?" *Indonesia and the Malay World*, 38 (112), 2010, 373–385.

Rich, D. *The Left's Jewish Problem: Jeremy Corbyn, Israel and Anti-Semitism.* London: Biteback, 2016.

Rokéah, Zefira Entin. "Money and the Hangman in Late-13th-Century England: Jews, Christians and Coinage Offences Alleged and Real (Part I)." *Jewish Historical Studies*, 1988, 31, 83–109.

Rokéah, Zefira Entin. "Money and the Hangman in Late-13th-Century England: Jews, Christians and Coinage Offences Alleged and Real (Part II)." *Jewish Historical Studies*, 1990, 32, 159–218.

Rose, Emily M. *The Murder of William of Norwich: The Origins of the Blood Libel in Medieval Europe.* Oxford: Oxford University Press, 2015.

Rosenfeld, Alan H. *Deciphering the New Antisemitism.* Bloomington: Indiana University Press, 2015.

Roth, Norman. *Conversos, Inquisition, and the Expulsion of the Jews from Spain.* Madison: University of Wisconsin Press, 2002.

Roy, Oindrila. "Religious Roots of War Attitudes in the United States: Insights from Iraq, Afghanistan, and the Persian Gulf." *Foreign Policy Analysis*, 12 (3), 2016, 258–274.

Rublack, Ulinka. *Reformation Europe.* Cambridge: Cambridge University Press, 2017.

Ruether, Rosemary. *Faith and Fratricide: The Theological Roots of Anti-Semitism.* New York: Seabury Press, 1974.

Sacks, Jonathan. *Not in God's Name: Confronting Religious Violence.* New York: Schocken Books, 2015.

Saiya, Nilay. "Blasphemy and Terrorism in the Muslim World." *Terrorism and Political Violence*, 29 (6), 2016a, 1087–1105, doi: 10.1080/09546553.2015.1115759.

Saiya, Nilay. "Religion, State, and Terrorism: A Global Analysis." *Terrorism and Political Violence*, 2016b, 1–20, doi: 10.1080/09546553.2016.1211525.

Saiya, Nilay. *Weapons of Peace: How Religious Liberty Combats Terrorism.* New York: Cambridge University Press, 2019.

Saiya, Nilay, & Anthony Scime. "Explaining Religious Terrorism: A Data-Mined Analysis." *Conflict Management and Peace Science*, 2014, 32 (5), 487–512, doi: 10.1177/0738894214559667.

Sanders-Phillips, Karen. "Racial Discrimination: A Continuum of Violence Exposure for Children of Color." *Clinical Child and Family Psychological Review*, 12, 2009, 174–195.

Sarkissian, Ani. *The Varieties of Religious Repression: Why Governments Restrict Religion*. New York: Oxford University Press, 2015.

Schoenberg, Harris O. "Demonization in Durban: The World Conference against Racism." *The American Jewish Year Book*, 102, 2002, 85–111.

Seaver, James E. "The Persecution of the Jews in the Roman Empire (300–428)." *Humanistic Studies*, 30, 1952, 1–101.

Sharansky, Natan. "3D Test of Anti-Semitism: Demonization, Double Standards, Delegitimization". *Jewish Political Studies Review*, 16 (3–4), 5–8, 2004.

Shindler, Colin. "Jeremy Corbyn's Anti-Imperial Nostalgia." *Foreign Policy*, January 26, 2018.

Sicher, Efraim. "The Image of Israel and Postcolonial Discourse in the Early 21st Century: A View From Britain." *Israel Studies*, 16 (1), 2011, 1–25.

Smith, Anthony D. "Ethnic Election and National Destiny: Some Religious Origins of Nationalist Ideals." *Nations and Nationalism*, 5 (3), 1999, 331–355.

Smith, Anthony D. "The Sacred Dimension of Nationalism." *Millennium*, 29 (3), 2000, 791–814.

Sorek, Tamir, & Alin M. Cebanu. "Religiosity, National Identity and Legitimacy: Israel as an Extreme Case." *Sociology*, 43 (3), 2009, 477–496.

Stark, Rodney. *One True God: Historical Consequences of Monotheism*. Princeton, NJ: Princeton University Press, 2001.

Stark, Rodney. *For the Glory of God*. Princeton NJ: Princeton University Press, 2003.

Stark, Rodney, & William Bainbridge. *The Future of Religion: Secularization, Revival and Cult Formation*. Berkeley: University of California Press, 1985.

Stark, Rodney, & Roger Finke. *Acts of Faith: Explaining the Human Side of Religion*. Berkeley: University of California Press, 2000.

Stark, Rodney, & Lawrence R. Iannaccone. "A Supply Side Reinterpretation of the 'Secularization' of Europe." *Journal for the Scientific Study of Religion*, 33 (3), 1994, 230–252.

Steinberg, Gerald M. "The Politics of NGOs, Human Rights and the Arab-Israel Conflict." *Israel Studies*, 16 (2), 2011, 24–54.

Sunstein, Cass R., & Adrian Vermeule. "Conspiracy Theories: Causes and Cures." *Journal of Political Philosophy*, 17 (2), 2009, 202–227.

Sutton, Robbie M., & Karen M. Douglas. "Conspiracy Theories and the Conspiracy Mindset: Implications for Political Ideology." *Current Opinion in Behavioral Sciences*, 34, 2020, 118–122, doi.org/10.1016/j.cobeha.2020.02.015.

Svensson, Isak. "Fighting with Faith: Religion and Conflict Resolution in Civil Wars." *Journal of Conflict Resolution*, 51 (6), 2007, 930–949.

Svensson, Isak, & Emily Harding. "How Holy Wars End: Exploring the Termination Patters of Conflicts with Religious Dimensions in Asia." *Terrorism & Political Violence*, 23 (2), 2011, 133–149.

Svensson, Isak, & Desiree Nilsson. "Disputes over the Divine: Introducing the Religion and Armed Conflict (RELAC) Data, 1975 to 2015." *Journal of Conflict Resolution*, 62 (5), 2017, 1127–1148, doi: 10.1177/0022002717737057, 1–22.

Swami, Viren. "Social Psychological Origins of Conspiracy Theories: The Case of the Jewish Conspiracy Theory in Malaysia." *Frontiers in Psychology*, August 6, 2012, https://doi.org/10.3389/fpsyg.2012.00280.

Swami, Viren, Rebecca Coles, Stefan Stieger, Jakob Pietschnig, Adrian Furnham, Sherry Rehim, & Martin Voracek. "Conspiracist Ideation in Britain and Austria: Evidence of a Monological Belief System and Associations between Individual Psychological Differences and Real-World and Fictitious Conspiracy Theories." *British Journal of Psychology*, 102 (3), 2011, 443–463.

Sweeney, Shawna A. "The Sacred and the Secular: Separation of Church (Mosque) and State & Implications for Women's Rights." *International Journal of Gender and Women's Studies*, 2 (1), 2014, 1–35.

Swisher, Clayton E. *The Truth about Camp David: The Untold Story about the Collapse of the Middle East Peace Process*. New York: Nation Books, 2004.

Tausch, Arno. "The New Global Antisemitism: Implications for the Recent ADL-100 Data." *Middle East Review of International Affairs*, 18 (3), 2014, 46–72.

Tausch, Arno. "The Return of Religious Antisemitism? The Evidence from the World Values Survey." Munich Personal RePEc Archive, November, 17, 2018. https://mpra. ub.uni-muenchen.de/90093/1/MPRA_paper_90093.pdf.

Taylor, Charles. *A Secular Age*. Cambridge, MA: Harvard University Press, 2007.

Toft, Monica Duffy. "Getting Religion? The Puzzling Case of Islam and Civil War." *International Security*, 31 (4), 2007, 97–131.

Topor, Lev. "Explanations of Antisemitism in the British Postcolonial Left." *Journal of Contemporary Antisemitism*, 1 (2), 2018, 1–14.

Topor, Lev. *Antisemitic Trends in the British Labour Party*. Doctoral dissertation, Bar Ilan University, Israel, 2019.

Topor, Lev. "The Covert War: From BDS to Delegitimisation to Antisemitism." *Israel Affairs*, 27 (1), 2021, 166–180.

Tsang, Ho-Ann, Michael E. McCullough, & William T. Hoyt "Psychometric and Rationalization Accounts of the Religion-Forgiveness Discrepancy." *Journal of Social Issues*, 61 (94), 2005, 785–805.

Uneal, Faith. "The Secret Islamization of Europe Exploring the Integrated Threat Theory: Predicting Islamophobic Conspiracy Stereotypes." *International Journal of Conflict and Violence*, 10 (1), 2016, 94–108.

van der Noll, Jolanda, Anette Rohmann, & Vassilis Saroglou. "Societal Level of Religiosity and Religious Identity Expression in Europe." *Journal of Cross-Cultural Psychology*, 49 (6), 2018, 959–975. doi: 10.1177/0022022117737302.

Van Prooijen, Jan-Willem, & Karen M. Douglas. "Conspiracy Theories as Part of History: The Role of Societal Crisis Situations" *Memory Studies*, 10 (3), 2017, 323–333, https://doi.org/10.1177/1750698017701615.

Van Prooijen, Jan-Willem, Andre P. M. Krouwel, & Thomas V. Pollet. "Political Extremism Predicts Belief in Conspiracy Theories." *Social Psychology and Personality Science*, 6 (5), 2015, 570–578.

Voicu, Malina. "Effect of Nationalism on Religiosity in 30 European Countries" *European Sociological Review*, 28 (3), 2011, 333–343, doi: 10.1093.

Waever, Ole. "Securitization and Desecuritization." In Ronnie Lipschutz, ed., *On Security*. New York: Columbia University Press, 1995, pp. 46–86.

Waever, Ole. "Politics, Security, Theory." *Security Dialogue*, 42 (4–5), 2011, 465–480.

Wainwright, Hillary. "The Remarkable Rise of Jeremy Corbyn." *New Labor Forum*, 27 (3), 34–42, 2018.

Wald, Kenneth D. *Religion and Politics in the United States*. New York: St. Martins, 1987.

Waldman, Lois. "Employment Discrimination against Jews in the United States, 1955." *Jewish Social Studies* xviii, 1956, 208–216.

Watt, Montgomorey W. "Muhammad." In P. Lambton Holt, A. Lambton, K.S., & B. Lewis, eds., *The Cambridge History of Islam: Islamic Society & Civilizations*, Vol. 1. Cambridge: Cambridge University Press, 1970, pp. 30–56.

Webman, Esther. "Rethinking the Role of Religion in Arab Antisemitic Discourses." *Religions*, 10 (7), 2019, 1–16.

Weil, Patrick. "The History and Memory of Discrimination in the Domain of French Nationality: The Case of Jews and Algerian Muslims." *HAGAR International Social Science Review*, 6 (1), 2005, 49–73.

Weitzman, Mark. "Transmigration of Antisemitism: Old Myths; New Realities." In Michael Berenbaum, ed., *Not Your Father's Antisemitism: Hatred of the Jews in the 21st Century*. St. Paul, MN: Paragon House, 2008, pp. 247–260.

White, Arnold. *The Modern Jew*. London: W. Heinemann, 1899.

Wistrich, Robert S., ed. *The Left against Zion: Communism, Israel and the Middle East*. London: Vallentine, Mitchell, 1979.

Wistrich, Robert S. A *Lethal Obsession: Anti-Semitism from Antiquity to the Global Jihad*. New York: Random House, 2010.

Wistrich, Robert S. *From Blood Libel to Boycott: Changing Faces of British Antisemitism*. Jerusalem: Vidal Sassoon International Center for the Study of Antisemitism, 2011.

Wistrich, Robert S. *Parallel Lines: Anti-Zionism and Antisemitism in the 21st Century*. Jerusalem: Vidal Sassoon International Center for the Study of Antisemitism, the Hebrew University of Jerusalem, 2013.

Wistrich, Robert S. *Between Redemption and Perdition: Modern Antisemitism and Jewish Identity*. Routledge, 2020.

Wodak, Ruth. "The Radical Right and Antisemitism." In Jens Rydgren, ed., *Oxford Handbook of the Radical Right*. Oxford: Oxford University Press, 2018, pp. 1–33. doi: 10.1093/oxfordhb/9780190274559.013.4.

Wood, Michael J., Karen M. Douglas, & Robbie M. Sutton. "Dead and Alive: Beliefs in Contradictory Conspiracy Theories." *Social Psychology and Personality Science*, 3 (6), 2012, 767–773.

Zellman, Ariel, & Jonathan Fox. "Defending the Faith? Assessing the Impact of State Religious Exclusivity on Territorial MID Initiation." *Politics & Religion*, 13 (3), 2020, 465–491, doi: https://doi.org/10.1017/S1755048319000488.

Zick, A., B. Küpper, & B. Hövermann. *Intolerance, Prejudice and Discrimination: A European Report*. Berlin: Friedrich-Ebert-Stiftung, 2011.

Zuckerman, Phil. "Jews and the Christian Right." *Journal of Jewish Communal Service*, 73 (1), 1996, 21–31.

Index

For the benefit of digital users, indexed terms that span two pages (e.g., 52–53) may, on occasion, appear on only one of those pages.

Tables and figures are indicated by *t* and *f* following the page number